The Forms and Orders

of

Western Liturgy

FROM THE TENTH
TO THE EIGHTEENTH CENTURY

The Forms and Orders

of

Western Liturgy

FROM THE TENTH
TO THE EIGHTEENTH CENTURY

A Historical Introduction and Guide
for Students and Musicians

JOHN HARPER

CLARENDON PRESS · OXFORD

Oxford University Press, Walton Street, Oxford OX2 6DP
Oxford New York Toronto
Delhi Bombay Calcutta Madras Karachi
Kuala Lumpur Singapore Hong Kong Tokyo
Nairobi Dar es Salaam Cape Town
Melbourne Auckland Madrid
and associated companies in
Berlin Ibadan

Oxford is a trade mark of Oxford University Press

Published in the United States
by Oxford University Press Inc., New York

British Library Cataloguing in Publication Data
Data available

Library of Congress Cataloging in Publication Data
The forms and orders of Western liturgy from the tenth to the
eighteenth century: a historical introduction and guide for
students and musicians/John Martin Harper.
Includes bibliographical references and index.
1. Liturgics. 2. Catholic Church—Europe—Liturgy. 3. Church of
England—Liturgy. 4. Church music—Catholic Church—History.
5. Church music—Anglican Communion—History. 6. Anglican
Communion—Liturgy. I. Title.
BV186.5.H37 1991   264'.02'009—dc20   91–7974
ISBN 0–19–816279–0

Typeset by Hope Services (Abingdon) Ltd.
Printed in Great Britain
on acid-free paper by
J. W. Arrowsmith Ltd., Bristol

For David Calcutt and
in memory of Ralph Dudley, priest,
who together helped me to realize
that church music is but a part
of Christian liturgy.

ACKNOWLEDGEMENTS

When I began to teach an introduction to medieval music at Birmingham University in the late 1970s I searched in vain for a guide to the liturgy of the period. In those days we made do with some primitive tables and with a visit to Worcester Cathedral where we tried to understand a medieval building, to see how it worked for the community who built it, and to see how its present order, use, and worship differed from those of the medieval period. Over ten years later, this is an attempt to provide the book I was looking for.

My own practical involvement in Christian liturgy as chorister, organist, and director of music through decades of rapid change in the Church has obviously been a continuing backcloth and influence, but four liturgical environments have been particularly important: the annual Festival in the Wiltshire village of Edington (a festival of music within the liturgy in a fourteenth-century monastic church) where over twenty years I was chorister, server, general factotum, administrator, and finally director; the Metropolitan Cathedral Church of St Chad in Birmingham where I directed the music and began to learn a little about the modern Roman liturgy; the Panel of Monastic Musicians to whom I am a musical adviser and through whom I have come to experience current English monastic liturgies; and the Chapel of Magdalen College, Oxford, where with a fine choir and supportive priests I have had opportunity for liturgical experiment and historical exploration.

A number of individuals have contributed to the book in important ways. One of the undergraduates who came on one of those visits to Worcester was Dr Sally Roper, whose own research on and knowledge of medieval liturgy has taught me much: she has also given me much counsel, support, and practical help. Through the Panel of Monastic Musicians I met Father George Guiver CR, whose own book on the Office (*Company of Voices*) has been instructive, and who has helped me to get into perspective the broad background of the liturgy in a historical context. Others have read, commented on, and corrected drafts of the text, and made suggestions: I am very grateful to Dr Roger Bowers, Dr Bojan Bujić, Professor Rudolf Flotzinger, Mr Christopher Hohler, Professor Andrew Hughes, the Reverend Dr Jeffrey John, Professor Richard Pfaff, Mr Henry Rees, and Dr Jerome Roche for their generous offerings of time, knowledge, and critical perception.

In tackling so large and complex a field of study in so compact a way I remain painfully aware of the dangers of oversimplification and overstatement, let alone of the lacunae in my knowledge and possible errors in my understanding. I am sure that this is a book that many will be able to improve on, and I look forward to their comments and corrections.

J.M.H.

Magdalen College, Oxford
Easter Eve, 1990

CONTENTS

LIST OF FIGURES

INTRODUCTION

As an introductory guide this book attempts to assist the study and understanding of formal Christian worship in the West, especially that of the Middle Ages. It extends beyond the sixteenth-century Reformation with those forms of worship that derive from medieval practice. Such are the liturgical orders established and standardized by the Roman Catholic Church in the Tridentine Rite, and by the Church of England in the Book of Common Prayer.

The need for a straightforward outline of liturgical forms and orders between the tenth and the eighteenth centuries is all the more necessary since the recent liturgical changes instituted in most Churches have been so far-reaching. The extent of these changes has made the connections with the practice of the medieval Western Church more tenuous. The great church buildings in which the liturgy was celebrated remain, though often much altered or reordered. The texts and music of the liturgy survive, at least in part. But the medieval communities of clerks, priests, monks, and nuns who animated these rich resources are gone. Gone too are the aesthetic, spiritual, and theological backgrounds, and the social framework that supported these communities. The modern awareness of the medieval Church, whether popular fascination or informed study, tends to be derived from the physical remains of buildings and books. This guide is concerned with the use of those church buildings and books for their principal function—Christian liturgy.

Though placed in a historical context, what is presented here is essentially practical in purpose. It should enable the reader to have an idea of how worship was conducted; to understand better how the surviving buildings were originally conceived and ordered. More especially it should enable the reader to discover where and how surviving texts and music were used in the liturgy.

Christian liturgical celebration is deeply rooted, and is almost a subculture with its own structures and conventions supported by their own terminology. For Christian readers some of that terminology (and its background) may be familiar, but others may have to bear with the use of unfamiliar terms which are (so far as possible) defined later in the text or else in the glossary. A Christian dictionary or encyclopaedia may also be a helpful adjunct.

In any culture with long ancestry, the reverence and worship of God (or gods) is central and often dominant. Early in Christian history, praise and prayer to God on a daily basis and at regular times throughout the day became a preoccupation of groups of devout Christians. With the codification of that worship it became both more regulated and more complex. The praise of the Almighty was for Christians the highest and most important of human activities, deserving the best of their energy, artistic endeavour, and wealth. The rich heritage of the medieval Church reflects this.

Though the worship of God remains central to Christians today its style, spirituality, and artefacts are rather different. Within the modern Church there is a lively interest in liturgy and especially pastoral liturgy. But if one consults current liturgical writing, even writing of a historical kind, the emphasis most often falls on the relationship of the early Christian centuries with present-day worship. Yet the period from which most great liturgical buildings, artefacts, books, and music survive in the West extends from the tenth to the eighteenth centuries.

The patterns of Christian worship codified in the West in the ninth and tenth centuries were evident in the liturgy of the Roman Catholic Church until the Second Vatican Council (1962–5). Since then the changes have been extensive. Before the 1960s the forms of worship used in the Roman Catholic Church were mostly those approved in the sixteenth century, the so-called Tridentine Rite. This Rite was closely related to the medieval ordering of liturgy, certainly far more closely than the reordered modern Rites. The new Rites attempt to reflect more of what is understood from the evidence of the earliest written sources of Christian worship. The long tradition of the use of the Latin language in worship has been overtaken by the widespread influx of the vernacular; and there have been fundamental changes of order, emphasis, style, and presentation, based on a revalued pastoral theology.

Those who try to understand earlier liturgical practices have to be aware of the changes of recent decades. The distance between medieval liturgy and what one can observe even in most Roman Catholic churches today has increased greatly since the 1960s. There are passages in the present study which address these differences, albeit at a basic level, in the hope that delineation may assist the reader to face this problem. It is perhaps worth emphasizing, however, that no value judgements are implied in drawing comparison between the old and the new.

In approaching the old we have to realize how our attitudes to liturgy have changed, and to be aware of the nature of our perception of what survives of earlier liturgies. Medieval liturgy was not only highly sophisticated, it was often the principal pursuit of communities of men or women whose whole lives (often from childhood) were dominated by daily worship. Many of the extant artefacts of that liturgy are now valued for their artistic worth in their own right—the churches, the sculptures and carving, the vessels, ornaments, and vestments, the texts and music, and the manuscripts in which they were written down. We are faced with the task of moulding all this evidence together, and of interpreting it in the context of highly developed social units which made great use of ritual and ceremony. Though we can only hope to sense the totality of medieval liturgy, we can go some way at least towards understanding its order and function. And this book sets its aims no higher than that. Reconstruction of liturgy is always partial. It may be better than nothing, but we have always to remember how much we lack of the basic grasp of medieval knowledge and thinking, let alone of belief, spirituality, and theology.

In conjuring up the richness of medieval liturgy with its sumptuous ceremonial, we must also beware of romanticizing: the medieval Church had its share of politics, power, greed, scandal, superstition, and disease, let alone such basic human failings as incompetence and sloth. But its stature, influence, and importance were indisputable. It was after all the only centrally organized, multinational corporation in the medieval world, with a substantial portion of the literate population of Western Europe in its service. Like all big organizations it required codification for its practices. That codification was complex and remains confusing. It was subject to amendment and interpretation over the centuries, and of course (particularly in an age of oral and manuscript transmission) central policy and local implementation did not always coincide.

This guide sets out the broad features of liturgical practice and relates them to the surviving materials. It is organized in four main parts.

PART I. LITURGY IN THE WESTERN CHURCH

It has seemed important to define the nature of liturgy, and to give a brief summary of the history of its formation in the Western Church. The liturgy makes no sense without an idea of the communities in which it was fostered and celebrated; and the second chapter of this part presents an outline of the principal groups of clergy and the kinds of church and chapel in which they served, further details of cathedral, collegiate, and monastic foundations, an introduction to the physical ordering of large church buildings, and a brief consideration of polyphony and polyphonic choirs.

PART II. MEDIEVAL LITURGY

The largest part of this guide deals systematically with the main features of medieval liturgy, and their interrelationship with one another. Beginning with the day, week, seasons, and year, there is a description of the principal liturgical books, with a special discussion of the Psalms, Old Testament texts that are central to Christian worship. There are then separate chapters on the order of the daily celebrations of Office and Mass, and on the special characteristics of processions, other additional observances, and Holy Week.

PART III. AFTER THE REFORMATION

The forms and orders of Western liturgy are essentially medieval. Nevertheless, the reaction of the Roman Catholic Church to the Protestant Reformation included liturgical revaluation and the establishment of a normative Roman Rite and Use after the Council of Trent. Its characteristics and consequences are considered here.

The reformed Churches formed separate denominations with their own liturgical practices. Apart from the Scandinavian Lutherans, only the Church of England produced a comprehensive, fixed liturgical order, derived from the medieval Rite. The principal services of the English Book of Common Prayer are described next, and questions of their musical celebration discussed.

PART IV. USING LITURGICAL SOURCES

Any attempt at establishing the order and content of a liturgical service needs care and caution. The basic process and problems of establishing such an order forms a chapter, which also raises questions of ceremonial. A longer chapter addresses the detailed order of specific medieval sources which survive and are generally accessible in modern editions or fascimiles. It should assist less experienced readers to find their way round these sources. They are predominantly English in origin, including books from the secular Uses of Salisbury, Hereford, and York, and from English monastic houses, but also the Breviary and Missal of the Use of the Roman (Papal) Curia.

There follows a series of practical sections listing the numbering and distribution of psalms, frequently used liturgical texts (in Latin and English), an annotated bibliography to assist the search for primary materials and further reading, and a glossary which either defines terms or refers to their discussion and definition in the text.

Much of the text is given over to the consideration of liturgical forms and orders between the tenth and the fifteenth centuries. These were the centuries when the Church's power, influence, and artistic patronage reached their zenith. After the ravages of the Dark Ages this was a time of liturgical continuity and stability, from the reforms of the Carolingian era (eighth and ninth centuries) until the Protestant Reformation (sixteenth century). And the richness of the liturgy in the later Middle Ages depended largely on flourishing communities committed to daily worship—canons, priests, and clerks in cathedral and collegiate churches; monks, friars, and nuns in religious houses. Their force was spent by the time of the Reformation, and the stability of liturgical order embodied in the Breviary and Missal of the Tridentine Rite and the Book of Common Prayer was very different. For the most part, the music and ceremonial of corporate worship were displaced in favour of functional (even private) daily recitation and occasional public celebration, resulting in a series of changed liturgical styles and values. Both before and after the Reformation kings and princes (not least the Pope as a prince) also maintained a religious establishment. Such a royal or noble chapel often assumed a status that extended beyond the spiritual needs of a court; its liturgy and music became an expression and embodiment of princely wealth, prestige, and power.

In the main this book is concerned with ordering of the liturgy rather than with individual items of music; and where there are specific references to sung texts these are generally associated with chant rather than polyphony. Musicians often tend to assume a higher profile for polyphony in the Middle Ages, because of the emphasis on it in musicological studies. But in most cathedrals, collegiate churches, and religious houses chant was the norm, and polyphony the exception. Where polyphony was used it was often regulated by ritual considerations. (As an instance, the ritual use of polyphony at Exeter Cathedral in the fourteenth century is tabulated in Frank Ll. Harrison, *Music in Medieval Britain* (London, 1958; 4th edn., Buren, 1980), p. 110.) Fortunately a great body of the chant is accessible in published form through the endeavours of scholars especially of the nineteenth and earlier twentieth centuries. Even more liturgical material from the Middle Ages can be found in printed editions without music published during the same period. (Some of these are introduced in Chapter 13.)

In spite of the passing of time and the ravages of religious upheaval in the West, large numbers of liturgical books survive from the tenth to the eighteenth centuries. Though consistent patterns are discerned in them (and this is especially so after the Tridentine reforms and the English Reformation), there was considerable variation from place to place and from century to century. Major variant Rites (such as the Ambrosian Rite still used—though reformed—in the Archdiocese of Milan, and the Mozarabic Rite which survives just in Toledo) have been omitted. There also have to be limitations on the extent of references and the noting of variants even within the mainstream of Western Latin liturgy. Of the non-Roman Churches only the Church of England is discussed. Other reformed Churches rarely compiled service books that were authorized or widely used, and they are not included.

While modern liturgists continue to concentrate on the formative periods of worship in the early Christian Church and their relation to present-day pastoral liturgy, the study of worship in the medieval, Renaissance, and Baroque eras remains somewhat neglected. Some of the best work on medieval Rites was done at the end of the last century: the scholarly integrity and method of many of these writers and editors were such that the value of their work is undiminished by time. Although current musical scholars and performers regularly address questions of liturgical order and practice, few can hope to emulate the knowledge and scholarly endeavour of such historical liturgists as W. H. Frere or J. B. L. Tolhurst, or of musicologists such as Peter Wagner and Frank Llewellyn Harrison. But this study makes an attempt to fill at least a part of the gap in our present understanding.

THE PRESENTATION OF LATIN TEXTS

The presentation of Latin varies, and readers need to be aware of possible confusions.

Medieval Latin sources have few capital letters and even less punctuation. They make frequent use of abbreviations and contractions of words. The letters *j* and *v* are rarely used as consonants (*i* and *u* appear instead), and diphthongs (i.e. *æ* and *œ*) are contracted to *e*.

Latin texts written after the Classical Renaissance are generally fuller and clearer in presentation. Capitals and diphthongs are used. More modern texts distinguish *j* and *v* as consonants.

Editors of Latin texts have varying policies. At one extreme, some may present a diplomatic (i.e. entirely literal) transcription; at the other, they may present a modernized edition. Most editors of medieval texts fall somewhere between the two, but it is important to be sure of their procedures.

The policy here is to use modernized Latin spelling with *j* (as initial letter), and *v*, and diphthongs in full. Capitals are used for initial words and proper names, but not for titles (thus, *Israel* but *deus* and *spiritus sanctus*). But what is presented here as *Jesus* may appear in original sources and printed editions as *iesus* (or *iesvs*), *ihesus*, *Iesus*, *Ihesus*, *jesus*, *jhesus*, *Jesus*, or *Jhesus*. This can be especially confusing when using an alphabetical index of texts in an edition.

English Texts

Where possible the English translations of Latin texts are taken from the Book of Common Prayer or the King James Authorized Version of the Bible. This seems most useful in a study related to Rites before the modern liturgical reforms, the more so since modern translations are often based on texts earlier than the medieval Latin sources. It also provides continuity between the translation of Latin texts and the English texts referred to in the chapter on the English Reformation and the Book of Common Prayer.

References and Bibliography

Though a broad pattern of Christian worship can be discerned, the specific nature of liturgical celebration is subject to historical and regional variations. Any general introduction has to be marked by caveats or qualified by detailed references. It has seemed more important to present an outline of the broad principles without extensive explicatory or qualifying footnotes which would have to be selective.

All the information relating to forms and orders of worship has been derived directly from primary sources (or from editions and facsimiles of them). For an English-speaking readership references are made most often to printed Roman books (especially from the fifteenth and sixteenth centuries) and to manuscript sources surviving from medieval foundations in England and generally available in printed editions and facsimiles. Further information about the order of many of these sources can be found in Chapter 13.

In the same way the Bibliography has been limited to an annotated list of selected primary and secondary sources that are particularly germane in basic study, and which will lead to other bibliographical information; a ready source for such additional information is Richard Pfaff's *Medieval Latin Liturgy: A Select Bibliography* (Toronto, 1982).

PART I.

Liturgy in the Western Church

What is Liturgy?

The ordered forms of Christian worship in the West emerged gradually during the first millennium, drawing on a variety of models, traditions, and influences. Western liturgy has never remained static in form or practice, but reached a crucial point of synthesis and stability in the tenth century. From this period it is possible to discern a consistency of liturgical observance supported by written sources that stretches to the present day. Two movements in the eighth and ninth centuries contributed to this: the reforms and codifications undertaken in the empire of Charlemagne and his successors, and the revitalization of Benedictine monasticism in northern Europe.

In spite of the constant flux and variation, it is possible to perceive six principal phases in the history of worship in the Western Church:

1. The formative period in the centuries immediately after Christ up to about the middle of the first millennium was a time when the main centres of influence were Mediterranean (e.g. Jerusalem, Antioch, Constantinople, Rome); here this period is referred to as 'early' or 'formative' (e.g. the early Church).

2. With the spread of Christianity to the outer limits of the Roman Empire (and beyond) important regional practices and repertories were established (e.g., in western Europe: Ambrosian, Beneventan, Celtic, Gallican, Mozarabic, Roman (known as 'Old Roman')); these emerged from the fourth century onwards, as did monasticism.

3. The attempt to codify and impose a unified pattern of ecclesiastical organization and worship in western Europe during the eighth and ninth centuries was a movement instigated in northern Europe by the Frankish emperor, Charlemagne, but based primarily on Roman practice. This was the Roman-Frankish Rite which became dominant throughout western Europe in the succeeding centuries; here it is referred to as 'medieval'.

4. A streamlined form of the medieval Rite (3 above) evolved to meet the needs of the Pope's chapel in Rome in the twelfth century, and

began to spread throughout Europe with the friars from the thirteenth century onwards. Sometimes referred to as Roman-Franciscan, here it is referred to as 'late medieval Roman' or 'the Use of the Papal Curia'.

5. In the later sixteenth century, after the Council of Trent, late medieval Roman Use (4) became the authorized, normative form of worship of the Roman Catholic Church internationally; this is the Tridentine Rite. Individual vernacular forms of worship were also established in the Protestant Churches that broke away from Roman authority in the sixteenth century (e.g. the Church of England, the Lutheran Church).

6. The principal Churches following 'Western' traditions (e.g. Roman Catholic, Anglican, Lutheran, etc.) have substantially revised their patterns of worship in the second half of the twentieth century; this is the modern liturgical movement, characterized in the Roman Catholic Church by the Second Vatican Council.

Partly as a result of these modern reforms, liturgy as a term and as an identified study has become more current in recent times. Its meaning and its parameters vary considerably. Derived from the Greek *leitourgia* (literally, the people's public service), in a Christian context it always relates to some aspect of formal worship. At its most limited it refers only to the celebration of the Eucharist (also known as the Mass or Holy Communion)—as in the fifth-century Liturgy of St James. More often it refers to the whole body and practice of corporate worship. Other current definitions exist: it may be specifically limited to the forms and orders of worship, or else identify the study of that worship.

In the context of this guide, liturgy embraces all the formal worship of a corporate Christian community. It embodies every aspect of that worship—the structure, the order, the text, the music, the movement, the vestments, the ornaments and vessels—and its relationship to the consecrated buildings in which it was enacted. Here, its consideration is limited to the period between the late tenth and the eighteenth centuries, and to the Western Church in Europe. The emphasis is on the mainstream Latin Rite derived principally from the liturgical practice broadly known as Roman. This Rite dominated Europe before the Reformation. Nevertheless there is reference to earlier liturgical formation. There is also consideration of the sixteenth-century provisions of the Tridentine Rite and the Book of Common

Prayer—orders of worship which draw on pre-Reformation models and practices (in the case of the Tridentine Rite very closely) and whose use extends into the twentieth century. In a written guide it is inevitable that there is more stress on orders and texts of the liturgy, rather than on ceremonial observance. And for the most part, pastoral, spiritual, and theological aspects of liturgy lie outside its scope.

Any perception of liturgy is coloured by personal experience (and probably prejudice). Those who have little knowledge of Christian worship or who belong to another religious culture will be largely alien to it. Those who are practising Christians may be conditioned by denominational outlook and local practices in all their contemporary diversity. Those brought up in the Church before 1960 may have memories of forms of worship that were far more rigid and consistent, and—in the case of Roman Catholics—celebrated in Latin.

In studying earlier liturgical practice one has to be receptive to contrasts of ethos and spirituality as well as of circumstance and style. It is tempting to assume that forms of worship in the undivided Western Church before the Reformation were consistent and static: though the language and basic structures were common, matters of detail, emphasis, and style varied over the centuries and from one place to another. Only with the advent of the authority and standardization afforded by printing and with the force of the Counter-Reformation did the Roman Catholic Church strive towards international uniformity in the sixteenth century, and even then with limited effect.

The variety and complexity of liturgical practice in the medieval Church required systematic codification. There was need for a written record of the content and manner of liturgical observance, very often in minute detail. It was important to do this in a medieval ecclesiastical foundation because the conduct of corporate worship was shared by the whole community from junior to senior, child to aged, often as many as a hundred or more men or women. Note had to be kept of what was to be done, (whether enacted, said, or sung); who was to do it; and when and how it was to be done.

Though the medieval books which include all this information are described in Chapter 4, it is important here to clarify three terms: *rite*, *ceremony*, and *use*.

Rite has a more limited connotation in Christian liturgy than in the anthropological sense. It relates specifically to order and content: it identifies what is to be said or done, and when. It may relate to a whole corpus of liturgical orders within a Church or denomination (e.g. Roman Rite), to a single order (e.g. Eucharistic rite), or to the elements of order and content (i.e. ritual elements). *Rite* (capital R) always refers to the whole liturgy of a Church. The Western Church has a Latin Rite, which by the sixth century may be subdivided into Roman Rite, Gallican Rite, Celtic Rite, and so on. From the eighth century onwards the Roman Rite dominated the Western Church. The use of *rite* (small r) is applied to all other uses of the word.

Ceremony is related to the conduct and style of an action or event. Ceremony can always be seen to be happening. It concerns the practical manifestation of the rite. It regulates who is to do something, and how they should do it. In later medieval liturgical books ritual and ceremonial instructions may be merged in *rubrics* (literally written in red) in the main body of the text.

Use identifies a regional, diocesan, or local variant of the Roman Rite. As a liturgical term it embraces all aspects of corporate worship; it may even extend to non-liturgical issues relating to duties and social order within the community. So, the Use of Salisbury indicates the liturgical observances followed in the cathedral at Salisbury (and in fact in the majority of English churches in the later Middle Ages). *Use* includes both *rite* and *ceremony*.

It is very important to be clear that the medieval Western Church was dominated by one Rite which may be described as Roman. Its liturgical structures were broadly comparable, and derived mostly from the Roman churches staffed by monks in the sixth and seventh centuries. It had two principal variant Uses, codified in the eighth and ninth centuries—often identified as secular and monastic. These two Uses are most readily contrasted by their differences in the order of the night Office of Matins. Within the two categories of secular and monastic there was a great variety of local Uses, many of them particular to a single diocese, region, or religious Order. Even in medieval Rome itself there was variety of liturgical practice. Because the Roman Use became synonymous with the Roman Rite in the centuries after the Counter-Reformation it can be tempting to impose the same concept of monolithic uniformity on the Middle Ages. Because the Use of Salisbury was widespread throughout medieval England, well documented, and comprehensively available in modern editions, it can be tempting to view it as a Rite rather than a Use, or as the main variant of Roman Use. Because monastic Use has received least attention in modern studies, it may easily be ignored in favour of its secular counterpart. It is important to be aware of these dangers, distortions, and oversimplifications.

All sources of instruction and information related to the conduct of the liturgy are concerned with establishing a series of norms, and qualifying them with variants and exceptions. Medieval liturgical practice is so rich and diffuse that norms are in themselves remarkably variable from Use to Use; and within Uses variants and exceptions differ from place to place, from manuscript to manuscript. Complexity, ambiguity, and confusion can deter the faint-hearted at every point in the struggle to piece together medieval liturgy. There is a tendency for sources to be frustratingly reticent on everyday matters which they take for granted. For the persistent, the stability of basic structures does become apparent, and the likely points of variance or inconsistency do emerge, but slowly and only after patient study!

I.

The Formation of Christian Liturgy: A Historical Summary

The Spread of Christian Worship

The earliest Christians were by race and religion Jews, and their worship was conducted in Jewish homes and in the Jewish synagogue and temple. They were familiar with the texts of the Old Testament, and the rites, ceremonies, and music they knew were Judaic. But the accounts of the Acts of the Apostles and the epistles of the New Testament underline the spread of Christianity to centres outside Palestine, to groups of people who had their own cultural and religious backgrounds. Jerusalem remained an influential centre until the seventh century. But expansion was rapid, and occurred predominantly within the bounds of the Roman Empire—to north and south around the Mediterranean Sea, and east towards Persia. The Roman Empire exerted its own influence, most importantly by extending recognition to the Christian religion by the Edict of Milan in 313. Christianity ceased to be a fragile, persecuted missionary religion: it achieved toleration and then widespread establishment in the Roman manner which implied order and codification.

The history of the formation of Christian liturgies in these early centuries is complex, difficult, and disputed. The relationship between early patterns of Christian prayer and Jewish worship is impossible to discern: no Jewish prayer-book survives from before the ninth century. The extant accounts of Christian worship in the first five centuries are scattered and often fragmentary. Nevertheless even by the sixth century it is possible to observe some common trends: the celebration of the Eucharist was separate from other formal public services; in other services the emphasis was on praise (especially in psalms) and prayer rather than on scriptural reading or teaching; daily attendance by the Christian community as a whole was most common at morning and evening prayer; monks and priests continued prayer at other times during the day and night.

Christian practice was exposed to local influences at every level, and this polarized in the two rival centres of the later Roman Empire—Rome and Constantinople (ancient Byzantium, modern Istanbul). The strength of the churches based in Rome under the leadership of the Pope and in Constantinople under the Patriarch led to growing independence and separation from the fifth century onwards, and total schism by the eleventh. The Latin Church was distanced from the Greek (Byzantine or Orthodox), as well as from the Syrian, Ethiopian, and Egyptian (Coptic) Churches, each imbued with individual traditions and styles.

The Latin Church dominated north-west Europe. But even here local and regional Rites prospered. In addition to the Roman Rite, important traditions emerged in the Ambrosian (Milan), Celtic (Ireland and northern Britain), Gallican (France), and Mozarabic (Spain) liturgies of the first millennium. These Rites were interrelated and overlapping, but distinct. In due course these independent Rites were either overtaken by Roman practice, or remained as isolated, local Rites. In Britain the northern Celtic Rites gave way to the Rite of Rome (at the Synod of Whitby (664) and the Council of Clovesho (747)); even so local Uses, and especially the ubiquitous Use of Salisbury, emerged and dominated the country's liturgical practice throughout the later Middle Ages.

Under Charlemagne and his successors the use of the Roman liturgy (albeit tinged with north European characteristics) was urged on the lands of the Frankish Empire during the eighth and ninth centuries. At its zenith, this empire, later known as the Holy Roman Empire, controlled most of central and northern Europe. The Roman Rite spread elsewhere: Spain was persuaded by the papacy to abandon the Mozarabic Rite in favour of the Roman from 1085, though it survives in Toledo. The Ambrosian Rite has continued to this day in the Archdiocese of Milan. The Gallican and Celtic Rites largely disappeared. Thus the Roman Rite, subjected to Frankish reform, dominated much of Europe, albeit with many regional, diocesan, and local Uses.

A second wave of Roman influence started to spread in the thirteenth century: this was the liturgy of the Papal Curia, the term now used to describe the court and administrative civil service of the Church based in Rome which worshipped in the Pope's chapel. Theirs was a liturgy intended for busy priests, cropped and streamlined for briefer recitation. It was conveniently compiled in Missal and Breviary, adopted by the new missionary order of Franciscan friars, and taken to every country in Europe.

MONASTICISM AND THE DAILY OFFICE

Within the Latin Church one movement was critically influential on liturgical formation—that of monasticism. Though the earliest monks lived alone as hermits in the Egyptian desert, it soon became their practice to live in community under a Rule (i.e. code of behaviour and practice), as was the case throughout the Western Church. (Hermits continued to be found throughout Christendom, but inevitably had little influence on medieval liturgy.)

In the fifth and sixth centuries, monks were important in Rome, where they conducted the liturgy in many of the Roman basilicas. Their liturgical practice in due course influenced the mainstream of Western liturgy, for monastic practice was the primary basis for the later medieval Roman Rite codified and promulgated under the Frankish emperors in the eighth and ninth centuries.

The figure who has come to be regarded as the father of Western monasticism is Benedict of Nursia (c.480–c.550). He drew up a Rule for his monks at Monte Cassino in Italy. It has proved the basis for the majority of monastic Orders—especially the most powerful and prolific Order, the Benedictines. St Benedict drew on earlier models, but his own Rule established most clearly and most humanely the principle of living in community under authority and with goods shared in common. The Rule also affirmed the centrality within the communal life of a constant pattern of daily prayer—*Opus Dei*, God's work, the so-called Divine Office—alongside study and manual work.

Benedict's Rule provides the most detailed account of the formation of the non-eucharistic cycle of daily prayer in the Western Church. It reflects both earlier and contemporary practices (including those of Roman basilicas served by monks), in the relationship of communal prayer to the natural cycle of the day. The monastic pattern in the West followed a sequence of prayer in the night (Matins), at dawn (Lauds), at four points in the day (Prime, Terce, Sext, and None—i.e. at the first, third, sixth, and ninth hours of the day), at dusk (Vespers) and before bed (Compline). The core of that daily prayer is the recitation of the Book of Psalms from the Old Testament. At each 'hour' (i.e. time) of prayer in the Divine Office the monastic Rules directed the recitation of a substantial portion of the psalter: the psalms constituted the major textual content of each service.

There were a number of monastic Rules in use during the sixth century. Benedict's was but one, though it was singled out in the centuries that followed. It was especially influential from the ninth century onwards. This was the time when the influence of the Frankish reformers was felt through much of the Western Church. While Alcuin (c.735–804) and Amalarius (c.780–850) turned to old Roman books for their reform of the 'secular' (i.e. non-monastic) liturgy, Benedict of Aniane (c.750–821) codified and extended the liturgical practice described in the sixth-century Rule of St Benedict. In turning to Rome, Alcuin and Amalarius drew on the liturgical practices used in churches staffed by monks in Rome during the fifth and sixth centuries. Thus, in the Middle Ages, the Roman (secular) and Benedictine (monastic) liturgies were related variants, both of earlier monastic origin. Monastic liturgical principles were adopted almost without exception throughout the Western Church. Their influence is evident even in modern forms of formal daily prayer.

THE MASS

Alongside the Divine Office the most important liturgical observance is that of the Mass. Again there is a complex and uncertain history of liturgical formation stretching back to Jewish practices. Within the Jewish Passover Christ instituted the celebration on the evening before the crucifixion ('Do this in remembrance of me'). Essentially the Mass is a fusion of two independent services of the early Church: a liturgy of readings and prayer, and a liturgy of thanksgiving with the blessing and sharing of bread and wine.

The formation of the order of Mass used in the medieval Western Church extended throughout the first Christian millennium. The evidence is piecemeal and still subject to scrutiny and controversy. However, the outline of the medieval Mass can be discerned in the document known as *Ordo Romanus Primus*, which describes Papal Mass as celebrated in a Roman basilica in the later seventh century. Such texts as *Kyrie, Gloria in excelsis, Sanctus*, and *Agnus dei* were assimilated into the order of the Mass, at least as celebrated in Rome, between about 325 and 700. *Credo in unum deum* (the Nicene Creed, compiled in its first form in 325) became a regular item of the Mass only in the eleventh century (as a measure against the risk of heresy). Its adoption marks the end of the process of liturgical codification stemming from the Frankish reforms of the eighth and ninth centuries.

LITURGICAL CHANGE IN THE LATER MIDDLE AGES

Though medieval liturgy continued to proliferate in form and detail, custom and text, the principal elements were stable by the tenth century, and a sufficient body of manuscript sources survives—both with and without music—to outline a framework which is relatively undisputed. But just as medieval architects and artists delighted in decoration and illustration, so too did liturgists—whether in cere-monial, text, or music. And for every movement that initiated new practices, there often followed a reforming zeal that imposed discipline or simplification: thus, within the broad movement of Benedictine monasticism, the rich and elaborate life of the monastery of Cluny (founded in 910 and influential throughout Europe in other 'Cluniac' monasteries) was embodied in its architecture and its liturgy, but this was countered later by the austerity and discipline of Cîteaux (founded 1098, the mother house of the Cistercian Order), whose reforming aesthetic extended to simplification and consistency in both buildings and liturgy.

The new regular Orders—not only Cistercian, but also Augustinian and Carthusian—exerted a reforming influence in the twelfth and thirteenth centuries. But it was a different religious movement that influenced the liturgy and spirituality of the Church more radically: this was the establishment of the mendicant Orders—the friars, the followers of St Francis of Assisi (1181/2–1226) and St Dominic (1170–1221). Though these Orders lived under a Rule and had communal houses, they were primarily missionaries; their preaching and teach-ing took place away from the enclosure; unlike monks or regular canons, the friars were often widely travelled. Like the busy administrators of the Papal Curia worshipping in the chapel of the Lateran Palace in Rome, the Franciscans (Order of Friars Minor) needed a compact form of daily prayer. The interaction of influences between Curia and Franciscans resulted in the late medieval form of the Roman Office, and in the portable Office book, the Breviary. The friars took both Roman Office and Breviary with them throughout Europe.

The Franciscans were influential in nurturing popular devotion, but intellectually and educationally the Dominicans were the more powerful, not least in the expanding medieval universities. Of the Dominicans, St Thomas Aquinas (c. 1225–74) deserves special mention. He revalued contemporary theological thinking in the light of the newly rediscovered (pre-Christian) philosophy of Aristotle. His writings proved a basis for much of the subsequent doctrine of the Roman Church (especially that of the Mass), and influenced its spirituality profoundly. The extent of his influence is remarkable in an age that relied on manuscript circulation of texts and oral transmission of ideas—modes of communication that encourage local variants and patchy reform.

Were Aquinas to be cited here only for the liturgical texts attributed to him (*Lauda Sion*, *Pange lingua gloriosi*, *Verbum supernum*), it would be to ignore the theology and spirituality that lie behind liturgy. Their consideration is beyond the scope of an outline like this, as too are the secular thinking and philosophy that underpin the contemporary intellectual and artistic revolution of the Renaissance. But taken together these intellectual trends, sacred and secular, represented a great threat to the late medieval Church.

REFORMATION AND COUNTER-REFORMATION

As an organization the medieval Church was enormous, complex, and disparate. Alongside the glories of its art, intellect, and prayer were the disputes, the corruption, the religious wars, and the scandal of the schismatic papacy of the fourteenth century (with rival papal courts at Rome and Avignon). Cross-currents of new thinking, reform, and revaluation caused healthy turbulence in the steady flow of the Church's life. But the dissatisfaction was widespread and the intellectual acerbity more incisive by the end of the fifteenth century. Printing accelerated the spread and enlarged the distribution of new ideas, bringing with it the authority of consistency unavailable in manuscript. With its aid the challenge of humanistic thought spread rapidly in northern Europe. Printing was also vital in the dissemination of new theological ideas. And in due course it was a means to achieving the uniformity and conformity that were characteristic of both the Reformation and the Counter-Reformation, and which extended to the liturgy.

Regular clergy and academics were among the prime movers in the reforming movements of northern Europe. Martin Luther (1483–1546), the instigator of the whole Protestant Reformation, was an Augustinian; Martin Bucer (1491–1551), influential in England as well as abroad, was a Dominican. The humanist thinker Erasmus (1469–1536) was also an Augustinian. And in England, the theological aspects of the Reformation were fired by intellectuals in the universities of Oxford and Cambridge. While both the Lutheran and English Churches retained some forms and items of the old rites, the simplification of liturgy and the new theological and scriptural emphases were radical. In England this was embodied in the Book of Common Prayer, a book which still remains the authorized prayer-book of the Church of England; but no book of equivalent authority and widespread use ever emerged in the Lutheran Church, except in Scandinavia.

Realignment, reform, and strengthening of the Roman Catholic Church also extended to the liturgy and its music. The drawn-out sessions of the Council of Trent (1545–63) and the subsequent directives from the Pope in Rome led to new authority, internal stability, and invigorated spirituality. Missionary and educational initiative moved from the friars to the newly founded, spiritually militant Order of the Jesuits (Society of Jesus, founded by St Ignatius Loyola (1491/5–1556)). New devotional and spiritual fervour was inspired by St Philip Neri (1515–95) and resulted in confraternities and congregations who met in oratories (hence the later musical genre of oratorio).

The new directions of teaching, devotion, and spirituality did not affect the liturgy overtly: the form and content were consolidated and enshrined in the printed Roman Breviary (1568) and Missal (1570). But the new spiritual climate did result in extraliturgical and paraliturgical observances, many related to devotion to the Blessed Sacrament and with their own musical repertory and traditions.

The stability achieved by the Tridentine liturgical reform is indisputable. But local variants were not entirely extinguished; indeed some reappeared, notably in France where, even in the eighteenth century, individual dioceses followed their own liturgical Uses. More generally the initial zeal was followed by progressive erosion of liturgical completeness. Corporate recitation of the Office was still expected, but it no longer dominated the life of the clergy as their principal occupation: elaborate musical and ceremonial celebration of the Office was often limited to Vespers on Sunday and great feasts. Though never formally sanctioned, private recitation of the Office out of church was often accepted as the norm for parish clergy. It also became common in the seventeenth century for motets with devotional eucharistic texts (or instrumental music) to displace the prescribed proper texts at sung Mass.

The fundamental patterns of liturgy established in the sixteenth century persisted until the second half of the twentieth century. But this book does not concern itself with the period after 1800. The power and the patronage of the Church waned: great composers, artists, and sculptors directed their efforts elsewhere for the most part. And throughout the nineteenth and earlier twentieth centuries there were signs of liturgical change: the suppression of French monasteries at the Revolution, the new interest in early sources of chant edited by the monks of Solesmes, the revisions to the Breviary under Pius X (1911); and in England the Oxford movement, and the attempt to produce a revised Prayer Book (1928). These and other factors pointed towards the watershed of liturgical revision and reformation that resulted in the new orders, language, and pastoral theology of the 1960s.

2.

Liturgy and the Medieval Church

MEDIEVAL CLERICS, RELIGIOUS, AND THEIR CHURCHES

The conduct of liturgy in the medieval Western Church was the prerogative of the clergy and religious. The manner in which they celebrated the liturgy depended on the community and church in which they served. Without attempting an outline or history of the organization of the Church, a summary examination of clerics and religious may help towards an understanding of liturgical practices.

The Secular Clergy

The ministers of the Church are known as the clergy. The secular clergy need to be distinguished from religious: the term 'secular' (first used in the twelfth century) properly denotes those who have access to the outside world, as opposed to those who are withdrawn from the world in a religious enclosure (i.e. monks and nuns). In practice, 'secular' identifies all those clergy who are not bound by vows to a religious Order.

The clergy receive their spiritual authority by ordination—the laying on of hands—a practice handed on from generation to generation, and originating with the apostles (hence the apostolic succession). There is a series of ranks of ordination, established in the earliest centuries of Christianity, and divided into two groups of clerical Orders—major and minor. The Major (or Holy) Orders are (in ascending rank) those of deacon, priest, and bishop. Each has specific sacramental authority: for instance, a deacon may baptize, a priest may celebrate the Eucharist and grant absolution, a bishop may confirm and ordain. In 1207 in the Western Church the order of subdeacon, previously regarded as a Minor Order, was added as the most junior of the Major Orders.

All those in Holy (i.e. Major) Orders were obliged to be celibate.

They were required to recite the full Divine Office daily, and from about the eleventh century it also became customary for every priest to celebrate Mass daily.

The Minor Orders were more obviously associated with practical tasks in the liturgy: in descending rank, acolyte (an assistant in the sanctuary at Mass), exorcist (an important function in the early Church), lector (or reader), and porter (or door-keeper). Those in Minor Orders (often referred to as 'clerks') were not bound to be celibate.

Distinction needs to be made between the Order to which a cleric was ordained, and the office or rank he held. When a priest was consecrated as a bishop his clerical Order changed. At the same time he was appointed to the office of bishop, generally with charge of a diocese (an area subdivided into small parishes staffed by clergy over whom he had authority). As a bishop his rank might change: he might be nominated a cardinal by the Pope, and as a cardinal he was an elector of a new Pope, and indeed might be a candidate for that election. But whether cardinal or Pope, his clerical Order remained that of bishop and his primary duty as pastor to clergy and people in his care was unaltered.

So far as the liturgical formation was concerned, the Pope and the local diocesan bishop were the most influential figures. The Pope had ultimate authority in the Western Church (and he, of course, remains supreme pontiff of the Roman Catholic Church). The mainstream of liturgical practice was centred on Rome, and it was the Pope and his senior ministers who instigated the major Councils (i.e. the sixteenth-century Council of Trent). The Roman Rite was the Rite of the Western Church.

At a local level, the bishop had authority over the secular clergy in his diocese. And it was in the dioceses that variants of the Western Rite flourished as local liturgical Uses. Such Uses were subject to the influence of the bishop, and normally reflected the practice of his cathedral church (i.e. the church where his episcopal throne was placed).

In due course, a third influence was critical in the Western Church. Around the Pope in Rome was a large and busy court (Curia), active in diplomacy as well as ecclesiastical administration. While other clergy could devote much of their time to the daily Office and Mass, the clergy in the Papal Curia had a busy life outside the liturgy. Consequently, during the thirteenth and fourteenth centuries, the liturgical practices of the Curia became more succinct (influenced by and influencing the burgeoning Order of Friars Minor—the Franciscans, discussed under 'The Friars' below). In due course this Use of the Papal Curia became the most significant Use in Rome, and the principal source of the sixteenth-century Tridentine Rite.

Secular Churches

Throughout medieval Europe two kinds of secular church building were prevalent: the parish church and the collegiate church.

Parish churches were the most numerous: each parish district was served by such a church, and there were often several hundred in every diocese. But their liturgical establishment was small—perhaps no more than a priest and an assisting clerk—and in most instances they followed the Use of a larger church (often the local cathedral) rather than instigating their own customs. Where a parish church had more elaborate liturgical provision this was often dependent on the resources of an associated foundation—chantry, college, confraternity, or guild—which used part of the building or an adjoining chapel.

Far more important in the Middle Ages were the collegiate churches. The tendency for holy people to group together and share daily worship dates back to the earliest days of the Church, and in the eighth century Chrodegang of Metz (d. 766) devised a code of conduct for priests who shared a common pattern of life and especially common worship. Colleges (i.e. communities) of priests and other clerics were founded throughout Europe, and often represented the largest and richest churches in a diocese.

A collegiate church was founded and governed by statutes, legal provisions which defined the nature and function of the institution. The community usually consisted of a group of canons (i.e. clerics bound by the provisions of the statutes) who shared responsibility for the running of the foundation, one of whom (often given the title of dean, *decanus*) presided over the liturgy and over business. Unlike a parish church whose priest had pastoral care of the people living in the parish, a collegiate foundation was self-sufficient and self-contained; it was primarily a praying community.

Smaller colleges might consist of no more than a dean and six canons. But the richer collegiate foundations had perhaps forty or more canons as well as a number of assisting clerics—minor canons and clerks. And because canons were frequently (sometimes permanently) absent from the liturgy, they employed substitutes—vicars—to undertake their duties in church. Though all the adults in a collegiate foundation were clerics, none were of necessity priests. In practice, a substantial number were priests, but there were canons who remained in Minor Orders: rank and clerical Order did not necessarily coincide. There were also young boys (often beginning an education for the priesthood) who had a place in the liturgy of a collegiate foundation. Often the community numbered well over a hundred.

A large collegiate church was commonly used as the cathedral in a diocese. Here the bishop had his throne, but the dean and canons were responsible for the running of the cathedral church and the direction of the liturgy. And in many great collegiate churches the liturgy and its chant were exceptionally fine. More details of their conduct are given in the second part of this chapter.

Other Secular Institutions

Some mention ought to be made of two other categories of institution which were effectively collegiate: the chantry and the household chapel. The chantry was normally a modest establishment, sometimes attached to or within the building of another church (a series of them often accounted for the many 'side' chapels in medieval cathedrals). A chantry was generally endowed by an individual or a family, and a priest or small group of clerics was engaged to say daily Mass and Office for the soul(s) of the patron(s). Where the group of clerics was large enough it was constituted as a college with a presiding officer (e.g. dean or warden), and was able to sing the daily observances corporately.

Kings, princes, and nobles often maintained an ecclesiastical retinue as part of their court or household. Such a household chapel normally accompanied the head of the house on his travels with the rest of his entourage. In some cases these chapels (and especially Chapels Royal) were prestigious musical foundations of considerable size. They were funded as a department of the household, but internally organized in the manner of a college with a dean (or equivalent) as superior. They were often important employers of professional lay musicians. One of the most significant household chapels was that of the Pope, subsequently based in the Sistine Chapel.

In England a third category of collegiate institution proved liturgically significant. During the later fourteenth century and especially during the fifteenth century a series of colleges was established which were primarily educational establishments. Though study was always an important feature of monastic life, and many monastic and secular institutions supported schools within or alongside the foundation, these new colleges were distinct. They effectively separated study and teaching (undertaken by fellows and scholars) from much of the preparation and conduct of the liturgy in the collegiate chapel (chaplains, clerks, and choristers). These chapel foundations provided much of the basis for the great flowering of polyphony in late fifteenth-century England.

The Religious

The religious consisted of both men and women. They included monks, nuns, regular canons, canonesses, and friars. All religious lived under the authority of a Rule (hence the term 'regular', from *regula*). They were bound to live according to the requirements of the Rule, and in obedience to an elected superior; monks, nuns, and friars (but not all regular canons) shared goods and life in common; all were celibate. The earliest monks (of the third and fourth centuries) were laymen committed to prayer. In subsequent centuries many more were ordained, but in the Middle Ages this did not include all religious (least of all any religious women). Each religious made a commitment to the Rule by vows, and progressed through a series of states of profession: postulant, novice, first profession (simple vows), final profession (solemn vows). The religious were organized as a series of Orders, each following a specific Rule.

Monastic Orders

The adjective 'monastic' is often used rather loosely. It can embrace both monks and nuns, and extend to regular canons and canonesses. In this sense it refers to those who live by a Rule and whose primary purpose is prayer (by contrast with active Orders such as friars).

The most important Orders of monks and nuns were the Benedictines, the Cluniacs, the Cistercians, and the Carthusians. Liturgically the most significant (and the most numerous) were the Benedictines, Cluniacs, and Cistercians, who all observed the Rule of St Benedict. Benedictine monasteries were autonomous, and although there were influences from one house to another, local customs and liturgical practices emerged in individual communities. The Cluniacs and Cistercians were centrally organized: each Order followed the customs and practices of the mother-house, respectively the rich elaboration of Cluny and the austere simplicity (at least in its first century) of Cîteaux. The Carthusians were the most severe: they evolved their own Rule and liturgical traditions. The liturgical formation of monasteries following the Rule of St Benedict is frequently referred to as 'monastic' Use (in contrast with secular Use, and regardless of the practices of Orders such as the Augustinians); it is another example of the range of application of the adjective.

A large number of foundations followed the Rule of St Augustine (of Hippo) but they are harder to categorize. The Rule of St Augustine is far less precise than that of St Benedict: it was based on a letter of guidance written in 423 to some nuns in North Africa. After its revival in the eleventh century, the nature of the communities which adopted the Rule varied considerably. Some were more strictly monastic in character (e.g. Premonstratensians), others were mendicant (Augustinian or Austin friars), but the majority were regular canons and canonesses—communities of men or women observing the full cycle of liturgical prayer. On the Continent the Augustinian canons staffed many of the cathedrals (in England they had charge of Carlisle). As their name suggests, the canons were all clerics.

The regular canons and canonesses may be distinguished from other 'monastic' Orders. First, although they were bound by the Rule of St Augustine, they also lived under the authority of the local bishop (whereas many monastic houses were less beholden or—in the case of Cistercians and some individual Benedictine houses—entirely exempt from diocesan authority). Second, many of the early communities of regular canons already existed as a group of clergy staffing a collegiate church. Third, unlike the majority of other monasteries, most Augustinian houses adopted the liturgical customs and practices of the local diocese, making minor adaptations for observances kept by the Order. Though the pattern of life and layout of buildings was much the same as in a Benedictine monastery, the liturgical Use of an Augustinian church was scarcely distinguishable from 'secular' Use.

Monastic communities, like collegiate institutions, could range from less than ten to well over a hundred monks. But a monk could not resign or move, unlike a secular canon or clerk. And the superior of a monastic community was not appointed but elected by the community (in theory at least). In larger monasteries the superior was generally an abbot (in convents of nuns, an abbess), but in smaller communities (or in cathedral monasteries where the bishop was titular abbot) the prior presided in church and chapter house. Cathedral monasteries were a particular feature in medieval England: almost half the cathedrals were staffed by Benedictine monks.

The business of the monastery was conducted by the whole community in the chapter house. Though the distinct ranks of canon, minor canon, and clerk were not found in monasteries, duties were allocated within the community and seating was arranged in church by seniority. The conduct of the monastic liturgy is discussed further below.

Some monastic Orders also included lay brothers or lay sisters, sometimes called *conversi*. These were often men or women from the lower social echelons, poorly educated and illiterate. They made limited vows and had their own, less complex, liturgy conducted in a separate part of the monastic church. Cistercian houses used them in great numbers to run their extensive farming operations.

The Friars

The importance of the new Orders of friars from the thirteenth century onwards has been observed in Chapter 1. Here it is important to distinguish them and their liturgical practices from other religious. Unlike the majority of religious, they abandoned the cloistered life and worked outside the community as pastors, preachers, and teachers. Though friars were based in a community with its own church, the liturgy was a basis for their pastoral mission outside the walls of the friary, rather than an end in itself. The principal Orders had strong associations with the papacy and with Rome. The friars were very strictly committed to poverty and held no endowments (corporate or individual): they relied on donations of money, and were thus known as mendicant (i.e. begging) Orders. They were dominated by the

Franciscans (Order of Friars Minor, sometimes known as Grey Friars), Dominicans (Order of Preachers, so-called Black Friars), Carmelites (Order of Our Lady of Mount Carmel, known as White Friars), and Augustinians (Austin Friars).

So far as liturgy is concerned, the long-term impact of Franciscan devotion and Dominican theology should not be underestimated. More specifically the close relationship with the Curia in Rome encouraged the Franciscans to adapt Roman (Curial) Use and mould the liturgy to their needs. The combined influence of Curia and Franciscans was critical in the formation of the so-called Roman Breviary, a self-contained portable Office book, and of a style of liturgy that was stripped of excess, and better suited for recitation by men with other important work besides *Opus Dei*. St Dominic adopted the Use of the Premonstratensian canons for his friary churches.

After the Reformation

So far as Protestant countries were concerned, monasteries, friaries, and chantries were dissolved in the process of Reformation, as were most collegiate foundations. Where the new denominations abandoned bishops and diocesan organization, the cathedral foundations were also disbanded. The parish became the primary unit of pastoral care and the liturgy was directed to the people of the parish. Within the Church of England the cathedrals were maintained as collegiate churches; indeed their number was increased. A relatively small number of collegiate foundations also survived: the colleges of Oxford, Cambridge, Eton, and Winchester, the medieval college of St George within Windsor Castle, and the newly founded college of St Peter in Westminster (formerly the abbey). Modest colleges were subsequently re-established in a few other institutions (e.g. Manchester, Ripon).

The impetus in the Roman Catholic Church moved away from collegiate and monastic foundations in the Counter-Reformation. Some of the most important movements in public worship were devotional rather than strictly liturgical and derived from the lay confraternities, especially in Italy, while the new Orders of clerks regular, notably the Society of Jesus, became far more powerful than the surviving monastic Orders.

Selected Examples of Medieval Ecclesiastical Institutions in England

Collegiate church	Beverley; Ripon; Southwell
Collegiate church serving as cathedral	Chichester; Hereford; St Paul's, London; Wells; York
Collegiate church combined with parish church	Manchester; Ottery St Mary, Devon; Tattershall, Lincolnshire
Educational college	King's College, Cambridge; Eton College; New College, Oxford
Chantry with collegiate organization	Fotheringhay, Northants; St William's College, York
Hospital with collegiate organization	St Mary in the Newark, Leicester
Monastic church:	
Augustinian	Bristol; Hexham; St Frideswide's, Oxford (now Christ Church); Southwark; Lacock, Wiltshire (canonesses)
Benedictine	Chester; Gloucester; Peterborough; St Albans; Tewkesbury; Romsey (nuns)
Carthusian	Mount Grace, North Yorkshire; Witham, Somerset
Cistercian	Fountains; Furness; Rievaulx; Kirklees (nuns)
Cluniac	Castle Acre, Norfolk
Monastic church serving as cathedral	Carlisle (Augustinian); Canterbury; Durham; Norwich; Winchester; Worcester (all Benedictine)
Monastic church with aisle or nave used as parish church	Dorchester, Oxfordshire; (Benedictine); Edington, Wiltshire (Augustinian)
Monastic church with hospital	St Bartholomew, Smithfield, London (Augustinian)

St Frideswide's, Oxford, Bristol, Chester, Gloucester, and Peterborough were refounded as secular collegiate churches serving as cathedrals in the early 1540s, after the dissolution of the monasteries. Other former collegiate and monastic churches did not become cathedrals until the nineteenth and early twentieth centuries: Manchester, Ripon, St Albans, Southwark, Southwell.[1]

---

[1] The most extensive archival work on English foundations has been undertaken by Roger Bowers. See his doctoral dissertation 'Choral Institutions within the English Church: Their Constitutions and Development 1340–1500', (University of East Anglia, 1975).

The Ordering of Collegiate and Monastic Buildings

Both collegiate and monastic foundations consisted of communities committed to corporate daily celebration of Mass and the Divine Office. However, as we have observed above, their constitutional and physical characteristics were different.

Monastic buildings are easily identified (see FIG. 2.1). They were closely grouped and self-contained, reflecting the communal pattern of existence. Placed around the cloister were all the main centres of monastic life: church (prayer), chapter house (business), refectory (sustenance), and dormitory (sleep). The cloister itself served for study and manuscript copying in many instances. Outside the main group of buildings were kitchen, store-houses, guest-houses, infirmary (for the sick of the monastic community), and often a separate lodging for the superior of the house. The whole site was normally enclosed by a gated wall. Though some Benedictine monasteries were established in towns and cities, many reformed Orders (e.g. Cistericans) set out to choose remote sites.

Unlike the monks, members of a collegiate foundation had individual accommodation around but not attached to the church. Because they had stipends and the right to personal wealth many lived in houses of considerable size. Collegiate churches tended to stand on their own, often in open spaces or squares with no other buildings close by (see FIG. 2.2). There was normally an adjoining chapter house and perhaps a cloister intended primarily for processions. The houses of the canons were the most substantial and were grouped around the church (often in a close). Those of the vicars and clerks were more modest: an outstanding surviving example may be seen at Wells where the medieval Vicars' Close consists of two parallel rows of terraced houses with a common hall at one end and a gateway with stairs to the cathedral at the other.

Whether monastic or secular, the dominant building was the church. Even where there was a large medieval community the scale of the church far exceeded the immediate needs of providing a sacred building for the daily Mass and Office. Though some churches were never completed (e.g. Beauvais) and many were subject to rebuilding and restructuring, they were most often planned to be cruciform with presbytery and choir in the east, nave in the west, and at least one pair

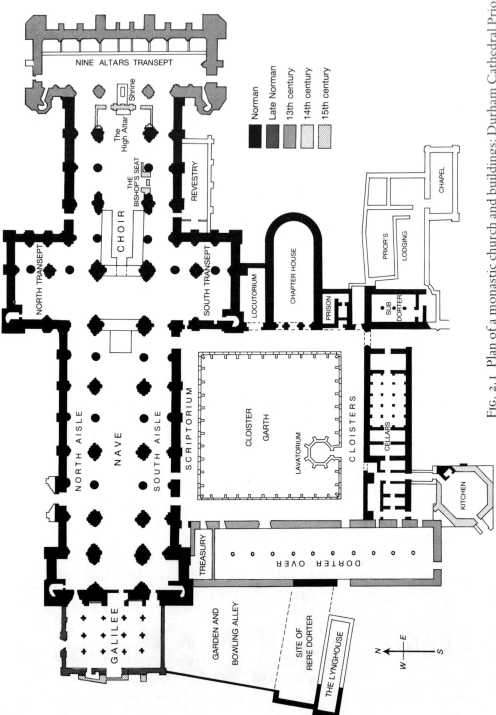

NINE ALTARS TRANSEPT

Shrine

The High Altar

THE BISHOP'S SEAT

CHOIR

REVESTRY

NORTH TRANSEPT

SOUTH TRANSEPT

LOCUTORIUM

CHAPTER HOUSE

PRISON

SUB DORTER

PRIOR'S LODGING

CHAPEL

NORTH AISLE

NAVE

SOUTH AISLE

SCRIPTORIUM

CLOISTER GARTH

LAVATORIUM

CLOISTERS

CELLARS

KITCHEN

GALILEE

TREASURY

DORTER OVER

GARDEN AND BOWLING ALLEY

SITE OF RERE DORTER

THE LYNGHOUSE

Norman
Late Norman
13th century
14th century
15th century

N
W — E
S

FIG. 2.1 Plan of a monastic church and buildings: Durham Cathedral Priory

Fig. 2.2 Plan of a secular collegiate church: Lincoln Cathedral

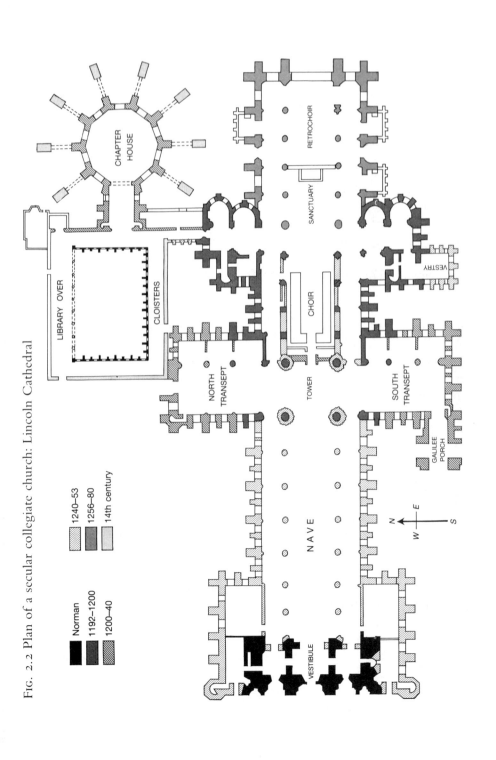

Norman
1192–1200
1200–40
1240–53
1256–80
14th century

LIBRARY OVER

CHAPTER HOUSE

CLOISTERS

RETROCHOIR

SANCTUARY

NORTH TRANSEPT

CHOIR

VESTRY

TOWER

SOUTH TRANSEPT

GALILEE PORCH

NAVE

VESTIBULE

N
W — E
S

of transepts forming the north and south. In this, Christian symbolism meets up with structural common sense (particularly where there is a central tower).

In many cases today, the appearance of the interior of a medieval church is misleading—even more so since the reordering effected by the liturgical changes since the 1960s. During the later Middle Ages, even small parish churches were divided by a screen, so that the eastern end of the church where the priest celebrated Mass and said the Office was only partly visible from the nave. The principal altar was at the far east beyond the screen. In the cathedral, collegiate, and monastic churches these screens were even more substantial, often made of stone, and more than ten feet deep. The vista now apparent in the secular cathedrals of Hereford and Salisbury, or in the monastic cathedrals of Durham and Winchester, is misleading: the choir screen has been removed. Though the secular cathedrals of Exeter and Wells and the monastic cathedral of Norwich each maintains its choir screen, it now bears a large organ. More typical of the medieval appearance are Chichester (secular) and Canterbury (monastic), where the choir screens are retained. However, it has to be said that this is not the case throughout Europe: as early as the twelfth century the great Abbot Suger had no place for a choir screen in his new monastery church of St Denis, and in the period after the Council of Trent, the late Renaissance and Baroque churches were more open in design. The basilica of St Peter's, Rome, is a classic example.

Apart from processions, the main *cursus* (i.e. cycle) of the daily Office and Mass was celebrated in the eastern part of the church—the choir (or quire) and presbytery (or sanctuary). When there, the whole community constituted 'the choir'. This was true of both monastic and secular foundations. It is important to understand the basic ordering of this part of the church, which was much the same in both kinds of community.

There were three important areas within this enclosed part of the collegiate or monastic church (see FIG. 2.3):

1. At the eastern end, there was the presbytery (sanctuary) with the high altar where Mass was celebrated by a priest (or bishop) and assisting ministers.
2. Adjoining the presbytery was the choir (quire). Here the community was ranged in two halves facing one another on the north and

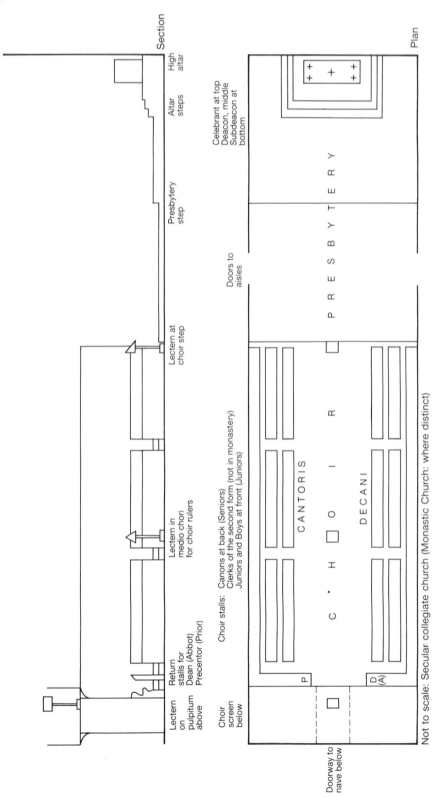

Section

High altar

Altar steps

Presbytery step

Lectern at choir step

Lectern in medio chori for choir rulers

Return stalls for Dean (Abbot) Precentor (Prior)

Lectern on pulpitum above

Choir screen below

Doorway to nave below

Celebrant at top Deacon, middle Subdeacon at bottom

Doors to aisles

Choir stalls: Canons at back (Seniors)
Clerks of the second form (not in monastery)
Juniors and Boys at front (Juniors)

PRESBYTERY

CANTORIS

C H O I R

DECANI

P

D
(A)

Plan

Not to scale: Secular collegiate church (Monastic Church: where distinct)

FIG. 2.3 Diagrams of a medieval choir and presbytery

south sides. On each side there were rows of stalls or benches, junior at the front, senior at the back. In monasteries there were normally two rows of stalls; in cathedrals there were three (the canons sat in the back row). At the south-west corner sat the senior member of the community (dean, abbot, or abbess); at the north-west corner sat the next senior (most often precentor, i.e. chief cantor). The two sides of the choir are named after these principal officers: *decani*, the side of the dean, and *cantoris*, the side of the chief cantor or precentor. There were two lecterns in the choir: one at the eastern end, generally at the choir step (used by readers and by soloists); the other in the middle of the choir (*in medio chori*) and mostly used by the ruler or rulers of the choir (*rector chori*), who began and directed much of the choral chant.

3. The third area was the choir screen at the western extremity of the choir. There was normally a platform (pulpitum) on top of the screen. On Sundays and feast-days the Epistle, Gradual, Alleluia, and Gospel of the Mass were sung from the top of the screen in some Uses. There was a staircase within the screen or an adjacent wall to give access to the upper level, and a lectern for the books.

THE RELATIONSHIP OF ORDER IN CHOIR AND MUSIC

There was clear delineation throughout medieval liturgical instructions as to who should sing each item and the place in the church where it should be sung.

Each item of the liturgy required someone to begin it. This varied according to the item, and according to the rank of the day. In the Mass a number of items were begun or recited by the celebrant, deacon, or subdeacon (see the description in Chapter 5). In the Office the minister's parts were mostly sung by the duty cleric for the week (*hebdomadarius*), though absolutions and blessings were generally given by the senior priest present. In both Mass and Office the choral chants were begun and the solo sections sung by members of the choir, often of different rank and seniority.

The 'beginners' and soloists were chosen by the precentor and set out on a weekly basis in the *tabula* (table). The two sides of the choir alternated for these duties each week (a practice still observed in some cathedral choirs where the music list may specify 'Verses: *Decani*' or 'Verses: *Cantoris*'). The number of beginners and soloists singing each item differed according to the rank of the day (from one or two to as many as four or five on principal feasts). The place from which they sang also varied: either their normal place in choir, or else one of the lecterns.

Thus the ritual ordering of the liturgy was articulated by ceremonial observance. Each member of the community had a part to play: it was in a very modern sense a corporate liturgy so far as the celebration in choir was concerned.

NUNS AND CANONESSES

The communities of women raise special liturgical problems. In the Middle Ages there were very large numbers of women in religious Orders—both nuns and canonesses; even the Franciscan friars had their counterpart in the Poor Clares (who remained enclosed). Many were daughters of great families, intelligent and well educated. Taking as an example the English Benedictine convent at Romsey (Hampshire), the surviving church is witness to the stature of the community, while the succession of abbesses underlines their high social rank, among them close relations of English kings.

While nuns and regular canonesses were usually well able to administer their communities and manage their endowments and lands, they were subject to limitations within the liturgy. No woman could be ordained even into Minor Orders: nuns therefore relied on clerics to undertake all the sacraments in their community. Most obviously, a priest and assisting ministers were required to celebrate Mass each day, as at most of the special ceremonies of Holy Week. There were fewer problems within the Divine Office: here a nun had the same status as an unordained monk.

The Ordinal of the Benedictine abbey of Barking (1404) shows how the nuns shared the duties with the priest and other ministers.[2] While the priest began the Office, other duties normally undertaken by the duty priest for the week (*hebdomadarius*) were carried out by the weekly duty nun (*hebdomadaria*) including the singing of the collect. The nuns also acted as rulers, beginners, and soloists: they carried out all the normal choir duties both at Mass and in the Office. The sharing

[2] Information derived from the text of *The Ordinale and Customary of the Benedictine Nuns of Barking Abbey*, ed. J. B. L. Tolhurst (2 vols., Henry Bradshaw Society, 65, 66; 1927–8).

of duties was particularly elaborate in Holy Week (at the end of which
the nuns acted out the Harrowing of Hell and the Easter Sepulchre
drama). Here it is clear that the abbess performed some duties normally
reserved for priests: on occasion she gave abbatial absolution and
blessing to members of the community.

In the main nuns wore only their choir habit. They did not vest in
surplices, albs, or copes for feast-days: these were clerical vestments.
However, the example of Barking seems to prove exceptional, for
there the convent dressed *in vestibus albis* (in white robes) on at least
four specified important saint's days.

In some instances communities of men and women lived in adjacent
monasteries. Though segregated, they shared the same church. This
so-called *Doppel-Kloster* was most prevalent among Augustinians on
the Continent. In England it was found only in the small number of
houses which belonged to the Augustinian-related Order established
by Gilbert of Sempringham in the twelfth century.

THE PLACE OF THE PEOPLE IN MEDIEVAL LITURGY

For the people the situation was very different. The medieval liturgy
had little place for the active involvement of the laity. Their role was
passive and devotional. Even in modest parish churches the priest was
distanced physically from the people at the east end. The principal
celebration took place behind the choir screen (a common feature by
the fifteenth century), partially if not totally obscured. Though the
Epistle and Gospel may have been proclaimed from the top of such a
screen, such crucial parts of the Mass as the consecration were private,
unheard. The people needed a bell to warn them that the Canon of the
Mass was beginning and that, in due course, the priest had blessed
the bread and wine, and (from the thirteenth century onwards) that he
was raising the consecrated bread for all to see (the elevation).

By the fifteenth century there was some response to the presence of
the people: in the Salisbury Use vernacular prayers were said towards
the end of the procession before the Mass (the Bidding of Bedes), and
in some churches there were vernacular prayers at the Offertory. But
for the most part the laity were excluded entirely from active participation in both Mass and Office, even in parish churches. Their
exclusion was more evident in the great churches where they might go

on pilgrimage or attend a major festival: they were generally confined to the nave where only the processions were visible.

Such a passive stance may seem unacceptable today, and it is important to understand the way in which medieval liturgy did involve the whole of a community in a monastery or collegiate church: the corporate body was the choir, not a selected group of able singers. But this celebration was effectively enclosed: those present from outside the immediate community could (perhaps) watch from the nave, and pray, but little more. Nevertheless, the fervour of devotion (especially to the Virgin and the Blessed Sacrament) and the spread of popular Offices (evident in surviving Books of Hours) attest to the liveliness of lay spirituality.

POLYPHONY AND POLYPHONIC CHOIRS

There is little mention of polyphony in Part II of this study. Medieval liturgy was sung predominantly to chant. Where there was polyphonic embellishment it was often restricted to solo sections of chanted items (see the repertory of *organa* from twelfth-century Paris). The choir (i.e. the community) sang the chant. Too often the remaining fragments of written medieval polyphony draw close attention at the expense of the vast repertory of the chant which they complemented and adorned. Much polyphony was in any case improvised and cannot be recovered.

The modern idea of a liturgical choir as a relatively small body of selected, trained (even professional) singers has its roots in three medieval practices: household chapels, absenteeism, and chapel choirs within larger foundations. First, household chapels became important centres of professional liturgical music. Here the distinction between the priests and the singers gradually became more marked. By the fifteenth century the singers were professionals and often laymen, and increasingly polyphony became the norm. By the sixteenth century in the Sistine Chapel they sang not in the body of the church but from a gallery to one side: their separation from the liturgical action was made quite apparent.

Second, in cathedral and collegiate churches the canons were commonly absent (those who held posts in plurality were often entirely absent) and they delegated their duties to vicars. By the sixteenth century these substitutes included laymen who were professional singers. In due course the musical responsibility for the liturgy fell to these singing men. And in England they alone were maintained after the Reformation, together with boys and a small group of priests and resident canons to staff the foundation. The term 'choir' was subsequently applied to the boy choristers and adult lay clerks.

Third, a number of communities designated a small group of priests and singers for specified observances in a separate chapel. Most often these duties were the singing of Mass in honour of the Blessed Virgin Mary (i.e. Lady Mass) as well as Vespers or a Marian antiphon in the chapel dedicated to the Virgin (Lady Chapel). This supplemented the main cycle of Mass and Office celebrated by the community in choir. In monasteries these special chaplains and clerks were often independent of the community and frequently included both boys (perhaps from the adjoining school) and laymen.

Comparable choirs of boys, clerks, and chaplains were established in the educational colleges of late medieval England. Here a separate musical and liturgical body had primary responsibility for the preparation of the liturgy, while the fellows and scholars devoted their time to study and learning. There was a distinction between the community and those responsible for singing in the liturgy.

By the mid-sixteeenth century the meaning of the word 'choir' was inverted: it ceased to refer to the community sharing the corporate celebration of liturgy 'in choir', and became the term for a body of trained singers responsible for much of the singing in the liturgy (while the remainder of the community was passive). In cathedral and collegiate churches and chapels they commonly occupied the stalls in the centre of the choir space close to the site of the choir lectern *in medio chori*. On the Continent they were often placed in galleries or on platforms.

By the same time the extent of polyphonic music in the liturgy had increased. Also boys had become more important as singers. In the fifteenth century, and especially in England, their musical potential was newly exploited; whereas they previously undertook minor responsibilities in the liturgy they now became statutory members of the newly constituted choirs, and major participants in the polyphonic repertory of the late fifteenth and sixteenth centuries.

PART II.

Medieval Liturgy

3.

The Liturgical Year and Calendar

The daily liturgy is regulated by four overlapping and interacting cycles:

the daily cycle of Office and Mass;
the weekly cycle;
the annual cycle of liturgical seasons (Temporale);
the annual cycle of feast-days (Sanctorale).

THE DAY

Except during the three solemn days at the end of Holy Week (the *Triduum*), the daily pattern of worship in the medieval Western Church consisted of the same elements: the Office and the Mass. Each will be dealt with in more detail in Chapters 6 and 7 respectively. In summary, the daily Office consists of the nocturnal service of Matins followed by Lauds, and of the six further liturgical hours sung between dawn and darkness: Prime, Terce, Sext, None, Vespers, and Compline (see Fig. 3.1).

By the eleventh century daily celebration of Mass was the norm (it had not always been so in earlier centuries). By that time Mass was celebrated individually by every priest: the older custom of the celebration of Mass by a group of priests was supplanted. (In part this explains the profusion of altars to be found in large medieval churches.) There was therefore at least one daily sung Mass in large churches, and more often two or even three.

The principal sung or High Mass was celebrated at some stage after Prime and before Vespers. The exact time depended on the season of the year. A typical medieval *horarium* (without the supplementary liturgical observances) included the following variants.[1]

---

[1] Derived from *The Ordinal and Customary of the Abbey of Saint Mary York*, ed. the Abbess of

Four Variants of the Medieval *Horarium*

Matins	Matins	Matins	Matins
Lauds	Lauds	Lauds	Lauds
Prime	Prime	Prime	Prime
Morrow Mass	Morrow Mass	Terce	Terce
Terce	Terce	Morrow Mass	Morrow Mass
High Mass	Sext	Sext	Sext
Sext	None	High Mass	None
None	High Mass	None	High Mass
Vespers	Vespers	Vespers	Vespers
Compline	Compline	Compline	Compline

The order was complicated further by the number and time of meals, especially in a monastic house. However, the most typical scheme for all Sundays and major feasts was that shown in the first column.

In addition to the main cycle of Office and Mass there were several supplementary liturgical observances commonly recited on a daily basis. Some consisted of a group of special psalms (e.g. Gradual Psalms, Penitential Psalms), others of complete liturgical services. Most significant were the daily Office of the Dead (Matins, Lauds, and Vespers) and the daily Little Office of the Virgin (the full cycle) which were appended to the main *cursus* of the liturgy in the later Middle Ages. In this later period Lady Mass and Mass of the Dead were also daily occurrences. Not all communities recited these additional observances corporately in choir: often there are detailed rubrics, and practice varies at certain times and seasons of the year.

THE WEEK

The weekly cycle was distinguished by Sunday, which began at Vespers on Saturday evening and ended with Compline on Sunday night. Sunday was always a festal day with a more extended form of Matins and (in the secular Uses) a longer series of psalms at both Matins and Prime. Every other day of the week was identified as feria,

Stanbrook (L. McLachlan) and J. B. L. Tolhurst, (3 vols., Henry Bradshaw Society, 73, 75, 84; 1936–51), iii. pp. vii–x, and *The Customary of the Cathedral Priory Church of Norwich*, ed. J. B. L. Tolhurst (Henry Bradshaw Society, 82; 1948), pp. xxviii–xxxi. The tables given in these sources present details of other activities during the day (e.g. meals, reading, manual work).

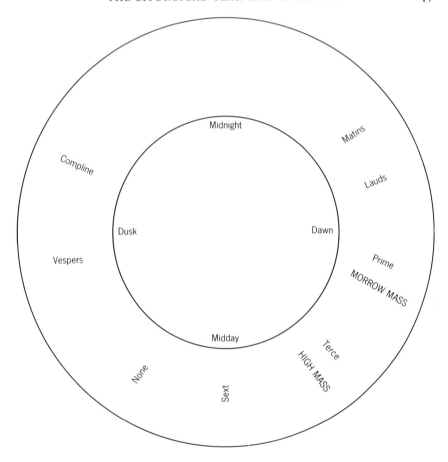

FIG. 3.1 An example of the medieval liturgical day

unless a feast-day fell on it (see 'The Ranking of Liturgical Days', below). In Latin liturgical books the week is presented thus:

Dominica	Sunday
Feria ii	Monday
Feria iii	Tuesday
Feria iv	Wednesday
Feria v	Thursday
Feria vi	Friday
Feria vii or *Sabbatum*	Saturday

In some medieval foundations there was a weekly series of special intentions. Such was the weekly cycle of Votive Masses established by Alcuin in the Frankish reforms. The Morrow Mass often followed this or a comparable cycle of votive observance. And Saturday was commonly singled out for special commemoration of the Blessed Virgin Mary at both Mass and Office. In some places there were other special commemorations on a weekly basis.

The celebration of the greatest festivals (notably Christmas, Easter, and Pentecost) also affected the weekly pattern, for the celebration of the feast was extended from the day itself to the week which followed (hence the Octave of Christmas, etc.).

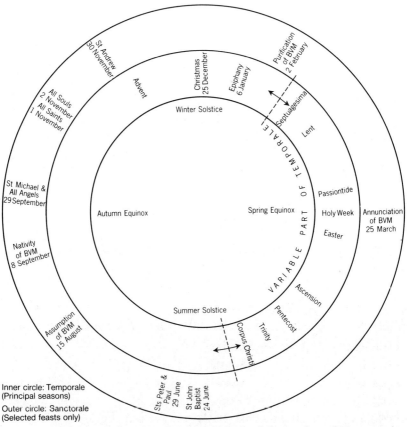

FIG. 3.2 Diagram showing the interaction of the cycles of Temporale and Sanctorale

The Calendar

The most important inflection of the daily pattern resulted from the annual cycle of the ecclesiastical Calendar. The Calendar (or Kalendar) established an annual diary for the observances of seasons and special feast-days; each day was ranked, and its rank affected the content of the liturgy and the manner in which it was conducted. Each church had its own Calendar with regional and local variants based on a common annual cycle. Most composite liturgical books include a Calendar.

The Calendar is not a simple, fixed diary: it consists of two overlapping cycles of seasons (Temporale, in part variable) and dated feast-days (Sanctorale) (see Fig. 3.2).

The Annual Cycle of Seasons (Temporale)

The seasonal part of the Calendar derives from the annual recollection of the life of Christ, the Proper of the Time (Temporale). The ordering of the Temporale is constant:

Preparation for Christ's coming	Advent
THE BIRTH OF CHRIST	CHRISTMAS
The revelation to the Gentiles	Epiphany
The forty days in the wilderness	Lent
The entry into Jerusalem	Palm Sunday
The last supper	Maundy Thursday
The crucifixion of Christ	Good Friday
THE RESURRECTION OF CHRIST	EASTER DAY
The ascension of Christ	Ascension Day
The gift of the Holy Spirit	Pentecost

The focal points of this seasonal cycle—the birth and resurrection of Christ (Christmas and Easter)—are fixed in different ways. Christmas is fixed by date (25 December) and falls on a different day of the week each year. Easter always falls on a Sunday, but the Sunday changes each year according to the phases of the moon (following the earlier practice of the Jewish Passover): it may be as early as 23 March or as late as 26 April. The period between Christmas and Easter can therefore vary by up to six weeks from one year to the next. In order to accommodate this, the Temporale has to allow flexibility in the number of Sundays after the Epiphany and the number of Sundays after Pentecost.

During the Middle Ages there were two important additions to the Temporale: the feast of the Holy Trinity on the Sunday after Pentecost, and the feast of Corpus Christi (the body of Christ) on the following Thursday. Both had been commemorated in special devotions for many centuries (Holy Trinity was included in Alcuin's weekly cycle of Votive Masses), but were officially given a place in the annual Calendar during the thirteenth and fourteenth centuries.

A more detailed Calendar for the medieval and Tridentine Temporale is given in Appendix 1, with both Latin and English titles. However the important features of the Calendar are as follows:

Advent	Four Sundays before Christmas, beginning between 27 November and 3 December; the Church's new year
Christmas	25 December
Epiphany	6 January
After Epiphany	A variable period depending on the date of Easter, with between one and five Sundays
Septuagesima	Seven weeks before Passiontide, nine weeks before Easter; the beginning of the penitential season
Sexagesima	
Quinquagesima	
Ash Wednesday	The beginning of Lent
Quadragesima	The four weeks before Passiontide
Passion Sunday	Two weeks before Easter, known as Passiontide
Holy Week	The week preceding Easter, and including
Palm Sunday	
Maundy Thursday ⎫	The most solemn three days of the Church
Good Friday ⎬	year, often referred to as the *Triduum* or
Holy Saturday ⎭	*Triduum sacrum*
Easter Day	Falling between 23 March and 26 April[2]

[2] In the Middle Ages: because of changes in the lunar phases, Easter from the seventeenth century to the present falls between 22 March and 25 April.

Eastertide	Easter Day to Saturday after Pentecost
Sundays after Easter	Five Sundays
Ascension Day	Thursday; forty days after Easter
Sunday after Ascension	The last Sunday in Eastertide
Pentecost (Whitsun)	Fifty days (seven weeks) after Easter
Trinity Sunday	Sunday after Pentecost (from 1334)
Corpus Christi	Thursday after Trinity Sunday[3] (from 1264)
After Trinity (until Advent)	A variable period, balancing that after Epiphany, and consisting of between twenty-two and twenty-seven Sundays

Broadly speaking about half the year (from Advent to Epiphany, and from Septuagesima to Corpus Christi) is seasonal, while the other half (from Epiphany to Septuagesima, and from Corpus Christi to Advent) is not. It is in the non-seasonal period, sometimes alluded to in Latin books as *per annum* or as the Ordinary Time, that the forms of Office and Mass follow a pattern that may be regarded as normative.

Some mention should be made of the penitential seasons. The first is that of Advent, beginning on the eve of Advent Sunday and ending on Christmas Eve. There are special ritual, ceremonial, and musical provisions for this season. The second penitential season is more extended, and becomes progressively more solemn. In the Latin Rite (until the recent reforms) it began at Septuagesima and was marked by liturgical changes at Ash Wednesday (the beginning of Lent), at Passion Sunday (the beginning of Passiontide), Palm Sunday (the beginning of Holy Week), and Maundy Thursday (the beginning of the solemn *Triduum*); it ends with the singing of *alleluia* at the Easter Vigil.

THE ANNUAL CYCLE OF FEAST-DAYS (SANCTORALE)

Both the seasonal and non-seasonal parts of the Temporale are punctuated by the cycle of individual feast-days found in the Sanctorale. In some respects this is a far more straightforward part of the Calendar: each feast is fixed by date. However, though the main feasts and their dates were common throughout the Western Church, lesser feasts and observances varied according to region, monastic Order, diocese, and

---

[3] The observance of the feast spread in northern Europe and especially in monasteries from the tenth century onwards.

individual church. They also varied over the centuries. The status of St Wenceslas is prominent in Bohemia, that of St Etheldreda ranked high around Ely in the English fenland. These saints do not normally occur in the same Calendar; indeed the Calendar (and especially the Sanctorale) often gives the strongest clues about the provenance of a medieval liturgical book. The chronological changes may be illustrated by the Feast of the Transfiguration of Our Lord (6 August), not formally adopted in the Western Church until 1457 (though found before this in some books).

The main difficulty with the Calendar is the interaction of the Sanctorale with that of the Temporale. There are generally two basic problems: the first occurs when a saint's feast-day coincides with a feast of the Temporale; the second occurs when a saint's day falls on a Sunday. As the medieval Sanctorale filled with observances so there was a need for rules to govern these coincident celebrations, rules which became progressively more elaborate.

At Christmas the Temporale (i.e. Christmas Day) is fixed by date, and the relationship to adjacent feasts of the Sanctorale is therefore unchanging:

25 December	Christmas Day
26 December	St Stephen
27 December	St John the Evangelist
28 December	The Holy Innocents
29 December	St Thomas of Canterbury (after 1173)
31 December	St Silvester

As a consequence of this stability, the feast-days in the Octave of Christmas (i.e. the week after Christmas) are often found in the Temporale.

The same is not true of feasts falling in the movable period between Septuagesima and Corpus Christi. This period may date, at one extreme, from 18 January to 21 May, or, at the other, from 3 March to 24 June. One of the best examples is that of the Feast of the Annunciation of the Blessed Virgin Mary, 25 March. This is an important feast falling awkwardly (if logically) nine months before Christmas. It may be in Lent, it may be in Eastertide; or it may fall in Holy Week. If it falls between Maundy Thursday and Easter Day it has to be transferred. Where it was transferred to differed. In the Middle Ages it commonly moved to Wednesday or Thursday of the following week; in the

Tridentine Rite it moved to Easter Monday; but at Norwich Cathedral Priory it moved to 18 December (following, as the thirteenth-century Customary notes, an instruction of a Council of Toledo).

The Annunciation can also serve to illustrate the second problem of a feast falling on a Sunday. This is one of the most complex areas of liturgical practice: by the fifteenth century it was such that Clement Maydeston published *Directorium Sacerdotum* (1487) to correct errors and lay out plainly all thirty-five possible orders of the annual Calendar according to the Use of Salisbury.[4] Using Maydeston's rules, the Annunciation would be transferred to Monday if it fell on a Sunday in Lent (unless it was the feast of a church's dedication) or on Palm Sunday (everywhere).

THE RANKING OF LITURGICAL DAYS

There are two fundamental liturgical categories for a day: feast and feria. In an ordinary week Sunday is ranked as festal, and the remaining days are ferial. But no single week in the medieval Calendar was as straightforward as that. The late medieval expansion of the Sanctorale in general, and the observance of Octaves of important feasts resulted in a dense Calendar with remarkably few ferial days. Maydeston's *Directorium* lists some 200 festal observances, and allowing for Sundays, special commemorative days, and transferred feasts, this leaves fewer than 100 ferial weekdays in a year. The contemporary Roman Missal (1474) has a Calendar that is even more crowded, with only six days without a festal observance in the whole year. (The Sanctorale was subject to extensive reform in the sixteenth century, in both the Protestant and Roman Catholic Churches: see Chapters 10 and 11.)

The majority of days were therefore feast-days, and these were classified in order of importance. Again there were two basic categories of feast—simple (*simplex*) and double (*duplex*), but the double feasts were further divided into as many as four separate ranks. The typical secular Latin scheme might include five categories of feast:

Principal double feast	*Festum principale duplex*
Double feast	*Festum duplex*
Semi-double feast	*Festum semiduplex*

[4] Maydeston's directory was subsequently revised by Clerke. See Chapter 13, pp. 208 f. for a summary of the thirty-five orders.

| Simple feast with nine lessons at Matins | *Festum simplex, ix lectiones* |
| Simple feast with three lessons at Matins | *Festum simplex, iii lectiones* |

Monastic Use often separated feasts by designating the wearing of copes or albs by those in choir:

Principal feast	*Festum principale*
Feast celebrated in copes	*Festum in capis*
Feast celebrated in albs	*Festum in albis*
Simple feast with twelve lessons at Matins	*Festum simplex, xii lectiones*
Simple feast with three lessons at Matins	*Festum simplex, iii lectiones*

More complex schemes exist in secular and monastic Uses. Some monastic customs have additional festal subdivisions (e.g. Mass in copes, Office in albs), and of the secular Uses that at Salisbury is suitably comprehensive:

Principal double feast	*Festum principale duplex*
Major double feast	*Festum maius duplex*
Minor double feast	*Festum minus duplex*
Lesser double feast	*Festum inferius duplex*
Simple feast of nine lessons at Matins with three cantors at the Invitatory[5]	*Invitatorium triplex ix lectiones*
Simple feast of nine lessons at Matins with two cantors at the Invitatory	*Invitatorium duplex ix lectiones*
Simple feast of three lessons at Matins with two cantors at the Invitatory	*Invitatorium duplex iii lectiones*
Simple feast of three lessons at Matins with one cantor at the Invitatory	*Invitatorium simplex iii lectiones*
Sunday (ranked as a double feast)	*Dominica*
Ordinary weekday	*Feria*

One of the most confusing observances is that of the Octave. Many major feasts had Octaves: their observance continued for the following week, and affected the liturgy during that period. The most important are the Octaves of Christmas, Easter, and Pentecost.

---

[5] The mode of celebration was identified by the first item of the day involving solo singers (here rulers or cantors).

Seasonal and Festal Observance

From the summary of Salisbury practice above, it becomes plain that the categories of simple feasts were identified by the number of lessons at Matins, and by the number of rulers or (on feasts of three lessons) other cantors who began the Invitatory to Psalm 94 *Venite exultemus* (also at Matins, but regulating the number of rulers/cantors throughout the day). Similarly there are designations in monastic Uses such as 'in copes' for major double feasts and 'in albs' for minor double feasts.

These forms of classification demonstrate how festal observances were distinguished in rite and ceremony: the order and content of the liturgy (rite) was affected by the rank of the day and also by the season; so too was the manner and conduct of the liturgy (ceremony). The detail of these matters is discussed in the relevant chapters below, but the principles can be summarized here.

So far as the rite was concerned, the most obvious distinction in the content of the liturgy from day to day was the use of special texts and chants—the Proper, which accounts for the greater part of the content in medieval liturgical books. The Proper extends not only to antiphons, hymns, responds, and prayers, but also to the choice of psalmody, especially at Matins and Vespers.

There were also changes in the normal order according to season and day. At Mass, *Gloria in excelsis* was not sung in Advent and Lent (except on double feasts), and the Alleluia was replaced by the Tract between Septuagesima and Easter. In secular Uses *Te deum* was omitted at Matins during Advent and Lent. During Eastertide itself *alleluia* was appended to many sung texts, and there were also special seasonal melodies (as also in other seasons).

On ferial days the most important contrast with Sunday was the omission of *Gloria in excelsis*, Sequence, and *Credo* at Mass, and the use of a shorter form of Matins (with three lessons and usually without *Te deum*). The simplest feasts also followed this short form of Matins, but on others the longer form was customary. Feasts of nine (or twelve) lessons also included *Gloria* and *Credo*, and there was very often a Sequence on principal and major feasts. Some Uses favoured processions (Salisbury is often cited, but is one of many) on Sundays and double feasts before Mass, and in some cases after the canticle and collect at Lauds and Vespers.

This is not the place to deal with the ceremonial observance of the liturgy. Already the distinction of choir dress (e.g. albs and copes) has been noted; to this may be added seasonal and festal liturgical colours used for vestments, altar frontals, and hangings. But most ceremonial observance governed the number of ministers and officiants (especially at Mass) and the nature and extent of their movement and action. It is quite impossible to summarize this or to single out a representative example.

In all these matters local practice was in some respect individual, and was subject to some change (often small) from one century to another. In a general summary it is only practicable to give general guidelines and to highlight the considerable complexities.

The Extent of the Liturgical Day

It can be confusing when using Office books to find that there are two ways of regarding the liturgical day.

Feria and Ordinary Sundays

In the ferial sections of the Office books (e.g. the Choir Psalter) the day begins with Matins and goes through each Office in sequence to Compline. Quite often Matins or Vespers for the whole week will be presented one after the other before going on to Lauds or Compline respectively. The Psalter presents the psalms for First Vespers for Sunday as part of the Saturday sequence, and Second Vespers is found in the Sunday sequence. When reference is made to 'Sunday Vesper psalms', it generally means those for Second Vespers celebrated on Sunday evening (i.e. the group of psalms beginning with Psalm 109).

Feasts

The pattern is different on feast-days. A feast begins not at Matins but at Vespers on the preceding evening. Thus, when (for instance) the Feast of St Agatha falls on Tuesday, 5 February, it is celebrated as follows: festal Vespers of St Agatha on Monday evening, Compline (as on a ferial day); Matins, Lauds, and Little Hours of St Agatha on Tuesday; Vespers with Tuesday's ferial psalms but Proper texts for

St Agatha. Similarly the weekly Commemoration of the Blessed Virgin Mary normally begins on Friday evening with Vespers and ends after None on Saturday; Vespers on Saturday is usually First Vespers for Sunday.

Double feasts (and Sundays) have two Vespers: thus, the Feast of St Luke falling on Tuesday, 18 October, begins with First Vespers of St Luke on Monday evening and continues to Second Vespers on Tuesday evening.

In some Uses the day before a major feast is accorded special festal observance as a Vigil or Eve of the following feast. Christmas Eve is an obvious example, but Salisbury Use (for instance) celebrated the Vigil of St Andrew as a feast with its own Propers for Mass and Office.

These two distinct patterns need to be grasped: Vespers of a ferial day is celebrated on that day; Vespers of a simple feast is celebrated on the evening before; First Vespers of a double feast is celebrated on the evening before, and Second Vespers on the feast-day itself.

4.

Books for the Liturgy

Books have always been a precious commodity of Christianity, for Christianity is predominantly a religion of the Word. The Word is the source of its authority and of its worship. When missionaries arrived in the first millennium they were frequently identified by a book (most often the Gospels) as well as a cross. And even cursory study of early medieval books reveals how precious they were, written as works of art on materials that would endure (witness the Celtic Gospel books of the seventh and eighth centuries).

Books were rare, especially before the twelfth century; and even in later medieval monasteries, the book cupboard (*armarium*) near the church door in the cloister was often very modest in size. Each book had to be copied by hand from an exemplar or exemplars; and often a liturgical book was individually adapted to the current needs of a particular church, allowing for local details of the Calendar or local practice.

Light was scarce. The need to capture more light is evident in the development of Gothic architecture: windows get larger, the tracery more delicate, sometimes stretched to structural limits. The choir was often situated near or in the crossing where light came from all four directions. Even so, the community was still some distance from the source of natural light, and moreover a substantial part of the Office was conducted at times of poor light or darkness (Vespers at dusk, Compline at bedtime, Matins and Lauds before dawn). The most important soloists (i.e. rulers of the choir) were placed in the middle of the choir where their books could be lit readily, especially on lecterns. Indeed the placing of lecterns at the choir step, in the middle of the choir, and on the choir screen identifies the use of books at these positions as well as acknowledging the ceremonial importance of these places in the choir.

Throughout the Middle Ages most of those in choir sang their parts of the Office and Mass from memory. Before the spread of the personal Breviary and Missal and the emergence of commercial workshops committed to bulk copying (especially in the fifteenth century), only those members of the community who needed a book had one. And it was common before the thirteenth century for a book to contain only those parts of the liturgy relevant to a single officiant in a service: at sung Mass the texts might therefore be shared out among the contents of as many as six to eight interdependent books. Most surviving liturgical books were source copies used only for reference, teaching, or copying.

For almost all the information required to understand medieval liturgical practice one has to rely on surviving contemporary books. Most of the English sources are manuscript, but a few printed books survive from the late fifteenth and sixteenth centuries. They may be placed in three broad groups:

books of information and instructions
books for use in the Office
books for use at Mass

There are some additional books which cut across this basic classification and a number of inconsistencies which have to be dealt with individually.

The titles and contents of a liturgical book vary over the period, and a familiar title may prove ambiguous: the thirteenth-century book now known as the Worcester Antiphoner includes Antiphonal, Gradual, and other materials, and does not survive complete. In the later Middle Ages the tendency towards private recitation of Office and Mass increased the need for conflated books (Breviary and Missal) which included all the texts but frequently without musical notation. Furthermore, these later books also subsumed many of the rubrics earlier confined to Ordinal and Consuetudinary. The field is specialized and confusing; caution is essential.

The ordering of books is described in more detail below (pp. 65 f.), but liturgical material is most commonly subdivided in four ways: daily (ordinary or ferial), seasonal (Temporale), specific to a particular feast-day (Sanctorale), and common to a group of feasts (Commune Sanctorum). For any Mass or Office it is necessary to draw material from more than one of these sections (see Chapter 12 for a more practical approach to this, and Chapter 13 for the ordering of some specific sources).

Books of Information and Instruction

Though not primarily a liturgical source, the Statutes established the constitution of a foundation, specifying membership, function, and organization, as well as conduct, discipline, and rank. They were particularly important for collegiate institutions (as opposed to monastic houses which followed a Rule). Statutes often designated the liturgical Use to be followed in the community, and even some local feasts and customs, but remained primarily legal in purpose.

The Calendar, Ordinal, and Consuetudinary (or Customary) were interlocking guides to the ordering of the liturgy; they established the *when*, *what*, and *how* of a foundation's worship. The Calendar has already been discussed in Chapter 3; it indicated which feasts were celebrated and often recorded their rank. There is a degree of overlap between Consuetudinary or Customary and Ordinal.

The Ordinal was a book for use in church. It prescribed the character, contents, and method of the services; it dealt with the rite. It was particularly important in the earlier medieval period when the content of the liturgy was divided between a number of separate books. A comprehensive book of instructions, it laid out the contents of the liturgy, showing precisely which text was to be used at each point on a particular day or during a specific season. The items were listed, mostly by textual incipit: it was therefore a summary of the content of the liturgy. In addition it might give instructions on the method of performance. However, even the most comprehensive Ordinals took certain normal practice for granted. (The problem of establishing the full content of any one service is explored in Chapter 12). In the later medieval liturgy many of the instructions of the Ordinal were absorbed into the text and rubrics of Breviary and Missal. At this period an Ordinal was often restricted to systematic instructions on the variants in the annual Calendar (discussed in Chapter 3); such a book is known as a Pie in England (more properly *Directorium Sacerdotum*).

The Consuetudinary and Customary derived from the chapter house rather than church. They might describe the structure of the community and the duties of each officer. So far as the liturgy is concerned, they explained the manner of conducting the services. If the Ordinal defined rite, the Customary (or Consuetudinary) delineated ceremonial. It established who said, sang, or did everything, and how it was to be done. It was a parallel book to the Ordinal and could not be used without it. It both provided a general pattern of ceremonial conduct, and gave details of variants throughout the year.

Some Customaries come closer to being Ordinals; some Ordinals include a substantial amount of ceremonial detail. A late medieval Missal or Breviary may present much detail from the Customary in rubrics (annotations in red ink) inserted throughout the book. In the sixteenth century the customs to be followed in those cathedral and collegiate churches which had adopted the Use of the Papal Curia were printed in the *Ceremoniale Romanum* (1516).

One last book of instruction was of particular musical importance. The Tonary (or Tonale) provided a musical companion to the Ordinal as a compendium of the chant repertory classified by mode and tone. Above all it demonstrated the matching of antiphon and psalm-tone, but also provided the repertory of melismatic endings (*neuma*) to be added to the last of a group of endings. It could also include instructions on their performance. Some gave indications of seasonal and festal melodies, including hymns and the Ordinary of the Mass. A Tonary may be found as an individual section in a later Antiphonal or Ordinal. Tonaries included within Breviaries and Missals gave the tones for the recitation of the priest's parts (i.e. prayers, readings, versicles).

BOOKS FOR USE IN THE OFFICE

By the end of the thirteenth century the Office books tended to be merged into three independent books: Breviary, Antiphonal, and Choir (or Ferial) Psalter.

The Breviary was primarily intended to be used by the officiating priest. It was generally a book without musical notation. The principal contents of the Breviary were the Proper items of the Office, but later medieval Breviaries were often sufficiently complete to contain the whole Office to allow for private recitation by the clergy. It conflated the earlier officiant's books (Collectar and Lectionary) with the choir books (Antiphonal and, often, Choir Psalter). Some later medieval

Breviaries included the chant. These are referred to as Noted Breviaries. Often large books intended for use in choir (they were especially suitable for a very small group of priests or religious), they are the most comprehensive sources with texts, music, and instructions for the conduct of the Office.

The Antiphonal was the principal choir book, and contained all the proper items. It included antiphons to psalms and canticles, responds, and often hymns; altogether it embraced the greater part of the choral repertory of Office chant. Later Antiphonals were even more complete, with Invitatories and even Psalter. The book was normally divided into the Proper of Time and Season, with an intermediate section of Commons—texts used for feasts that shared the same basic repertory of proper items (e.g. Evangelists, Apostles, Martyrs, Confessors, Virgins, and the Virgin Mary).

The Choir (or Ferial) Psalter complemented the Antiphonal, and contained the ferial (unchanging) items of the Office. In it could be found not only the psalms but such regularly used items as the ferial texts and music for Invitatories, antiphons, canticles, chapters, and short responsories. A Hymnal, containing the hymns for the Office, was a frequent appendage to the book.

Earlier medieval books frequently separated the constituent parts of the Office. The Collectar included prayers, chapters, versicles and responses, preces and benedictions. The Lectionary contained the lessons at Matins (sometimes only as a summary list). The Benedictional included blessings. The Hymnal, Psalter, and Invitatorium (antiphons for use with Psalm 94, *Venite exsultemus*) are self-explanatory. Even in early books the Invitatorium was normally only a separate section of a larger book.

BOOKS FOR USE AT MASS

Before the thirteenth century the constituent parts of the Mass were often copied into separate books. For the ministers there were the Sacramentary (containing prayers and Prefaces), the Lectionary (including Epistles and Gospels, sometimes as two separate books), and the Ordo Missae (the priest's unchanging texts for the Mass). In choir there were the Kyriale (the chants of the Ordinary), the Gradual (choral chants of the Proper, on occasion omitting the solo sections), the Cantatory (solo sections of the Proper, notably the Gradual and Alleluia), the Troper (additional interpolated solo sections), and Sequentiary (the Sequences sung after the Alleluia).

By the fourteenth century most of the Mass chants were conflated into two books: the Missal and the Gradual. In the Missal were to be found all the proper items said or sung by the celebrating priest and his assistants, including the readings for Epistle and Gospel. The texts of the choir Proper (Introit, Gradual, Alleluia, Offertory, and Communion) were also included. The priest's texts of the Ordinary (including Prefaces) were presented as a separate section, Ordo Missae. Few Missals contain music (except perhaps the intonations for *Gloria in excelsis*, Preface, and the Dismissal), and those that do are generally designated as Noted Missals. As with Noted Breviaries, these can be very comprehensive sources of texts, chant, and rubrics.

The choral repertory of the Proper was compiled in the Gradual (sometimes known as *Antiphonale Missarum*). Here were included all the chants for Introit, Gradual, Alleluia, Offertory, and Communion, together with the Tract for penitential times. Later Graduals also tended to include the choir chants of the Ordinary of the Mass (Kyriale)—*Kyrie, Gloria, Credo, Sanctus, Agnus dei*, Dismissal—in a separate section, comparable with the Ordo Missae in the Missal. Sequences and tropes are not often found in sources copied before the eleventh century; and even in the later Middle Ages when they were common they were often copied in separate books or sections. The Sequence and trope repertories reflect the tendencies to proliferation, diversity, accretion, gloss, and commentary, especially typical of the eleventh to the thirteenth centuries.

OTHER BOOKS

In monastic and secular foundations chants to be sung during processions were most often contained in a separate book, predictably known as the Processional.

Most special rites (e.g. those particular to Holy Week and Easter) were contained in the principal liturgical books. However, two further books were important in parish and diocesan liturgy. The Ritual (abroad) or Manual (England) was intended primarily for parish priests, and provided for such occasional rites as baptism and

marriage; the *Rituale Romanum* was first printed in 1614, but there are
earlier printed examples from other Uses (in Germany such books are
often called *Agenda*). The Pontifical included services conducted by a
bishop, including annual rites held in cathedrals (e.g. ordination and
the blessing of oils). Neither of these books was significant in the daily
liturgy of a cathedral, collegiate, or monastic church; nor were the
special Books of Hours with their selected Offices of the Blessed
Virgin Mary and the Dead, often intended for private devotions.

After the Reformation and the Council of Trent

The books produced after the sixteenth-century upheaval are mostly
printed, fewer in number, and more uniform. So far as the reformed
Churches were concerned, only the Church of England and the
Lutheran Church in Scandinavia compiled vernacular liturgies that
were firmly codified in a manner comparable with the medieval and
Tridentine liturgies. The Book of Common Prayer is discussed in
detail in Chapter 11.

The Roman Church relied substantially on the priest's Breviary and
Missal and the choir's Gradual and Antiphonal. The suppression of
many medieval accretions (processions, Sequences, tropes) rendered
many early books obsolete.

One of the most convenient and accessible printed sources for study
is *Liber Usualis*. The nature of this book needs to be understood. Its
title is best translated as 'the useful [liturgical] book' rather than 'the
book of [liturgical] use'. It is a modern compilation (1896) from the
larger liturgical books for Mass and Office, and is only selective. It
includes only those services commonly sung in the Roman secular
Church in the last days of the Tridentine Rite: Mass and Vespers on
Sundays and feast-days. Other services are provided for, especially on
principal feasts and in Holy Week. But it is in no way liturgically
complete. Later editions follow the Calendar, Lectionary, and Psalter
issued by Pope Pius X in 1911. The melodies of the chant are those
edited in the nineteenth century and thereafter by the monks of
Solesmes: though closer to the earliest surviving manuscript sources
these melodies frequently differ in detail from the readings found in
medieval and Tridentine books. *Liber Usualis* is nevertheless quite as
useful as its title suggests, with chants for every item of Mass and

Office. But it does need to be used with awareness and understanding of its purpose and nature: it is no more than a convenient liturgical anthology.

THE ORDERING OF LITURGICAL BOOKS

Anyone unfamiliar with Latin liturgical books may easily be confused by their ordering. With the exception of the special services for the *Triduum* of Holy Week, even the most comprehensive and self-contained liturgical books present their contents in a fragmented form: they may assume a norm that is never clearly laid out; variants may be tucked away in rubrics with incipits; there will very likely be no index. The problem of facing these difficulties in a practical way is considered in the discussion of establishing a liturgical order in Chapter 12. The specific ordering of selected medieval sources is presented in Chapter 13.

Medieval liturgical books are not laid out in a consistent order, but are generally grouped in identifiable sections.

Office Books

Breviary:	Calendar, Psalter, Temporale, Commune Sanctorum, Sanctorale
Antiphonal:	Temporale, Sanctorale, Commune Sanctorum
Choir Psalter:	Psalms, Canticles, Invitatories, Hymns

Some sources separate Winter (1 November to Easter) and Summer. A few sources merge Temporale and Sanctorale in one sequence: these tend to date from before the thirteenth century. Post-Tridentine Breviaries are commonly subdivided into four volumes (Winter, Spring, Summer, and Autumn). Some Antiphonals include Invitatories and hymns, and British examples often include Calendar and Psalter as well. Tonaries may be found in Noted Breviaries and Antiphonals. The Common section (mostly Commune Sanctorum) may include Offices of Dedication, the Virgin, and the Dead, or these may be separated from it.

Mass Books

Missal: Calendar, Temporale, Ordo Missae, Sanctorale, Commune
          Sanctorum, other special Masses (Dedication, Dead, Votive),
          Sequences

Gradual: Temporale, Sanctorale, Commune Sanctorum, other special
          Masses, Ordinary chants (i.e. Kyriale), Sequences

The Ordo Missae may be placed in the middle of the Missal (generally just before Easter Day), and there are some Missals and Graduals which combine Temporale and Sanctorale. Noted Missals may include the Ordinary (Kyriale) along with Ordo Missae.

A far more detailed analysis of the ordering and content of liturgical books for Mass and Office may be found in Andrew Hughes's study of *Medieval Manuscripts for Mass and Office* (Toronto, 1982). He also outlines the use of illuminated and capital letters as structural markers in manuscripts, and includes a summary catalogue of manuscripts consulted, with indications of their principal subdivisions.

5.

The Psalter

THE BOOK OF PSALMS

Of all the books in the Bible, none has so fundamental a part in the liturgy as the Book of Psalms. In spite of their strong roots in Jewish history, the themes and the spirituality of the Psalms have transcended cultural and theological barriers throughout Christendom.

A collection of 150 Hebrew poems grouped together in the Old Testament, the Psalms were always intended to be sung. They form an important bridge between Jewish and Christian traditions. From at least the fourth century onwards Christians used selections from the Psalter in daily public prayer, singing them together: sources from this early time sometimes disguise their identity by calling them 'hymns'. Alongside them they used other songs (canticles) drawn from other parts of the Bible, as well as non-scriptural texts (e.g. *Te deum* and *Gloria in excelsis*).

If a few selected psalms sung regularly (even daily) formed a major part of 'lay' public worship in the early Church, the whole collection recited successively provided a basis for meditation for the early solitary monks. In due course monks gathered together in groups, and so the recitation of psalms developed as a shared practice. And from the monks the custom of successive recitation spread throughout the Church in the West. It was the corner-stone of the medieval Office, and the principle continues in most lectionaries even today.

PROBLEMS OF NUMBERING AND NATURE

There are problems in referring to individual psalms because two numbering systems are in current use. When the Bible was translated into Greek (known as the Septuagint) and Latin (the Vulgate) some of the divisions of the psalms were altered from the Hebrew text, with consequent changes in numbering. At the Reformation the vernacular translators (including the English) favoured the old Hebrew numbering.

The divergences of numbering occur at four points: Hebrew Psalms 9 and 10 are treated as one psalm in the Vulgate (9), as are Psalms 114 and 115 (Vulgate 113); but Hebrew Psalms 116 and 147 were each subdivided into two separate psalms in the Vulgate (respectively 114, 115 and 146, 147). In both numberings there is a total of 150 psalms.

HEBREW (AND PROTESTANT)	LATIN (VULGATE)
1–8	1–8
9, 10	9
11–113	10–112
114, 115	113
116	114, 115
117–146	116–145
147	146, 147
148–150	148–150

All the Latin Rites use the Vulgate numbering, as do the new vernacular translations from the Latin. Vulgate numbering is adopted as a norm in this book, except in the consideration of the reformed English Rite found in the Book of Common Prayer, where Hebrew numbering is followed (Chapter 11). Appendix 2 contains an index of all the psalms in numerical order (Hebrew and Vulgate), including their normal place in the *cursus* of the Office (monastic and secular). They are also listed in alphabetical order (Latin).

The psalms vary greatly in length; most are between ten and twenty verses long; the shortest (116) is only two verses; some are in several sections, including the longest (118) which consists of twenty-two sections, each of eight verses; a few extend to over seventy verses without break (e.g. 77). Some of the psalms composed in sections have very strong contrasts of text and theme.

The problem of the nature of the Psalter as a medieval book has been raised in the preceding chapter. Suffice it to reiterate here that in medieval times the term 'Psalter' generally identified a book with contents additional to the psalms: though many surviving examples are Choir (or Ferial) Psalters, some are private devotional books akin to Books of Hours.

THE PSALMS IN THE MASS

The structure and order of the Mass are discussed in detail in Chapter 7 below. Broadly speaking the texts of the Mass may be divided into two categories—those that are constant (the Ordinary) and those that change day by day according to season and feast (the Proper); all these texts may further be divided into those said or sung by the priest and ministers, and those intended for all present (the community).

The psalms are prominent in the communal parts of the Proper. In the early Church they were sung at important ceremonial points in the Mass: at the entrance of the celebrant (Introit), as a response to the proclamation of the scriptures (Gradual and Tract), at the offering and preparation of gifts (Offertory), and while the people received communion (Communion). It is plain that originally these psalms were sung in their entirety, but in medieval sources what remains is often no more than a verse or two. This truncation is the result of changes in the ceremonies: the curtailing of entrance and offertory processions, musical rather than textual elaboration in the Gradual and Tract, and the disappearance of regular communion by all present.

At the Introit, Gradual, Offertory, and Communion the psalm was originally recited in full and with a refrain after each verse or pair of verses. The musical nature of these refrains (antiphon and respond) is discussed below. Textually they normally consist either of a verse extracted from the psalm (e.g. the Easter Introit and Gradual: *Resurrexi* and *Haec dies*) or of a short text from another biblical book (e.g. the Christmas Introit *Puer natus est* from Isaiah, and the Ascension Introit *Viri Galilaei* from Acts). In their medieval form these psalms have dwindled, often to a single verse at Introit and Gradual, or disappeared, as in most cases at the Offertory and Communion: it is the refrain which has become the principal feature.

The Tract, by contrast, consists of a psalm sung through successively without refrain—so-called direct psalmody.

THE PSALMS IN THE OFFICE

In the Office the psalms retained their pre-eminence even in the Middle Ages. A group of psalms was sung at the beginning of each of the Hours, and at the beginning of every section (nocturn) of Matins. The choice of these psalms reflects the two traditions of the early Church mentioned above: the non-monastic use of a regular, well-known selection chosen to suit the time and the day, and sung in an established pattern; and the monastic practice of singing the psalter from beginning to end in numerical order regardless of theme. The monastic principle established in the sixth century was prevalent in the Middle Ages, and the whole psalter was recited each week. Nevertheless even here vestiges of the older practice of reciting a fixed group of psalms (a practice derived from the early, so-called cathedral Office) can be seen in the cycles of psalmody codified by the medieval secular and monastic Uses. Each can be examined in Appendix 2.

Certain psalms were constant each day in both the secular and monastic Uses. Matins included Psalm 94 in the introductory section. Lauds had a group of unchanging daily psalms (66, 148–150); Psalm 62, recited daily in the secular *cursus*, was sung on Sunday in the monastic cycle; and Psalm 50, recited every day in the monastic cycle, was included on weekdays in the secular *cursus*. Compline was unchanging in its use of Psalms 4, 90, and 133, though the secular Use also included the first part of Psalm 30. The secular cycle also had a regular daily pattern for the little hours of Prime, Terce, Sext, and None (partly echoed in monastic Use). The numerical sequence is most evident in Matins and Vespers: broadly speaking Psalms 1–108 form the *cursus* at Matins, while Psalms 109–150 occur at Vespers (allowing in each case for the extraction of psalms used at other Hours).

In the Middle Ages there emerged a separate selection of psalms for use on particular feast-days. These proper psalms displaced the regular weekly cycle at Matins and Vespers. By the late Middle Ages this disruption totally distorted the principle of weekly recitation of the psalter. Because the choice of proper psalms was not standardized it is harder to present tables of them in relationship to medieval practice. However, the reform of the Roman Breviary in the sixteenth century and its widespread adoption within the so-called Tridentine Rite led to greater uniformity. Some of the proper psalms are listed in Appendix 2, and those for Vespers in the Tridentine Rite are discussed in Chapter 10.

As in the Mass the Office psalms were originally sung with refrains between the verses. However, in the Middle Ages a refrain (antiphon) was sung either at the beginning and end of each psalm, or at the beginning and end of a group of psalms. (Details of these practices can be found set out for each individual Office in Chapter 6.) As in the Mass the texts of the Office antiphons were frequently drawn from the psalm it framed or else from another scriptural source apposite to the season or feast. The repertory of psalm-antiphons was very large: whereas the psalms were largely constant from one week to another, the antiphons changed week by week, season by season, and feast by feast. Some of the texts duplicated those found in the Mass repertory, but their musical setting in the Office was far more perfunctory.

One further use of psalmody needs to be noted. Though in the medieval Office the bulk of the psalmody was sung early in each service, extracts from psalms provided a response to scriptural readings or the texts of dialogues in intercessions. The extent of the response varied: perfunctory dialogues (a single versicle and response, a form also used in intercessions); short responds (refrain—psalm verse—refrain—*Gloria patri*—refrain, set to a simple musical formula); and highly elaborate responds (similar in structure to the short responds, but markedly more extended in their musical treatment). The extended responds are found predominantly in Matins, where they followed each of the readings (lessons).

THE FUNCTIONAL DISTINCTIONS OF PSALMODY

It is already apparent that the psalms were used in a variety of different ways within the liturgy. There is comparable variety in their musical treatment and manner of performance.

Every textbook on medieval music elucidates the differences between antiphonal and responsorial psalmody. In fact it is often hard to distinguish between the two types in a musical context since both employ the principle of refrain in their earliest manifestations. Both types also occur set to elaborate and to simple melodies. It is easiest to distinguish them by function: responsorial psalmody always follows a reading—it is a response to that reading; antiphonal psalmody stands in its own right whether as an accompaniment to the ceremonial actions of the Mass, or as praise and prayer near the beginning of each Office. By the Middle Ages these two basic types had changed in their format (especially those with truncated texts) and in their manner of performance. The original principle of both was comparable: a psalm whose verses are separated by the repetition of a refrain sung by all. Their individual distinctions may be summarized as follows:

Responsorial Chants

Ritual characteristics: Always follow a reading from scripture.
  Gradual and Alleluia at Mass;
  extended responds at Matins;
  short responds at other hours.
  Beginning and psalm verse(s) sung by soloists.
Musical characteristics: Stylistic consistency, either highly melismatic or
  syllabic (in either case an element of musical formula).
Formal ordering: Refrain—Verse—Refrain, *or* Refrain—Verse—
  Refrain—*Gloria patri*—Refrain. These are simplified; there are
  many variants, including partial repetition of the refrain (see below,
  Chapter 6).
Ceremonial distinction: Soloists sing their parts from lectern at choir step
  or pulpitum; implied spatial dialogue between soloists and choir.

Antiphonal Psalms and Chants

Ritual characteristics:
  Psalms and canticles in Office most often performed by two sides of
  choir singing alternate verses.
  Invitatory at Matins;
  Introit, Offertory, Communion at Mass—antiphon sung by choir,
  verses (where used) by selected members of choir.
  All begun by members of choir.
Musical characteristics: Psalm and canticle texts sung to simple formulas
  (tones) repeated each verse; antiphons freely composed (melismatic
  in canticle antiphons and Mass chants)—implicit stylistic contrast
  between antiphon and psalm.[1]
Formal ordering: Most often Refrain—Psalm—Refrain but Invitatory
  and some Introits retain older practice of Refrain—Verse—Refrain
  —[etc. to] *Gloria patri*—Refrain.[2]
Ceremonial distinction: All solo portions of antiphonal chant sung either
  in stalls or by rulers at lectern in mid-choir; they are chants sung
  within the choir, without spatial dialogue.

---

[1] The small number of Offertory chants with verses have melismatic chant throughout. In this way they are musically (but not ritually or ceremonially) closer to responsorial chants.

[2] Invitatory refrain sung complete at beginning and end, but only half in between pairs of psalm verses, and by alternate sides of the choir.

6.

The Divine Office

The Office Before the Eighth Century

Morning and evening prayer were the main daily services celebrated by Christians in the early Church. Morning prayer began as a service of sung praise including the 'Laudate' psalms (Psalms 148–150)—hence its later Latin name, *Laudes matutinales* (morning praises), anglicized as Lauds. Evening prayer (Vespers) was marked by the ceremonial lighting of lamps (*lucernarium*). The custom disappeared in the medieval Western liturgy.

By the fourth century in Jerusalem there was a monastic service before dawn—the forerunner of the night Office of Matins, sometimes known as Vigils. The monks and nuns also met to pray during the day—a practice later formalized in the Offices of Prime, Terce, Sext, and None. (Much valuable information comes from the account of the Spanish nun, Egeria, who described the liturgy in Jerusalem during her visit there, *c.*380.)

The classic formation of the Western Office is most clearly expounded in the Rule of St Benedict, compiled in the first half of the sixth century. But, as outlined in Chapter 1, Benedict's is just one of a group of monastic Uses found at this time. The liturgical sections of his Rule (mainly chapters 8 to 20) describe the times and order of daily corporate worship in the monastery, including the recitation of the Psalter. Though intended for his own monastery at Monte Cassino in central Italy, Benedict's Rule has been adopted in monasteries through-out the Western Church, especially since the ninth-century revival. Its counterpart, the 'secular' Office in the West, is also derived from monastic practice; in this case from the Roman churches staffed by monks in the sixth and seventh centuries. Monastic liturgy has therefore provided the basis for the mainstream of the Western Office.

The Medieval Office

The sixth-century monastic Rules set forth seven hours (i.e. times) of prayer, together with the night Office of Matins. The basic timetable and order of these services were adopted throughout the medieval Western Church, though some aspects of internal structure and details (i.e. distribution of psalmody) varied. Throughout Europe there are two principal liturgical traditions—monastic and secular; only the local Rites of Milan (Ambrosian) and Toledo (Mozarabic) remained significantly distinct in their liturgical orders and chant. Nevertheless the Frankish reforms of the eighth and ninth centuries, the constant flux of local observance throughout the Middle Ages, and the alterations made by the Papal Curia in Rome in the thirteenth and fourteenth centuries all contributed to changes which make clear-cut outlines or definitive summary difficult. In spite of this, it is possible to go some way to providing a reliable summary of the basic structure of the Office.

The Office was conceived for sung, corporate prayer. It was dominated by the recitation of the psalms. Only in Matins was there a substantial quantity of scriptural reading. In the other services a single short extract was recited, often no more than a reminder of the larger biblical context. Extended scriptural reading at morning and evening prayer became a feature of the reformed Protestant churches: medieval practice favoured periods of private scriptural reading and study, but this obviously excluded the illiterate.

The celebration of the Office extended throughout the day and night. Though the timetable varied in winter (All Saints to Easter) and summer, and was affected by geographical latitude, a typical northern European community would have celebrated Vespers in late afternoon. Compline was sung in mid-evening and followed by a period of sleep. Matins began shortly after midnight. In most cases Lauds followed directly, although in monastic churches there was a short break between the two services. A second period of sleep followed Lauds. Prime was sung at around six or seven in the morning. The working (or praying) day was punctuated by Terce, Sext, and None. What began in the monastic churches of Benedict's time as four or five hours each day in church proliferated after the tenth century to perhaps as many as ten or twelve hours in church, certainly on great feast-days.

See Fig. 3.1 for a diagram showing the liturgical day. A summary of the order of the medieval daily Office is laid out in Table 1.

THE MATERIALS OF THE OFFICE

The classification of materials within the Office needs brief explication. Four categories of text and music are referred to: ferial, seasonal, proper, and common. Items used as a norm throughout the year are ferial. Those that vary in Advent, Christmas, Lent, Easter, or other times of the year are seasonal. Those that are particular to a specific Sunday or feast are proper. Where a group of related feasts (e.g. feasts of apostles, martyrs, the blessed Virgin Mary) share a repertory of proper material this is identified as common. It should be noted that some writers identify ferial items as 'common' in discussing the Office, but this can cause confusion with the materials of the Common of the Saints (Commune Sanctorum—the proper items shared by a number of saint's feast-days). Nevertheless, it needs to be stressed that not all ferial items are limited to ferial days; they are, however, frequently found in the Ferial (Choir) Psalter.

Text and music do not necessarily coincide in their classification: a ferial text may have a seasonal melody (e.g. the hymn at Compline); equally, a seasonal, proper, or common text may use a ferial melody (e.g. a short respond or versicle and response). Some of the most elaborate patterns of the incidence of these categories are listed in the discussion of psalms and antiphons below (pp. 78 f.).

The Opening Versicle

Almost every Office began with the first verse from Psalm 69 sung as a versicle and response:

v. *Deus in adiutorium meum intende*
r. *Domine ad adiuvandum me festina*
(O God make speed to save me: O Lord make haste to help me.)

The exception was the night Office of Matins which began with a verse from Psalm 50:

TABLE I. *Summary of the order of the medieval daily office*

	Matins (longer form)	**Lauds**

Key:
CHOIR CHANTS
  (i.e. sung by
  the community)
Minister's chants
  or recitations
Dialogues between
  Minister or
  Cantor(s) or
  Soloists and
  Choir
	Opening Versicles
	INTRODUCTORY PSALM(S)
	HYMN
	First nocturn:
	
	PSALMS
	Prayer and Blessing
	Readings with *Responds*
	Second nocturn:
	PSALMS
	Prayer and Blessing
	Readings with *Responds*
	Third nocturn:
	
	PSALMS
	Prayer and Blessing
	Readings with *Responds*
	
	TE DEUM LAUDAMUS
	Lauds followed[a]
		Opening Versicle
		PSALMS and CANTICLE
		Sentence from scripture
		[Monastic Use: *Respond*]
		HYMN
		Versicle
		CANTICLE (BENEDICTUS)
		Prayer
		Blessing

Notes: The table is highly simplified, and shows none of the variants found on other days, especially at Matins. Though not indicated here, psalms and canticles are almost all sung with antiphons before and after them.

[a] Monastic Use: Old Testament CANTICLES replaced psalms in third nocturn; after TE DEUM there followed Gospel reading, TE DECET LAUS, and Prayer. There was a break before Lauds.

V. *Domine labia mea aperies*
R. *Et os meum annuntiabit laudem tuam*
(O Lord open thou my lips: and my mouth shall show forth thy praise.)

This was normally followed by *Deus in adiutorium*. However, in some Uses *Domine labia mea* replaced *Deus in adiutorium*; in others it followed *Deus in adiutorium* and *Gloria patri*. St Benedict instructed that *Domine labia mea* should be sung three times after *Gloria patri* at Matins.

On a few occasions in some Uses *Deus in adiutorium* was replaced by a proper versicle and response.

TABLE I (*cont.*):

Prime, Terce, Sext, None	Vespers	Compline
		Secular Use:
Opening Versicle	*Opening Versicle*	*Opening Versicle*
HYMN	PSALMS	PSALMS
PSALMS	Sentence from scripture	Sentence from scripture
Sentence from scripture	*Respond* (not always included)	*Respond*
[Secular Use: *Respond*]	HYMN	HYMN
Versicle	*Versicle*	*Versicle*
[Prime in secular, and all four	CANTICLE (MAGNIFICAT)	CANTICLE (NUNC DIMITTIS)
hours in monastic Use:	Prayer	*Preces*
Preces]	*Blessing*	Prayer
Prayer		*Blessing*
Blessing		**Monastic Use:**
		Opening Versicle
		PSALMS
		HYMN
		Sentence from scripture
		Versicle
		Preces
		Prayer
		Blessing

Gloria patri

Gloria patri et filio et spiritui sancto
Sicut erat in principio et nunc et semper et in saecula saeculorum. Amen
(Glory be to the Father and to the Son and to the Holy Ghost: As it was in the
beginning is now and ever shall be world without end. Amen.)

The short doxology (*Gloria patri*) was one of the most frequently
recited texts. It followed *Deus in adiutorium* at all Offices. It was recited
at the end of every psalm (or portion of a psalm) and canticle. The first
section (*Gloria patri . . . sancto*) was sung in many responds. It was not
sung on the solemn days of Holy Week (see Chapter 9).

Alleluia

The acclamation *alleluia*, a Hebrew cry of joy, was also very frequently used. It followed almost every sung text in Eastertide. It was never proclaimed at all in the penitential season between Septuagesima and Easter.

At the beginning of the Offices it was sung after *Gloria patri*. But at this point in the penitential season it was replaced by *Laus tibi domine rex aeternae gloriae* (Praise be to thee O Lord, king of eternal glory).

Psalm and Antiphon

The psalms are discussed in detail in Chapter 5. Their recitation formed the core of every Office. Most psalms were sung with an antiphon, either in the sequence

Antiphon 1—Psalm 1—Antiphon 1, Antiphon 2—Psalm 2—Antiphon 2, etc.,

or

Antiphon—group of psalms—Antiphon.

In the Middle Ages it became increasingly common for only the beginning of the antiphon to be sung before the psalm by the appointed singer(s) except on feast-days: the complete antiphon was sung after the psalm by the whole community.

A psalm was begun (intoned) by the appointed singer(s) and then sung alternately by each side of the community. Evidence is not always clear but it appears that each side normally sang a whole verse (rather than half a verse) in turn, including *Gloria patri* (which counts as two verses). Most often the first verse was sung by the duty side, though a Salisbury rubric implies that the first verse was sung by *decani* (see Chapter 2). Normally, the opening intonation was sung only at the beginning of the psalm; thereafter each verse began on the reciting note.

The pattern for the daily recitation of psalms is presented in Appendix 2.4. There are two main forms of the *cursus*, monastic and secular. The normal ferial pattern was often broken on double feasts when special series of psalms were designated at Matins, Lauds, and Vespers (rarely at the other hours).

The Choir (or Ferial) Psalter often included ferial antiphons for the psalms. There was a vast repertory of proper antiphons for Sundays, seasons, feasts, and special observances (e.g. Rogation, the Dead). Again these were mostly for Matins, Lauds, and Vespers.

The combination of psalms and antiphons can therefore be as follows:

Psalms ferial: antiphons ferial;
Psalms ferial: antiphons proper;
Psalms proper: antiphons proper

Many of the sequences of proper psalms can be found in the Commune Sanctorum (Common of the Saints) in Breviary, Antiphonal, and Ordinal.

The melodies of the antiphons were characteristic, and each was classified into one of the eight church modes and then into one of a series of subcategories. For every mode there was a corresponding basic melodic formula (known as a tone) for the recitation of the psalms, together with a series of variants to match the melodic subgroups of the antiphons. The tone to which a psalm was sung had to correspond with the mode of the antiphon sung with it. In some Uses there were solemn forms of the psalm tones for principal feasts. There was also a repertory of *neuma* (melismatic endings) to be sung at the end of the last antiphon of a group of psalms: these had also to be matched by modal classification.

Some commentaries refer to 'anthem' rather than antiphon. In the Latin liturgy there is no distinction.

There were a few exceptional ways of singing psalms in the Office.

1. A psalm could be sung without an antiphon (e.g. Psalm 3 at the beginning of monastic Matins, and Psalm 66 in monastic Lauds).

2. The antiphon could be repeated after each verse or group of verses in the manner of early Church practice. The Invitatory at Matins (Psalm 94) was the only common example of this practice. This psalm was divided into five sections sung by soloists (normally the rulers or cantors); the Invitatory (i.e. antiphon) was sung (whole or in part) at the beginning and end and after each section and the *Gloria patri*. One form of performance was:

a1–2/A1–2/v1–2/$A1$/v3–4/$A2$/v5–7/$A1$/v8–9/$A2$/v10–11/$A1$/Gloria/
$A1$.a1.$A2$

(Key: a, v, Gloria-soloists; A-full choir; A-half choir, alternately; a, A, A is antiphon; v is psalm verse(s).)

Hymn

Hymns consist of non-scriptural Christian texts, normally written in stanzas in stressed metre and sung to a repeated melody stanza by stanza.

Already specified in the sixth-century Rule of St Benedict, hymns were included in all the Offices by the eleventh century throughout the secular and monastic Uses. Many were written in the early centuries of the Latin Church, though the repertory continued to expand during the Middle Ages.

At Matins and the Little Hours the hymn preceded the main body of psalmody; at Lauds, Vespers, and secular Compline the hymn followed the psalmody and reading; at monastic Compline the hymn, somewhat unusually, followed the psalmody but preceded the reading.

The hymn at each of the Little Hours and at Compline scarcely varied throughout the year. The text was generally unchanging (though sometimes there were seasonal variations), but the melody was often seasonal.

At Matins, Lauds, and Vespers there were common, seasonal, and proper hymns, selected according to the season and day. The common hymns could have seasonal melodies. A number of proper hymns for feasts were compiled in the Common of Saints (Commune Sanctorum).

In some Uses the hymn was replaced by a Sequence (or *Prosa*) on certain principal or double feasts.

Versicle and Response

A simple dialogue (indicated in books as v. and r.) between an officiant (not necessarily a priest) and the rest of the community was frequently used. The opening dialogue of the Office (*Deus in adiutorium*) is typical. A versicle and response were also sung after most hymns (though not at Matins nor at monastic Compline). Other instances are noted in the detailed lists below. Some were proper; most were verses extracted from psalms. They were sung to one of a small group of simple melodic formulas, some of which might vary according to the rank of the day.

Lesson or Chapter

A reading from the scriptures or from the Church Fathers was designated lesson (*lectio*) or chapter (*capitulum*). Except at Matins, the reading (*capitulum*) was often very short—little more than a single verse. Many were evidently recited from memory. They were often seasonal or proper, but there were also groups common to each Office for selection *ad libitum*. Those at the Little Hours and Compline changed least.

Longer readings (*lectiones*) were used at Matins. Before each lesson the reader sought and received a blessing. In the longer form of Matins there were three groups of lessons, one group in each nocturn; the first group scriptural, the second patristic or hagiographical, the third from a homily on the Gospel text of the day (the relevant verse was recited before the lessons). In secular Use there were three lessons in each group (nine in all); in monastic Use there were four (a total of twelve). The scriptural readings (*historia*) worked through the whole Bible (excluding the Gospels) during the year. During the Sundays after Pentecost, Breviaries commonly separated the lessons of the first two nocturns (listed by biblical book) from those of the third nocturn (listed by Sundays). Proper readings were designated for many feasts.

On lesser days the number of lessons at Matins varied according to Use (secular or monastic), rank of day, and season. This complex matter is dealt with in the detailed descriptions of the forms of Matins later in the chapter.

Both chapters and lessons were recited to one of a small group of designated tones (melodic formulas), in a manner comparable to the Epistle and Gospel at Mass. Both forms of reading at the Office frequently ended with the versicle and response:

v. *Tu autem domine miserere nobis*
r. *Deo gratias*
(But thou O Lord have mercy upon us. Thanks to be God.)

The practice varied: in some instances only the response *Deo gratias* was said; in Advent and Lent, only the versicle *Tu autem* was said at Matins; in Holy Week and at the Office of the Dead both were omitted. When the reading was from the Old Testament the versicle could be *Haec dicit dominus convertimini ad me et salvi eritis* (Thus saith the Lord, turn to me and ye shall be saved).

In the monastic Use the longer form of Matins also included the Gospel after *Te deum laudamus*. The text was that of the Mass of the day, and also corresponded with the Gospel verse before the lessons from the homily, but here it was recited in full. It was announced as at Mass with the greeting *Dominus vobiscum* (see 'Greeting' below) and title. It was recited to a Gospel tone and ended with the choir response *Deo gratias*. It was followed by the short prose hymn (in some sources called canticle) *Te decet laus*.

Respond

In addition to the versicle and response said at the end of most chapters and lessons, there was a more formal response to the reading. In some instances this was a versicle and response; more often it was a respond. In both cases the text was usually scriptural, and frequently taken from the psalms.

The characteristics of the respond have already been outlined in Chapter 5, but given their complexity it is worth expanding on this. The forms and musical setting of the respond vary considerably, but the principle is unchanging: a choral refrain preceding and following a solo verse. There may be more than one verse, in which case the refrain may be subdivided and repeated only in part after each verse.

Some writers refer to the form as responsory, and use the term respond to identify the refrain.

The short respond was used at most Offices, especially in secular liturgies. The performance of the short respond at Compline in the Roman Use is typical:

Soloist(s):   *In manus tuas domine, commendo spiritum meum*
Choir: *In manus tuas domine, commendo spiritum meum*
Soloist(s):   *Redemisti nos domine deus veritatis*
Choir: *Commendo spiritum meum*
Soloist(s):   *Gloria patri et filio et spiritui sancto*
Choir: *In manus tuas domine, commendo spiritum meum*
(Into thy hands O Lord I commend my spirit. For thou hast redeemed me O Lord thou God of truth. Glory be to the Father . . . [Psalm 30: 6])

No more than the first word of a repetition may be shown in sources.

At Matins the responds were more extended, especially in their musical treatment. Here the soloist(s) intoned the opening of the refrain and the choir continued with it immediately. In its simplest form the performance took the form rR—v—R (where r is solo beginning of refrain, R is choral refrain, v is solo verse).

More elaborate responds often had several verses, and the last respond of each nocturn included *Gloria patri*; the refrain itself could be subdivided. A common pattern is

rR1–2/v/R2/Gloria/R2,

but a more complex pattern can be

rR1–3/v1/R2–3/v2/R3/Gloria/R3.

Gloria patri was omitted during Passiontide and there was often provision for the repetition of the whole refrain at the end of the respond (referred to as doubling).

Canticle and Antiphon

The principal canticles are those from St Luke's Gospel. *Benedictus* (the song of Zacharias, Luke 1: 68–79) is sung daily at Lauds; *Magnificat* (the song of Mary, Luke 1: 46–55) is recited daily at Vespers. They are invariable. Each canticle could be sung to a more solemn (i.e. elaborate) form of the psalm tones. Each was sung with an antiphon. The canticle-antiphons are musically among the finest in the repertory, more extended than the psalm-antiphons. They were almost always proper to the day, or at least to the Sunday and the week following. Sources frequently identify the antiphon as *ad evangelium*, i.e. for the gospel canticle; the text is often taken from the Gospel of the day. As with the psalms, the tone of the canticle had to be matched to the antiphon: some Antiphonals include an incipit or summary ending to show the tone of the chant.

The third gospel canticle, *Nunc dimittis* (the song of Simeon, Luke 2: 29–32) was sung at secular (but not monastic) Compline. Its antiphon was most often *Salva nos domine* and changed rarely.

Other canticles taken from the Old Testament were sung at Lauds and in the third nocturn of monastic Matins. These were treated as part of the *cursus* of psalmody, and are listed in Appendix 2.3.

Though not strictly a canticle, the prose hymn *Te deum laudamus* (the song of Ambrose and Augustine) was sung at the end of Matins on Sundays and on feasts of nine (or twelve) lessons. It was sung without antiphon. In some Uses (e.g. the English secular Uses) *Te deum* was omitted during the penitential seasons of Advent and Septuagesima to Easter; in such cases it was often customary for the last respond to be 'doubled' (i.e. the whole refrain was sung through complete at the end of the normal respond sequence). In some Uses (e.g. later medieval Roman and Tridentine) *Te deum* replaced the ninth respond, except during the penitential seasons.

After the Canticle

This was the most variable part of every Office, and the order on Sunday or a feast often differed from that of a ferial day. At some Offices on Sunday and feasts it consisted only of Collect and Blessing. However, other items were commonly interpolated, resulting in the sequence: Lesser Litany, Lord's Prayer, Preces, Collect, and Blessing. A series of memorials or suffrages could follow the collect at Lauds and Vespers.

Lesser Litany and Lord's Prayer

An extended litany was said in the early Church, but by medieval times this was truncated to the Greek petitions *Kyrie eleison, Christe eleison, Kyrie eleison* (Lord have mercy upon us, Christ have mercy upon us, Lord have mercy upon us) which were sometimes sung three times. The exact manner of performance varied, but there was a dialogue between officiant and choir.

The Lord's Prayer followed. The officiant either intoned *Pater noster* (the remainder of the text was then prayed silently, possibly with *Ave Maria*), or else he sang the whole prayer. In either case the conclusion was sung as versicle and response:

v. *Et ne nos inducas in tentationem*
r. *Sed libera nos a malo*
(And lead us not into temptation, but deliver us from evil.)

Preces

A series of psalm verses sung as versicle and response between officiant and choir was referred to as preces. At Prime and Compline the preces generally included a confession, and even a whole psalm (or psalms). The texts were normally ferial (i.e. unchanging).

Greeting

It was usual to include the liturgical greeting before prayers and blessings. It was unchanging in text, though there were different tones in some Uses.

v. *Dominus vobiscum*
r. *Et cum spiritu tuo*
(The Lord be with you. And with thy spirit.)

Its use was assumed and will rarely be included in the Breviary.

Collect

Every Office ended with a collect (*oratio*). There is a large corpus of such prayers, many of them ancient. Most were proper either to the day or to Sunday and the week following; proper collects often corresponded with those used at Mass. They are found in the Breviary. The collect was recited by the officiant, and all responded *Amen*. Collects were recited on a single note with inflections (as in the readings); these tones might vary according to the rank of the day. A collect was prefixed by *Oremus* (Let us pray).

Memorials and Suffrages

In the later Middle Ages additional intentions were included at the end of Lauds and Vespers. Some were proper (memorials) and some were chosen from a fixed repertory (suffrages). Each consisted of a self-contained liturgical unit: antiphon, versicle and response, collect. They are discussed in detail in Chapter 8.

Blessing

The Office normally ended with a blessing in the form of a versicle and response:

v. *Benedicamus domino*
r. *Deo gratias*
(Let us bless the Lord. Thanks be to God.)

This was preceded by the greeting (*Dominus vobiscum*) and could be followed by a short, spoken prayer for those absent or departed.

At Lauds and Vespers some Uses included *Benedicamus* after the collect and again after the memorials and suffrages. In other cases where two Offices were celebrated successively (e.g. Matins and Lauds) *Benedicamus* was sung only at the end of the second Office.

There were special melodies for *Benedicamus* at some Offices, according to season and rank of the day. Solemn blessings (benedictions) were provided, especially for abbots and bishops: these were generally reserved for principal feasts and followed the *Benedicamus* dialogue.

THE DAILY OFFICE IN DETAIL

Even detailed lists of the order of the daily Office have to be viewed with caution. The Uses of secular and monastic churches were distinct in the order as well as the content of the Office. Within each of the two Uses there were often two versions of an Office, one for Sundays and greater feasts, the other for minor feasts and ferial weekdays. Matins was even more complex because of additional categories in the monastic Use. Most Offices were also subject to seasonal alteration (notably in Advent, Lent, and Easter), as well as to the influence of local customs and changes over the centuries.

THE STRUCTURE AND ORDER OF MATINS (*Ad Matutinas*)

The night Office of Matins is also known as Vigils or Nocturns. It was the only Office to include substantial readings. Its form varied considerably according to the rank of the day and (in monastic Use) season. Distinct characteristics of both content and form separated Matins in secular and monastic Uses. Nevertheless a common structure can be discerned:

Introduction
Nocturns (one, two, or three)
Conclusion

Each of these sections is discussed separately in relation to both secular and monastic Matins.

Secular Matins

1. The Introduction to Secular Matins

The introductory section of Matins consisted of three elements: opening dialogue, Invitatory, and hymn.

v. *Domine labia mea* . . . R. *Et os meum* . . .
v. *Deus in adiutorium* . . . R. *Domine ad adiuvandum* . . .
Gloria patri . . . *in saecula saeculorum. Amen*
Alleluia (*Laus tibi domine* . . . from Septuagesima to Holy Week)

Invitatory (ferial, seasonal, common, or proper) together with Psalm 93 (*Venite exsultemus*)

Hymn (seasonal, common, or proper)

The hymn was a relatively late addition. Though found in most medieval sources it was omitted on certain feasts (e.g. Epiphany, Easter, and the week following) in some sources.

2. The Ordering of the Nocturns at Secular Matins

The nocturns formed the heart of Matins and followed the same order in secular Use. Each full nocturn consisted of:

Psalmody
    3, 6, or 12 psalms (according to the Use and the day) with antiphons;
    psalms—ferial, common, or proper;
    antiphons—ferial, seasonal, common, or proper

Versicle and response—seasonal, common, or proper
Lord's Prayer (*Pater noster*)
Absolution (not found in all Uses, especially earlier ones)

Blessing—Lesson 1—Respond 1
Blessing—Lesson 2—Respond 2
Blessing—Lesson 3—Respond 3

The blessings were taken from a limited selection. The lessons and responds were drawn from the vast annual cycle found in Temporale, Sanctorale, and Commune Sanctorum.

    In the third nocturn the lessons were taken from a homily attributed to one of the Church Fathers or a Pope. The homily was based on a Gospel text taken from the Mass of the day. This Gospel verse was recited before the first lesson in the third nocturn.

From this basic pattern three variant orders emerge for the nocturns in secular Matins:

A. At Matins on Sundays, Double Feasts, and Simple Feasts of Nine Lessons

First nocturn

3 psalms (on Sunday 3 groups of 4 psalms) with 3 antiphons
Versicle and response—*Pater noster*—Absolution
Blessing—Lesson 1—Respond
Blessing—Lesson 2—Respond
Blessing—Lesson 3—Respond [Lessons from scripture]

Second nocturn

3 psalms with 3 antiphons
Versicle and response—*Pater noster*—Absolution
Blessing—Lesson 4—Respond
Blessing—Lesson 5—Respond
Blessing—Lesson 6—Respond
  [Lessons from patristic or hagiographical writings]

Third nocturn

3 psalms with 3 antiphons
Versicle and response—*Pater noster*—Absolution
Blessing—Gospel verse—Lesson 7—Respond
Blessing—Lesson 8—Respond
Blessing—Lesson 9—Respond
  [Lessons from homily of Church Father or Pope]

B. At Matins on Simple Feasts of Three Lessons

One nocturn

9 psalms with 9 antiphons
Versicle and response—*Pater noster*—Absolution
Blessing—Lesson 1—Respond
Blessing—Lesson 2—Respond
Blessing—Lesson 3—Respond [Lessons from scripture]

C. At Matins on Ferias

One nocturn

6 groups of 2 psalms, with 6 antiphons
Versicle and response—*Pater noster*—Absolution
Blessing—Lesson 1—Respond
Blessing—Lesson 2—Respond
Blessing—Lesson 3—Respond [Lessons from scripture]

To these may be added two other orderings of the nocturns:

D. At Matins on Easter Day and Pentecost

One nocturn

3 psalms with 3 antiphons
Versicle and response—*Pater noster*—Absolution
Blessing—Lesson 1—Respond
Blessing—Lesson 2—Respond
Blessing—Lesson 3—Respond [Lessons from scripture]

E. At Matins for the Daily Little Office of the Virgin

One nocturn

3 psalms with 1 antiphon
Versicle and response—*Pater noster*—Absolution
Blessing—Lesson 1—Respond
Blessing—Lesson 2—Respond
Blessing—Lesson 3—Respond [Lessons normally from scripture]

3. The Conclusion of Secular Matins

The conclusion to secular Matins was brief, but again there were several orders:

At the end of secular Matins on Sundays, double feasts, simple feasts of nine lessons (outside the penitential seasons):

Te deum laudamus (sung after the last respond)

At the end of secular Matins on Sundays, double feasts, simple feasts of nine lessons in the late medieval Roman (Papal Curia) and Franciscan Uses (outside the penitential seasons):

Te deum laudamus (sung instead of last respond)

During the penitential seasons (Advent and Septuagesima to Easter) there was generally no *Te deum*. Instead, some Uses specified that the last respond should be 'doubled' on Sundays, double feasts, and feasts of nine lessons: the whole of the refrain was sung again at the end of the normal sequence of the respond.

On all days (whether *Te deum* was sung or not) there was a versicle and response (seasonal, common, or proper) before Lauds. Lauds followed immediately.

Monastic Matins

Though the underlying structure of monastic Matins was related to secular Use, it possessed a number of individual features which affected its forms.

1. The Introduction to Monastic Matins

In the monastic forms of Matins the order of the opening dialogue was commonly reversed, and Psalm 3 preceded the Invitatory and hymn.

v. *Deus in adiutorium . . .* R. *Domine ad adiuvandum*
Gloria patri . . . in saecula saeculorum. Amen
Alleuia (Laus tibi domine . . . from Septuagesima to Holy Week)
v. *Domine labia mea . . .* ⎫
                                    ⎬ this pair sung three times
R. *Et os meum . . .* ⎭
Psalm 3 (*Domine quid multiplicati*, recited without antiphon)
Invitatory (ferial, seasonal, common, or proper) together with Psalm 94
   (*Venite exsultemus*)
Hymn (seasonal, common, or proper)

2. The Ordering of the Nocturns at Monastic Matins

Nocturns

The contrasts between monastic and secular Matins are most marked in the structure of the nocturns. The monastic forms are those laid down by St Benedict in the Rule.

The psalmody of the monastic schemes was consistent: there were always two groups of six psalms (though the number of antiphons varied). Matins with three nocturns included three Old Testament canticles in the third nocturn (often known as the monastic canticles). The other forms of Matins had two nocturns. In the first nocturn, the winter form had three lessons, but that for summer just one (because of the shorter night); both have just a chapter (not in the lectionary and recited from memory) in the second nocturn.

A. AT MATINS ON SUNDAYS, DOUBLE FEASTS, AND SIMPLE FEASTS OF TWELVE LESSONS

First nocturn

6 psalms with 6 antiphons
Versicle and response—*Pater noster*—Absolution
Blessing—Lesson 1—Respond
Blessing—Lesson 2—Respond
Blessing—Lesson 3—Respond
Blessing—Lesson 4—Respond [Lessons from scripture]

Second nocturn

6 psalms with 6 antiphons
Versicle and response—*Pater noster*—Absolution
Blessing—Lesson 5—Respond
Blessing—Lesson 6—Respond
Blessing—Lesson 7—Respond
Blessing—Lesson 8—Respond
    [Lessons from patristic or hagiographical writings]

Third nocturn

3 canticles with 1 antiphon
Versicle and response—*Pater noster*—Absolution

Blessing—Gospel verse—Lesson 9—Respond
Blessing—Lesson 10—Respond
Blessing—Lesson 11—Respond
Blessing—Lesson 12—Respond
  [Lessons from homily of Church Father or Pope]

B. At Matins on Simple Feasts of Three Lessons and on Winter Ferias

First nocturn

6 psalms with 1, 3, or 6 antiphons
Versicle and response—*Pater noster*—Absolution
Blessing—Lesson 1—Respond
Blessing—Lesson 2—Respond
Blessing—Lesson 3—Respond [Lessons from scripture]

Second nocturn

6 psalms with 1, 3, or 6 antiphons
Chapter—Versicle and response

C. At Matins on Summer Ferias (Easter to 1 November)

First nocturn

6 psalms with 1, 3, or 6 antiphons
Versicle and response
Short Lesson—Short Respond [Lesson from scripture]

Second nocturn

6 psalms with 1, 3, or 6 antiphons
Chapter—Versicle and response

3. The Conclusion of Monastic Matins

The end of Matins was more extended in monastic Use, especially
when there were twelve lessons. Two forms were used throughout
the year.

AT THE END OF MATINS WITH TWELVE LESSONS

Te deum laudamus
Gospel (introduced as at Mass; *Deo gratias* at the end)
Te decet laus
Collect (of the day)

Lauds then followed, normally with only a short break when the ministers revested (if necessary) and the others of the community could leave the church to answer the call of nature (Rule of St Benedict, chapter 8).

AT THE END OF OTHER FORMS OF MATINS

Kyrie eleison
Pater noster
Preces
Collect (of the week or of the day)
Benedicamus domino

There was a gap before Lauds, occupied with other devotions. However, there were monasteries (e.g. St Mary's York) where Lauds followed Matins without a break on weekdays. In such circumstances *Benedicamus domino* was omitted, and the choir proceeded directly to the first psalm of Lauds (Psalm 66) after the Matins collect.

A Summary Comparison of Secular and Monastic Matins

SECULAR MATINS ON SUNDAYS, DOUBLE FEASTS AND SIMPLE FEASTS OF NINE LESSONS	MONASTIC MATINS ON SUNDAYS, DOUBLE FEASTS AND SIMPLE FEASTS OF TWELVE LESSONS
Domine labia mea aperies	
Deus in adiutorium	*Deus in adiutorium*
Gloria patri	*Gloria patri*
Alleluia	*Alleluia*
	Domine labia mea aperies (thrice)
	Psalm 3 (without antiphon)
Invitatory and Psalm 94	Invitatory and Psalm 94
Hymn (seasonal, common, or proper)	Hymn (seasonal, common, or proper)

First nocturn	*First nocturn*

Psalmody
  3 psalms (on Sunday 3 groups of 4 psalms) with 3 antiphons (common or proper)
	Psalmody
	  6 psalms with 6 antiphons (common or proper)

Versicle and response (common or proper)	Versicle and response (common or proper)
Pater noster	*Pater noster*
Absolution	Absolution (or versicle and response)
Blessing	Blessing
Lesson 1 (ending *Haec dicit*, or *Tu autem* with R. *Deo gratias*)	Lesson 1 (ending *Haec dicit*, or *Tu autem* with R. *Deo gratias*)
Respond 1	Respond 1
Blessing	Blessing
Lesson 2	Lesson 2
Respond 2	Respond 2
Blessing	Blessing
Lesson 3	Lesson 3
Respond 3 (with *Gloria patri*)	Respond 3
	Blessing
	Lesson 4
	Respond 4 (with *Gloria patri*)
(Lessons from daily, common, or proper lectionary; responds from Sunday, common, or proper sequence)	(Lessons from daily, common, or proper lectionary; responds from Sunday, common, or proper sequence)

Second nocturn	*Second nocturn*

Psalmody
  3 psalms with 3 antiphons
	Psalmody
	  6 psalms with 6 antiphons

then all as first nocturn above until Respond 6	then all as first nocturn above until Respond 8

Third nocturn	*Third nocturn*

Psalmody
  3 psalms with 3 antiphons
	Psalmody
	  3 lesser canticles (seasonal rota) with 1 antiphon (common or proper)

Versicle and response (common or proper)
Pater noster
Absolution

Blessing
Gospel verse
Lesson 7
Respond 7

Blessing
Lesson 8
Respond 8

Blessing
Lesson 9
Respond 9 with *Gloria patri* [omitted in late medieval Roman Use]

Te deum laudamus

Versicle and response (common or proper)
Pater noster
Absolution (or versicle and response)

Blessing
Gospel verse
Lesson 9
Respond 9

Blessing
Lesson 10
Respond 10

Blessing
Lesson 11
Respond 11
Blessing
Lesson 12
Respond 12 with *Gloria patri*

Te deum laudamus
Gospel of the day
Te decet laus
Kyrie, Pater noster, Preces
Collect (of the day)

SECULAR MATINS ON SIMPLE FEASTS OF THREE LESSONS AND FERIAS

Domine labia mea aperies
Deus in adiutorium
Gloria patri
Alleluia

Invitatory and Psalm 94
Hymn (seasonal, common, or proper)

MONASTIC MATINS ON SIMPLE FEASTS OF THREE LESSONS AND WINTER FERIAS

Deus in adiutorium
Gloria patri
Alleluia
Domine labia mea aperies (thrice)
Psalm 3 (without antiphon)
Invitatory and Psalm 94
Hymn (seasonal, common, or proper)

Nocturn

Psalmody
 Feasts: 9 psalms (ferial or
  common)
   with 9 antiphons
   (common or proper)
 Ferias: 12 psalms (ferial)
   with 6 antiphons
   (ferial or seasonal)
Versicle and response (of week,
 common, or proper)
Pater noster
Absolution

Blessing
Lesson 1 (ending *Haec dicit*, or *Tu
 autem* with R. *Deo gratias*)
Respond 1

Blessing
Lesson 2
Respond 2

Blessing
Lesson 3
Respond 3 (with *Gloria patri*)
(Lessons from daily, common, or
 proper lectionary; responds from
 Sunday, common, or proper
 sequence)

First nocturn

Psalmody
 6 psalms (ferial or common) with
  1, 3, or 6 antiphons (ferial,
  seasonal, common, or proper)

Versicle and response (of week,
 common, or proper)
Pater noster
Absolution

Blessing
Lesson 1 (ending *Haec dicit*, or *Tu
 autem* with R. *Deo gratias*)
Respond 1

Blessing
Lesson 2
Respond 2

Blessing
Lesson 3
Respond 3 (with *Gloria patri*)
(Lessons from daily, common, or
 proper lectionary; responds from
 Sunday, common, or proper
 sequence)

Second nocturn

Psalmody.
 6 psalms with 1, 3, or 6 antiphons
Chapter (seasonal, common, or
 proper)
Versicle and response (of the week or
 common)
Kyrie, Pater noster, Preces
Collect (of the day or week)
Benedicamus domino

In the monastic form of Matins on summer ferias the psalms and versicle (as on winter ferias) were followed immediately by the short lesson and short respond (both from a weekly cycle). The second nocturn then followed, as in the winter form, with chapter selected from the seasonal series and versicle and collect of the week.

Lauds (*Ad Laudes Matutinales* or *In Laudibus*)

Lauds had its roots in the morning prayer of the early Church. It retained some of the ancient fixed psalmody. Its structure was related to Vespers. Secular and monastic Use were much closer, and there was more stability of form (here and in the other hours) than at Matins. In secular Use it normally followed Matins without a break.

In monastic churches there was at least a short break before Lauds on Sundays and feast-days when the longer form of Matins was celebrated (see above, monastic Matins). On other days Matins and Lauds may have been separated or Lauds may have followed on directly. For instance, at Norwich in the thirteenth century, additional psalms and (in winter) both Matins and Lauds of the Dead were recited after Matins of the day but before Lauds; yet at St Mary's, York (*c.* 1400) Lauds followed on immediately, beginning not with *Deus in adiutorium* but with Psalm 66.

Secular Lauds	Monastic Lauds
Versicle and response (seasonal, common, or proper)	
Deus in adiutorium	*Deus in adiutorium*
Gloria patri	*Gloria patri*
Alleluia	*Alleluia*
Psalmody	Psalmody
(5 psalms with 1 or 5 antiphons)	(First psalm without antiphon; then 5 psalms with 1 or 5 antiphons)
Psalm 92 (Sunday and feasts; Psalm 50 on other days)	Psalm 66 (no antiphon)
	Psalm 50 (92 on some Sundays and feasts)

(SECULAR LAUDS)	(MONASTIC LAUDS)
1 variable psalm	2 variable psalms
Psalms 62 and 66 (as one psalm)	
Old Testament canticle	Old Testament canticle
Psalms 148–150 (as one psalm)	Psalms 148–150 (as one psalm)
Chapter (seasonal, common, or proper) with response *Deo gratias*	Chapter (seasonal, common, or proper) with response *Deo gratias*
	Short Respond (seasonal, common, or proper)
Hymn (seasonal, common, or proper)	Hymn (seasonal, common, or proper)
Versicle and response (seasonal, common, or proper)	Versicle and response (seasonal, common, or proper)
Benedictus with antiphon (most often proper; Temporale text frequently from Gospel at Mass)	*Benedictus* with antiphon (most often proper; Temporale text frequently from Gospel at Mass)
[*Kyrie*, *Pater noster*, Preces on specified ferias and vigils]	*Kyrie*, *Pater noster*, Preces (ferial)
Collect (of the day or week)	Collect (of the day or week)
Benedicamus domino	*Benedicamus domino*

In both Uses there were commonly additional memorials and suffrages (see Chapter 8). These would follow the collect and precede *Benedicamus*. However, in many foundations they followed *Benedicamus*; a second *Benedicamus* was then sung at the end of the memorials and suffrages.

Where the Little Office of the Virgin (see Chapter 8) was recited in choir the sequence was often thus: Office of the day to *Benedicamus*, Little Office to collect, other memorials and suffrages, concluding *Benedicamus*.

While five psalm-antiphons were most common at Lauds, a single psalm-antiphon was sung on certain ferias and in some votive or commemorative Offices. Some Uses also allowed for seven antiphons (thus treating Psalms 148–150 separately) on specific important feasts.

PRIME (*Ad Primam*)

Prime was the first of the lesser hours, though more substantial than Terce, Sext, and None. Each of these lesser hours was characterized by the singing of the hymn before the psalms, and by the absence of a canticle. A more extensive group of psalms (especially in secular Use on Sunday) was laid down for Prime, including the Athanasian creed, *Quicumque vult*. As with the other lesser hours, much of Prime was unchanging, and any proper materials were usually borrowed from Lauds.

SECULAR PRIME	MONASTIC PRIME
Deus in adiutorium	*Deus in adiutorium*
Gloria patri	*Gloria patri*
Alleluia	*Alleluia*
Hymn (*Jam lucis orto sidere*, ferial— seasonal doxologies and melodies)	Hymn (*Jam lucis orto sidere*, ferial— seasonal doxologies and melodies)
Psalms with one antiphon (ferial rota; antiphon ferial, seasonal, or borrowed from Lauds)	Psalms with one antiphon (ferial rota; antiphon ferial, seasonal, or borrowed from Lauds)
Chapter (repertory of three texts according to season, with ending *Deo gratias*)	Chapter (repertory of three texts according to season, with ending v. *Tu autem* . . . R. *Deo gratias*)
Short Respond (fixed refrain, but seasonal, common, or proper verse)	
v. *Exsurge domine adiuva nos*	v. *Exsurge domine adiuva nos*
R. *Et libera nos propter nomen tuum* (occasional seasonal variants)	R. *Et libera nos propter nomen tuum* (occasional seasonal variants)
Kyrie, Pater noster, Credo in deum	*Kyrie, Pater noster, Credo in deum*
Preces	Preces
Confession, Absolution	Confession, Absolution
Preces	Preces
Collect (of the hour)	Collect (of the hour)
Benedicamus domino	*Benedicamus domino*

The psalmody needs some comment. On weekdays the secular Use had three psalms (53, 118 vv. 1–16, and 118 vv. 17–32) each concluding with *Gloria patri*. On Sunday the nine secular psalms were sung in five groups (21, 22; 23, 24; 25, 53; 117, 118 vv. 1–16; 118 vv. 17–32), each group ending with *Gloria patri*. In monastic Use Psalm 118 was sung in portions of eight rather than sixteen verses (this distinction also applied at the other lesser hours).

Quicumque vult followed as a final psalm on Sundays, double feasts, and simple feasts of nine lessons. In some Uses it had a separate antiphon. In monastic Use, if not sung here, it was sung after the second series of preces.

The rules for the recitation of preces varied according to place and date. In most cases they corresponded to the sequence recited at Compline but individual rubrics need to be consulted.

TERCE, SEXT, NONE (*Ad Tertiam, Sextam, Nonam*)

All three hours followed an identical pattern:

SECULAR TERCE, SEXT, AND NONE	MONASTIC TERCE, SEXT, AND NONE
Deus in adiutorium	*Deus in adiutorium*
Gloria patri	*Gloria patri*
Alleluia	*Alleluia*
Hymn	Hymn
Terce: *Nunc sancte nobis spiritus*	Terce: *Nunc sancte nobis spiritus*
Sext: *Rector potens verax deus*	Sext: *Rector potens verax deus*
None: *Rerum deus tenax vigor*	None: *Rerum deus tenax vigor*
(few textual variants;	(few textual variants;
seasonal melodies)	seasonal melodies)
Psalms with one antiphon	Psalms with one antiphon
3 portions of Psalm 118 (16 verses	Fixed rota—3 psalms or 3 portions
each with *Gloria patri*); antiphon	of Psalm 118 (each of 8 verses);
ferial, seasonal, or borrowed	antiphon ferial, seasonal, or
from Lauds	borrowed from Lauds
Chapter (seasonal, common, or	Chapter (seasonal, common, or
proper; could correspond with	proper; could correspond with
Lauds or Second Vespers)	Lauds or Second Vespers)
Short Respond (seasonal, common,	
or proper)	
Versicle and response (seasonal,	Versicle and response (seasonal,
common, or proper)	common, or proper)
	Kyrie, Pater noster, Preces
Collect (of the day or week)	Collect (of the day or week)
Benedicamus domino	*Benedicamus domino*

Vespers (*Ad Vesperas*)

Vespers derived from the principal evening service of the early Church. Celebrated at dusk, it may also be known as evensong or evening prayer. Vespers complemented Lauds in structure, though the psalms (unlike those at Lauds) all varied daily.

SECULAR VESPERS	MONASTIC VESPERS
Deus in adiutorium	*Deus in adiutorium*
Gloria patri	*Gloria patri*
Alleluia	*Alleluia*
Psalmody	Psalmody
5 psalms with 1 or 5 antiphons	4 psalms with 1 or 4 antiphons
Chapter (seasonal, common, or	Chapter (seasonal, common, or
proper) with response *Deo gratias*	proper) with response *Deo gratias*
[Respond (on certain Sundays and	[Respond (on certain Sundays and
feasts—common or proper)]	feasts—common or proper)]
Hymn (seasonal, common, or	Hymn (seasonal, common, or
proper)	proper)
Versicle and response (seasonal,	Versicle and response (seasonal,
common, or proper)	common, or proper)
Magnificat with antiphon (most often	*Magnificat* with antiphon (most often
proper; Temporale text frequently	proper; Temporale text frequently
from Gospel at Mass)	from Gospel at Mass)
[*Kyrie, Pater noster*, Preces on	*Kyrie, Pater noster*, Preces (ferial;
specified ferias and vigils;	sequence often as at Lauds)
sequence often as at Lauds]	
Collect (of the day or week)	Collect (of the day or week)
Benedicamus domino	*Benedicamus domino*

In both Uses there were commonly additional memorials and suffrages as at Lauds (see Chapter 8). These might follow the collect and precede *Benedicamus*. However, in many foundations they followed *Benedicamus*; a second *Benedicamus* was then sung at the end of the memorials and suffrages.

Where the Little Office of the Virgin (see Chapter 8) was recited in choir the memorials and suffrages often followed that Office.

COMPLINE (*Ad Completorium*)

This was the last Office of the day before the community retired to bed.

The monastic form was preceded by Collatio (a short Office centred on a reading), normally conducted in chapter house or cloister. It is frequently included in the Office books. In both Uses there was a versicle before the Office (as at secular Lauds).

The Office was distinct in the two Uses. Secular Compline was close to Lauds and Vespers in structure, but monastic Compline was individual in its ordering. The sequence of preces usually corresponded with that at Prime.

SECULAR COMPLINE	MONASTIC COMPLINE
	Collatio
	Blessing of reader
	v. *Jube domne benedicere*
	Blessing *Noctem quietam et vitam aeternam tribuat nobis omnipotens et misericors dominus*. R. *Amen*
	Lesson (ending *Tu autem . . .* R. *Deo gratias*)
	v. *Adiutorium nostrum in domine domini*
	R. *Qui fecit caelum et terram*
	Compline
v. *Converte nos deus salutaris noster*	v. *Converte nos deus salutaris noster*
R. *Et averte iram tuam a nobis*	R. *Et averte iram tuam a nobis*
Deus in adiutorium	*Deus in adiutorium*
Gloria patri	*Gloria patri*
Alleluia	*Alleluia*
Psalms 4, 30 vv. 1–6, 90, 133, with one antiphon (ferial or seasonal)	Psalms 4, 90, 133, no antiphon

Chapter
> *Tu autem in nobis es domine at nomen*
> *tuum sanctum invocatum est super nos*
> *ne derelinquas nos domine deus noster*
> (with response *Deo gratias*)

Short Respond (ferial or seasonal
  text; recited only in Lent in some
  Uses)

Hymn (ferial or seasonal, most often *Te lucis ante terminum*)	Hymn (ferial or seasonal, most often *Te lucis ante terminum*)
	Chapter (text as secular Use)
v. *Custodi nos domine ut pupillam oculi*	v. *Custodi nos domine ut pupillam oculi*
r. *Sub umbra alarum tuarum protege nos*	r. *Sub umbra alarum tuarum protege nos*
Nunc dimittis with antiphon (ferial or seasonal, most often *Salva nos*)	
Kyrie, Pater noster, Credo in deum	*Kyrie, Pater noster, Credo in deum*
Preces	Preces
Confession, Absolution	Confession, Absolution
Preces	Preces
Collect of the hour (*Illumina quaesumus domine*)	Collect of the hour (*Visita quaesumus domine*)
Benedicamus domino	*Benedicamus domino*
	Benedictio dei omnipotentis patri et filii et spiritus sancti descendet et maneat super nos r. *Amen*

If Compline of Our Lady was said in choir it could follow here, but more often there was just the Antiphon of Our Lady (consisting of antiphon, versicle and response, collect). Both are discussed in Chapter 8.

Important Seasonal Variants

Advent

Secular Use: Omission of *Te deum laudamus* at Matins; last respond doubled (i.e. the refrain is repeated in full at the end).

Secular and monastic Uses: Series of Great Antiphons (the 'O' antiphons) for *Magnificat* at Vespers from 16 December, the first often marked in the Calendar (*O sapientia*).

Septuagesima to Holy Saturday

Alleluia omitted at all times, except (in some Uses) on double feasts and simple feasts of nine or twelve lessons.

Alleluia after *Gloria patri* at beginning of Office replaced by *Laus tibi domine rex aeternae gloriae* (Praise be to thee O Lord, king of eternal glory).

Secular Use: Sunday Matins, omission of *Te deum laudamus*; last respond doubled (late medieval Roman Use: ninth respond replaces *Te deum*). Sunday Lauds, replacement of Psalm 92 by Psalm 50. Sunday Prime, replacement of Psalm 117 by Psalm 92.

Lent (normally from Ash Wednesday)

Seasonal texts and chants. The penitential season originally began at Quadragesima (first Sunday in Lent). It was extended back to Ash Wednesday, and then (in the ninth century) to Septuagesima. Nevertheless some special texts and chants were used from Lent rather than from Septuagesima, and in some cases the change was made on the Monday immediately after Quadragesima (as at Barking Abbey).

Passion Sunday to Holy Saturday (Passiontide)

Omission of *Gloria patri* at beginning of Office, after psalms, canticles, hymns (rhymed doxologies), and from responds. Where the *Gloria patri* was omitted from a respond, the respond was doubled.

Maundy Thursday to Holy Saturday (Triduum)

Monastic Use usually followed the secular order (*mores canonicorum*) of the Office for these three days.

In some foundations some of the hours were said (rather than sung) or else recited privately out of choir.

During the *Triduum* the Office was pared down to its essentials. The introductory sections, chapters, responds, hymns, and proper versicles and responses were omitted. There was only a small number of antiphons. Each Office began with the first psalm; the last psalm was followed directly by the canticle at Lauds, Vespers, and Compline. There were special lessons in the first nocturn at Matins (known as

Tenebrae) with their own tones, and special forms of preces at some hours. All of this is dealt with in more detail in Chapter 9.

Easter Day and the Week Following

Alleluia was used prolifically as an appendage to many sung texts.

Secular Use: Short form of Matins throughout the week. Vespers and Little Hours incorporated material from Easter Mass. This is discussed further in Chapter 9.

Eastertide

Seasonal texts and chants, many with suffix of *alleluia*.

THE OFFICE OF THE DEAD (*Officium Defunctorum*)

The Office of the Dead consisted only of Vespers, Vigils (i.e. Matins), and Lauds. It was frequently recited on a daily basis as a Votive Office, especially in chantries, but its principal use was at the time of funerals. There were alternative texts for the prayers when a corpse was present in the church.

Like the rites of the *Triduum*, the Office of the Dead was remarkably unchanging across the centuries and from Use to Use. As with the Office during the *Triduum*, monasteries followed the secular Use. There are other parallels: the omission of the opening and ending of the Office, the omission of hymns, preces, and memorials, the suppression of the absolutions and blessings at Vigils, and in most instances the omission of *Gloria patri*. The latter was most often replaced by *Requiem aeternam dona eis domine: et lux perpetua luceat eis* (Rest eternal grant unto them O Lord, and let light perpetual shine upon them). The earlier texts of the Office of the Dead made less use of *Requiem aeternam*: even as late as the sixteenth century, the Use of Salisbury continued instead to double the last respond in each nocturn at Vigils.

The order presented here is derived from the Breviary of the Roman Curia (Venice, 1522; see Chapter 13, pp. 221 ff.). Minor variants can be found in other medieval Uses and in the post-Tridentine Roman Breviary (notably in the ordering of responds and versicles at Vigils).

VESPERS OF THE DEAD (*Placebo*)

Antiphon *Placebo domino*   Psalm 114 *Dilexi*
Antiphon *Heu mihi*   Psalm 119 *Ad dominum cum tribularer*
Antiphon *Dominus custodit*   Psalm 120 *Levavi oculos meos*
Antiphon *Si iniquitates*   Psalm 129 *De profundis*
Antiphon *Opera manuum*   Psalm 137 *Confitebor tibi*

v. *Audivi vocem* r. *Beati mortui*
Antiphon *Omne quod dat mihi*   Canticle *Magnificat*
Pater noster [silently until v. *Et ne nos* r. *Sed libera nos*]
Psalm 145 *Lauda anima mea* [without *Requiem aeternam*; omitted on All Souls'
   Day and on day of funeral]
v. *A porta inferi* r. *Erue domine*
v. *Requiescant in pace* r. *Amen*
v. *Domine exaudi* r. *Et clamor meus*
v. *Dominus vobiscum* r. *Et cum spiritu tuo*
Collects: Three prayers from a series of alternative cycles, according to the
   occasion.
v. *Requiem aeternam* r. *Et lux perpetua*
Dismissal *Requiescant in pace* r. *Amen*

VIGILS OF THE DEAD (*Dirige*)

Unusually, at Vigils of the Dead all nine readings were from the Old
Testament book of Job. When recited as a Votive Office it was
common for only one of the three nocturns to be used (on a rota basis,
i.e. first nocturn on Monday and Thursday, etc.).

[Invitatory *Regem cui omnia*   Psalm 94 *Venite exsultemus*]
   (sung only on All Souls' Day and day of funeral)

First nocturn

Antiphon *Dirige domine*   Psalm 5 *Verba mea*
Antiphon *Convertere domine*   Psalm 6 *Domine ne in furore*
Antiphon *Nequando rapiat*   Psalm 7 *Domine deus meus*

v. *A porta inferi* r. *Erue domine*
Pater noster [silently until v. *Et ne nos* r. *Sed libera nos*]
Lesson 1 *Parce mihi domine* (Job 7: 16–21)
Respond 1 *Credo quod redemptor*
Lesson 2 *Tedet animam meam* (Job 10: 1–7)

Respond 2 *Qui Lazarum*
Lesson 3 *Manus tuae* (Job 10: 8–12)
Respond 3 *Domine quando veneris*
  [with *Requiem aeternam* instead of *Gloria patri*]

Second nocturn

Antiphon *In loco pascuae*   Psalm 22 *Dominus regit*
Antiphon *Delicta juventutis*   Psalm 24 *Ad te domine levavi*
Antiphon *Credo videre*   Psalm 26 *Dominus illuminatio*

v. *Collocet eos* r. *Cum principibus*
Pater noster
Lesson 4 *Responde mihi* (Job 13: 22–8)
Respond 4 *Memento mei deus*
Lesson 5 *Homo natus* (Job 14: 1–6)
Respond 5 *Hei mihi domine*
Lesson 6 *Quis mihi hoc* (Job 14: 13–16)
Respond 6 *Ne recorderis* [with *Requiem aeternam*]

Third nocturn

Antiphon *Complaceat tibi*   Psalm 39 *Expectans expectavi*
Antiphon *Sana domine*   Psalm 40 *Beatus qui intelligit*
Antiphon *Sitivit anima mea*   Psalm 41 *Quemadmodum desiderat*

v. *Ne tradas bestis* r. *Et animas pauperum*
Pater noster
Lesson 7 *Spiritus meus* (Job 17: 1–3, 11–15)
Respond 7 *Peccantem me*
Lesson 8 *Pelli meae* (Job 19: 20–7)
Respond 8 *Domine secundum actum*
Lesson 9 *Quare de vulva* (Job 10: 18–22)
Respond 9 *Libera me domine de morte aeterna* [with *Requiem aeternam*]
  [*Libera me domine de viis inferni* when only the third nocturn was recited.]

LAUDS OF THE DEAD

Lauds of the Dead normally followed Vigils without a break.

Antiphon *Exaltabunt domino*   Psalm 50 *Miserere mei*
Antiphon *Exaudi domine*   Psalm 64 *Te decet hymnus*
Antiphon *Me suscepit*   Psalm 62 *Deus deus meus* [with Psalm 66]

Antiphon *A porta inferi*   Canticle *Ego dixi* (Ezekiel 38: 10–20)

Antiphon *Omnis spiritus*   Psalms 148–150 *Laudate dominum*

v. *Audivi vocem* r. *Beati mortui*

Antiphon *Ego sum resurrectio*   Canticle *Benedictus*

Pater noster [silently until v. *Et ne nos* r. *Sed libera nos*]

Psalm 129 *De profundis* [without *Requiem aeternam*; omitted on All Souls' Day and on day of funeral]

v. *A porta inferi* r. *Erue domine*

v. *Requiescant in pace* r. *Amen*

v. *Domine exaudi* r. *Et clamor meus*

v. *Dominus vobiscum* r. *Et cum spiritu tuo*

Collects: Three prayers (as at Vespers), from a series of alternative cycles, according to the occasion.

v. *Requiem aeternam* r. *Et lux perpetua*

Dismissal *Requiescant in pace* r. *Amen*

7.

The Mass

The Mass, like the Office, has a consistent form and structure. It includes texts that are constant (the Ordinary of the Mass) and texts that vary (the Proper of the Mass). What distinguishes it from the Office services is the action of the Mass: the elements of bread and wine are prepared, consecrated, and consumed. The words of institution are those spoken by Christ at the Last Supper before the Crucifixion ('This is my body . . . This is my blood . . .'), and for Christians (in the Middle Ages and in many denominations today) Christ's presence is real in the consecrated bread and wine.

The Contrast Between Medieval and Modern Eucharistic Liturgy

The Mass (also known as the Eucharist, Holy Communion, or the Lord's Supper) remains as the central corporate liturgy of the modern Church. For those studying liturgy, the Mass is easily accessible as a regular celebration, but its modern, revised form is not a ready means to discover earlier practices.

One problem is the change in the relationship between Mass and Office. In the Middle Ages the Mass and the Office coexisted: they were part of the constant daily round of corporate prayer in collegiate and monastic communities. By the later fifteenth century Mass and Vespers were often celebrated more elaborately than the other Offices: certainly most of the surviving liturgical polyphonic music was written for Mass and Vespers.

The Mass has never ceased to be the principal act of worship in the Roman Catholic Church. As in the Middle Ages every Roman Catholic priest says Mass daily, and for the modern Roman Catholic laity attendance at Mass on Sundays and Holy Days remains an obligation. But the daily Office is more often said privately or informally today in the Roman Church (except in monasteries and choral foundations). Similarly, weekly eucharistic worship has become prevalent in the Anglican Communion since the 1960s, displacing Morning and Evening Prayer (i.e. Mattins and Evensong) in many parishes.

Even more misleading for those exploring medieval practice than the emphasis on the Mass at the expense of the Office in public worship is the new pastoral direction evident in eucharistic celebration. Modern liturgical revision relates more closely to the understanding of worship in the early Church than to medieval or post-Tridentine practice. The Mass is presented as a corporate celebration shared by the assembly, over which the priest presides. The action of the Mass is visible and participation of all is encouraged. It is taken for granted that those present will receive communion, as members of one body partaking in a shared meal.

For Roman Catholics this is a very recent development. Until the changes instituted by the Second Vatican Council in the 1960s Mass was heard rather than shared. It was primarily a celebration by the priest who offered a sacrifice on behalf of the people. In almost all medieval churches the priest celebrated Mass at an altar distant from the people, often hidden by a substantial screen; surrounded by his assisting ministers he faced east, away from the people, for much of the celebration; he spoke in Latin; on most occasions he alone received communion. This pattern, still evident in 1960, has its roots in early medieval practice.

The new order of the Mass is much further removed from the medieval rites than was its Tridentine predecessor in style, emphasis, and detail. Only in a very small number of Roman Catholic Churches can one observe the celebration of Mass in the 'old' manner.

The Formation of the Mass Between the Second and Eleventh Centuries

The new modern orders of eucharistic celebration hark back to the mid-second century, and the eucharistic rites of the time of Hippolytus and Justin. There are two distinct liturgical forms in these early rites: the Liturgy of the Word (or Mass of Catechumens) and the Liturgy of the Eucharist (or Mass of the Faithful). Much has been written recently about the origins and history of the Mass, but it is important to establish here the relationship of earlier forms with the medieval Mass.[1]

What had begun in the early Church as two flexible units, the one centred on scriptural readings, the other on the blessing and sharing of the bread and wine, had changed substantially by the end of the seventh century. The document known as *Ordo Romanus I* (late seventh century) is a description of a Papal Mass celebrated at a church in Rome: it may be considered a prototype of the form of Mass that came to be codified in the Middle Ages.

The transition to the liturgical order described in *Ordo Romanus I* was gradual. Its contents encompass a compilation of items adopted, expanded, or truncated over at least 400 years. A crude summary shows something of this process: Entrance psalm (for Papal Mass procession in basilicas, *c.*430), *Kyrie* as Litany (*c.*495, later truncated), *Gloria in excelsis* (at Lauds, *c.*350; at Mass, *c.*500), Collect (*c.*440), Readings (originally three or four, but only two by about the fifth century), Psalm between readings (by fourth century), Alleluia (spreads from Eastertide use, sixth century); Homily (from earliest times, but disappeared by seventh century), Dismissal of Catechumens (formalized in fourth century, disappeared in sixth century); Prayers of the Faithful (solemn prayers of second century, displaced by opening Litany in *c.*495); Peace (before Offertory in second century, transferred to before Communion by fifth century); Offertory (wide range of offerings before fourth century); Thanksgiving (eucharistic prayer, earliest texts from second century); inclusion of *Sanctus* in eucharistic prayer (*c.*400); Lord's Prayer (fourth century); Communion (with psalms from fourth century); Prayer after Communion (fourth century).

The lists which follow overleaf present a rudimentary comparison of the orders of Eucharistic celebration that may be reconstructed from the writings of Justin and Hippolytus (second century), from the description of the Papal Mass found in *Ordo Romanus I* (seventh century), and from eleventh-century liturgical sources.

---

[1] A comprehensive introduction to many of these issues is provided by C. Jones, *et al.* (eds.), *The Study of Liturgy* (London, 1978). There is also the compact study by J. D. Crichton, *A Short History of the Mass* (London, 1983). However, the classic study remains that of J. A. Jungmann, *The Mass of the Roman Rite* (New York, 1951–5).

A Summary of Selected Orders of Mass
as Celebrated in the Second, Seventh, and Eleventh Centuries

SECOND CENTURY	SEVENTH CENTURY	ELEVENTH CENTURY
	Entrance of ministers (antiphonal psalm)	Introit (antiphon and psalm verses)
	Litany	*Kyrie eleison*
	Gloria in excelsis	*Gloria in excelsis*
Scriptural Readings as long as time allows; with psalmody and ending with Gospel reading	Lesson	Epistle
	Responsorial psalmody and alleluia	Gradual (respond)
		Alleluia
		Sequence
	Gospel	Gospel
Homily		
Intercessions		*Credo*
Dismissal of Catechumens		
Rite of Peace		
Preparation of gifts	Preparation of gifts (antiphonal psalm)	Offertory (antiphon and prayer)
Eucharistic prayer (blessing of bread and wine)	Eucharistic prayer with *Sanctus*, intercessions, and commemorations	Preface
		Sanctus and *Benedictus*
		Canon of the Mass
	Lord's Prayer	Lord's Prayer
	Rite of Peace	Versicle and response (*Pax*)
		Agnus dei
		Rite of Peace
Communion of all present	Communion (antiphonal psalm)	Communion of priest (Communion antiphon)
	Concluding prayer	Postcommunion (prayer)
	Dismissal	*Ite missa est*

THE NATURE OF THE MEDIEVAL MASS

The medieval rite demonstrates two distinct features: first, the truncation of actions which became priestly rather than corporate, restricted
to the sanctuary around the altar rather than encompassing the whole
church (i.e. entrance, offertory, and communion); second, the proliferation, formalization, and codification of texts and ceremonial. The
musical consequences may be seen in the curtailment of Introit,
Offertory, and Communion: whole psalms intended to accompany
extended actions were reduced to an antiphon, or else an antiphon and
residual psalm verse (or verses). The extended Litany before the
readings and before communion became stereotyped in the nine-fold
Kyrie eleison and the three-fold *Agnus dei*.

The celebration of the medieval Mass centred on the priest. Corporate
elements of the early Church's celebration were omitted or abbreviated:
in addition to the shortening of Introit, Offertory, and Communion,
the Homily and Intercessions disappeared (the Creed was introduced
in the eleventh century on certain days to counter heresy); and the rite
of peace originally shared by the whole assembly was restricted to a
symbolic gesture and a brief, formal versicle and response.

All this reflects the impact of the rise of the ordained clergy from the
sixth century in both the monastic and secular Church. Where a
community consisted entirely or largely of priests, each said his own
Mass daily: in that sense the eucharistic assembly ceased to exist. All
Masses became principally individual or 'private' (hence the large
numbers of altars in great cathedral and monastic churches to accommodate daily Masses said by all priests in the community as well as
additional chaplains at endowed chantries).

It is easiest to understand sung Masses in cathedrals, collegiate
churches, and monasteries of the Middle Ages as 'private' Masses at
which the whole community was present. For, though there may
have been more assisting ministers, the celebration in the sanctuary
was much as in a 'private' Mass; it was separate and distinct from the
community in their stalls in choir. There were texts which were
audible only to the celebrating priest, and ceremonies restricted to
those in the sanctuary. Furthermore what was sung by those in choir
did not always coincide with what was said and done in the sanctuary.
For instance, at the beginning of Mass the celebrant and his assisting

ministers recited prayers, censed the altar, and continued to say the texts of Introit and *Kyrie*, while those in choir sang Introit and *Kyrie*: not until the beginning of the *Gloria in excelsis* (or on ferial days at the greeting before the Collect) did celebrant and choir coincide.

The action of the Mass took place in the sanctuary: the choir's part was far more akin to the conduct of an Office. The duality of what amounts to two celebrations (one sacramental, the other primarily consisting of choral chant) is more difficult for us to grasp today, as is the lack of coincidence in content and synchronization. It is easiest, perhaps, for musicians to understand this by analogy with the medieval motet, where different texts are sung simultaneously, bound together by the underlying orders of mensuration and *cantus firmus*. From a modern standpoint we assume one event will follow another successively, we expect texts to be comprehensible and actions to be functional; we have to identify anew with medieval acceptance of non-coincident events, of overlaid texts, and of non-functional, emblematic, or symbolic actions.

The Order of the Medieval Mass

The medieval Mass is more straightforward than the Office. There was little fundamental variation between regional rites or between monastic and secular Uses. Structure and order were relatively stable from the mid-eleventh century, though the detailed content of the Proper varied, as might be expected. In describing the Mass the most difficult aspects are the interaction of text and action, and of those events in the sanctuary with those in choir. While the Office can be understood from texts and rubrics, the ceremonial of the Mass requires an additional grasp of the visual and the spatial.

It is best to begin with an exposition of the main texts of the Mass, those items which would be heard. Envisage, perhaps, medieval pilgrims attending the celebration in a great church, standing in the nave where the whole action of the Mass in choir and sanctuary was invisible beyond the stone screen. In the list which follows the Ordinary and the Proper are presented in separate colums. The distinctions of typography indicate CHANTS SUNG BY THOSE IN CHOIR, texts intoned by the celebrant or an assisting minister, and *dialogues between the celebrant (or minister) and those in choir*.

Sung Mass on Sunday or a Feast-day Outside the Penitential Season: Texts which were Audible

ORDINARY	PROPER
	INTROIT
KYRIE ELEISON	
GLORIA IN EXCELSIS	
	Collect(s)
	Epistle
	GRADUAL
	ALLELUIA
	SEQUENCE
	Gospel
CREDO IN UNUM DEUM	
	OFFERTORY
	Secret (conclusion heard)
Sursum Corda	
Preface (with proper interpolations)	
SANCTUS *with*	
BENEDICTUS	
Conclusion of Canon of the Mass	
Pater noster	
Pax domini	
AGNUS DEI	
	COMMUNION
	Postcommunion prayer
Ite missa est	

THE CONTENTS OF THE MEDIEVAL MASS IN DETAIL

Introit (or Officium)

Originally an antiphonal psalm to accompany an extended procession in the Roman basilicas, this was curtailed normally to an antiphon (A), psalm verse (V), *Gloria patri* (G) and repeated antiphon (A). In most cases the order was A—V—G—A, but there were instances of A—V—A—G—A, recalling the original antiphonal practice. (See Chapter 5, p. 72.)

Kyrie eleison

Many of the medieval *Kyrie* settings were troped (i.e. additional texts which expanded on, and made more specific, the general petition of 'Lord have mercy'). Groups of ordinary chants are still known by the interpolated text of the *Kyrie* trope (e.g. *Lux et origo*, *Orbis factor*, *Cunctipotens genitor deus*)

Gloria in excelsis

An early popular hymn of the Church (one of the so-called *psalmi idiotici*), it was first used in the Office. Within the Mass it was sung on Sundays and at least on feasts of nine or twelve lessons. Some rites included *Gloria in excelsis* (Glory be to God on high) on feasts of three lessons and ferias. It was omitted in Advent and from Septuagesima (or Ash Wednesday) to the end of Holy Week (though some Uses allowed it on feast days in those seasons). Most Missals specified the melody of the intonation of *Gloria in excelsis* according to the rank of the day or the intention of the Mass. The beginning was intoned by the celebrant.

Collect(s)

The repertory of Collects includes some of the most ancient Christian prayers. The priest introduced the prayer in the usual way (v. *Dominus vobiscum*. ℟. *Et cum spiritu tuo. Oremus.*) It was intoned (a formula can be found in *Liber Usualis*). All responded *Amen*. A group of collects was often recited: often they brought together a variety of intentions (e.g. collect of the day, a memorial collect of a coincident lesser feast, a collect for a special intention).

Epistle (or Lectio)

In the early Church there were two or three readings, but only on a few exceptional days were there more than two readings in the medieval liturgy. Though the first reading was normally taken from the Epistles of the New Testament, some came from the Acts of the Apostles, Revelation, or the Old Testament. The Epistle was intoned by the sub-deacon who began the text of the reading *Fratres* . . .

(Brothers): a series of introductions and lesson tones may be found in
Liber Usualis. Medieval Ordinals with music sometimes included the
relevant tones.

Gradual

In the early Church the verses of the responsorial psalm were sung by a
cantor and all sang the response after each verse. Like the responds in
Matins the medieval Gradual was a much shortened form of the
original psalm. The florid melisma of the solo singers remained, but
normally only one psalm verse was sung. On ferial days when there was
no Alleluia the Gradual was sung: Response—solo verse—Response.
When the Alleluia followed it was common to omit the repetition of
the response and to sing the Alleluia immediately after the Gradual
verse. In the Easter season the Gradual response is *alleluia*.

Alleluia

Alleluia, the Church's expression of joy borrowed from the Hebrew,
is sung before the Gospel. Though originally sung without any other
text a verse was added, and in medieval times the Alleluia was
normally sung thus: solo (first strain of *alleluia*)—choir (whole *alleluia*)—
solo verse (concluded by choir)—choir (whole *alleluia*). When a
Sequence followed the Alleluia the repetition of *alleluia* was curtailed:
after the verse the soloists sang the beginning of the repetition of
alleluia but then went on to the Sequence. Ferial masses do not include
the Alleluia, and it was not sung during the penitential season (Septuagesima to Easter Eve) nor on certain occasional penitential days
during the year.

Sequence (or Prosa)

Sequences were sung on a number of greater feasts effectively as an
extension of the Alleluia. These were medieval compositions written
from the tenth century onwards, metrical, strophic, and often rhymed;
set syllabically to periodic melodies, they are reminiscent of the
hymn and secular *lai*, and therefore belong to a rich corpus of medieval
literary writing in verse. They continued to be written throughout the
Middle Ages, though all but four were suppressed in the Tridentine

reforms (see Chapter 10). They belong broadly to the repertory of tropes, for they provided a gloss or commentary that related the Alleluia more closely to the feast. Musically set in paired verses they were normally sung by alternate sides of the choir.

Tract

A psalm (or verses from it) sung without antiphon or respond (i.e. direct psalmody), it replaced the Alleluia during the penitential season and on other penitential days during the year. The melodies employ a repertory of standardized phrases (a practice known as centonization), and only a limited number of modes are used (modes 2 and 8).

Gospel

The second reading (last in the early Church) was taken from one of the four New Testament Gospels. It was sung by the deacon. It was announced by him, and all responded *Gloria tibi domine*. The reading was prefaced by the opening words *In illo tempore* . . . (At that time). The alternative tones for the Gospel are printed in *Liber Usualis*. Again medieval examples may often be found in an Ordinal.

Credo

The Nicene Creed became a standard element of the Ordinary of the Mass only in the eleventh century. It was sung on Sundays and feasts. In some Uses (e.g. Salisbury) there was only one melody. As with *Gloria in excelsis* the celebrant intoned the opening.

Offertory

Like the Introit and Communion this was a truncated antiphonal psalm. A number of Offertories retained between one and four verses (often with elaborate chant in the style of a respond), but in the majority only the antiphon has survived. The style of chant contrasts with the Introit and Communion: there is sometimes repetition of text (and melody in some instances), and the melodies are far more extended and melismatic.

Secret

The offertory prayer belongs to the Proper, but only the conclusion of the doxology at the end of the prayer was sung aloud by the celebrant (the remainder was silent as the name suggests). All sang *Amen*.

Sursum corda and Preface

A dialogue between celebrant and those present marks the beginning of the eucharistic prayer. The chant and text are Ordinary. The celebrant then intoned the Preface. Though there are special forms for certain seasons and feasts these are included in the Ordo Missae. The Preface always ended in the same way: *Et ideo cum angelis et archangelis . . . sine fine dicentes* (Therefore with angels and archangels . . . evermore praising thee and saying).

Sanctus and Benedictus

Sanctus (Holy, holy) is the culmination of the Preface, one of the oldest of the choral texts in the Mass. At a very early date it became customary to follow *Sanctus* with *Benedictus qui venit* (Blessed is he that cometh). By the late fifteenth century there are instances of the replacement of *Benedictus* with a polyphonic motet for the elevation.

Canon

In the eucharistic prayer (or prayer of consecration) the bread and wine are blessed and consecrated by the celebrant. This ancient prayer has a long and complex history, and consists of a number of sections: commendation of the offerings, commemorations, invocation (*epiclesis*) over the offerings, narrative of the institution, memorial of Christ, invocation of the Holy Spirit, intercessions, and concluding doxology. The Canon was recited silently: only the last phrase of the doxology was intoned by the celebrant, and all responded *Amen*.

Pater noster

The celebrant continued to intone the introduction to the Lord's Prayer, and then sang all of the prayer until *Et ne nos inducas in tentationem* to which all responded as usual *Sed libera nos a malo*. The priest also sang the conclusion to the doxology *Per omnia saecula saeculorum*, all responding *Amen*.

Pax domini

A simple versicle and response between celebrant and those in choir: v. *Pax domini sit semper vobiscum*. R. *Et cum spiritu tuo* (The peace of the Lord be with you always. And with thy spirit). (While intoning this the celebrant made the sign of the cross three times over the chalice: it was no longer a greeting of peace to the assembly.)

Agnus dei

The repeated melodies which often characterize the three petitions of *Agnus dei* (O Lamb of God) recall its origin as a more extended litany. There was a time when only one petition was sung (and this is found again much later in some sixteenth- and seventeenth-century polyphonic Masses), but three was the medieval norm.

Communion

Of the three antiphonal chants in the Mass this is the most perfunctory. The psalm has entirely disappeared and in most cases the antiphon is brief. No more was needed when the priest alone received communion.

Postcommunion

This proper prayer was preceded by the usual greeting and intoned in the same way as the Collect, all responding *Amen*.

Dismissal

The greeting was repeated and then the deacon sang *Ite missa est* (Go, the Mass is ended), all responding *Deo gratias* (Thanks be to God). At Masses where the *Gloria in excelsis* was omitted the deacon sang *Benedicamus domino* (Let us bless the Lord) with the response *Deo gratias*. The melodies for the dismissal were part of the Ordinary of the Mass and were designated according to the season or day.

Medieval Celebration of the Mass

In summarizing the order of texts and chants, and classifying them into Proper and Ordinary it is possible to start to understand the sequence of the medieval Mass. But that is a very incomplete summary, and not least because it ignores the action of the Mass. In a great church this may have been invisible to the laity attending in the nave, but east of the choir screen the interaction of those in choir with those celebrating the Mass in the sanctuary was paramount.

First, the importance of the two groups involved in the sung Mass should be stressed. Those in choir were in their usual stalls and remained there throughout the liturgy (unless they moved to one of the lecterns). Those who were designated to celebrate and assist in the sanctuary had a more active role to play. At Mass celebrated in choir there were three principal ministers: a celebrant (priest), assisted by a deacon and a subdeacon. In some Uses on great feasts there would have been two deacons and two subdeacons. Also present in the sanctuary were a number of other assistants commonly known as servers. The number varied according to the size and practice of the community, the rank of the day, and the consequent complexity of the ceremonial. A normal minimum was four: an acolyte (clerk) responsible for the vessels, a thurifer in charge of the incense, and two taperers who each carried a candlestick.

Second, it is important to remember that the outline which follows is entirely rudimentary. It is impossible to summarize the high art of medieval ceremonial in all its complexity, but at least this may assist readers to find their way round the books that give full details. It is related specifically to the Use of Salisbury, the variant of the Roman Rite used in the largest number of secular English churches. This is chosen because texts and descriptions are available not only in modern editions and facsimiles but also in English. Many of the Salisbury books are introduced in Chapter 13. However, by far the most accessible detailed account of the celebration of Mass at Salisbury (in English and with all the chants) is that edited by Nick Sandon, *The Use of Salisbury, i. The Ordinary of the Mass* (Newton Abbot, 1984). On the one hand this allows ready access for those wishing to pursue the matter in detail. On the other hand the information has to be used with caution: though the principles may hold good for many Uses within the Roman Rite, it represents only one Use at one time.

The Celebration of the Mass on Sunday
A Summary of the Use of Salisbury *c.*1400

Item	Choir	Ministers in Sanctuary
Introit	Begun by rulers, continued by choir Verses sung by rulers	Entry of ministers Private prayers Blessing of incense and censing of altar
Kyrie eleison	Begun by rulers, continued by all in choir	Introit and *Kyrie* recited privately by celebrant
Gloria in excelsis	Sung by all in choir	Intoned by celebrant
Collect(s)		Intoned by celebrant
	Amen	Subdeacon goes to pulpitum
Epistle	Soloists for Gradual move to pulpitum	Intoned by subdeacon from lectern on pulpitum Taperers leave to conduct acolyte back to the sanctuary with chalice and paten
Gradual	Begun by appointed soloists from the lectern on the pulpitum Soloists to sing the Alleluia vest in copes and move to pulpitum	Subdeacon returns Bread and wine prepared by subdeacon in paten and chalice
Alleluia	Begun by appointed soloists from the lectern on pulpitum	Deacon censes altar and seeks blessing from celebrant Procession for Gospel forms and moves to pulpitum

Sequence (on some Sundays)	Begun by rulers, sung *alternatim* by two sides of choir	
Gospel		Sung by deacon at lectern on pulpitum, facing north
Credo		Intoned by celebrant
	Sung by all in choir	Gospel procession returns to sanctuary
Offertory	Begun by rulers, sung by all in choir	Chalice and paten are brought to altar where they are prepared and censed by celebrant
		Censing of celebrant, ministers, and all in choir in order
		Celebrant washes his hands while deacon censes the altar
Secret		Said privately by celebrant, who sings the last phrase aloud
	Amen	
Sursum corda		Intoned by celebrant
Preface	All in choir respond	
Sanctus and *Benedictus*	Begun by rulers, sung by all in choir	Said privately at altar
Canon		Celebrant continues while choir sings *Sanctus*; the long prayer is not heard, but bells are rung to signal the moments of blessing and the elevation of the bread
Pater noster		Sung by celebrant
	All in choir respond	
		Celebrant breaks bread into three pieces (fraction of the host)

ITEM	CHOIR	MINISTERS IN SANCTUARY
Pax domini		Celebrant sings conclusion of prayer and following versicle
	All in choir respond	
Agnus dei		Kiss of peace symbolically and solemnly passed from celebrant to deacon to subdeacon
	Kiss of peace brought by deacon to rulers who pass it to all in choir in order	Celebrant consumes consecrated bread and wine
		Assisted by subdeacon he then washes chalice
Communion	Begun by rulers, sung by all in choir	Celebrant washes his hands while deacon covers chalice and paten and passes them to acolyte
Postcommunion		Intoned by celebrant
	Amen	
Dismissal		Acolyte takes chalice and paten out of sanctuary
		Celebrant greets those in choir, then deacon sings Ite missa est
	All in choir respond	
	Deo gratias	Ministers leave sanctuary, celebrant reciting the first fourteen verses of St John's Gospel

It is important to observe how the chant was distinguished by ritual. Antiphonal chants (Introit, Offertory, and Communion) were begun in choir by the rulers; responsorial chants were begun by soloists at the lectern at the choir step or on the pulpitum (Gradual, Alleluia); Ordinary chants were begun either in the sanctuary (*Gloria* and *Credo* by celebrant, *Ite* by deacon) or in choir by the rulers (*Kyrie, Sanctus, Agnus dei*). The Sequence was begun by the rulers as a choral not a solo chant.

What happened in the Use of Salisbury is probably a fair indication of the kind of practice used in great medieval churches until about the late fourteenth century, though variants will be found everywhere. But whereas Salisbury upheld its ceremonies, the direction of the Papal Chapel in the Lateran (and subsequently in the Vatican) in Rome was rather different. Here there was progressive pruning of ceremonial: there was no procession of bread and wine, and the pulpitum was not used; duplication of ministers (e.g. more than one deacon or subdeacon) did not normally occur. Mass at Salisbury and the late medieval Mass of the Roman Curia present extremes of ceremonial observance (though both Uses remained very elaborate by modern standards). Between the two a whole range of ceremonial observance may be discovered by investigating other local Uses and practices.

MASS OF THE DEAD (*Requiem*)

One of the most frequently recited medieval Masses was the Requiem, offered privately in chantries daily by chaplains for the souls of benefactors and in churches for the souls of departed members of the community, as also at funerals. This was a period when Christians desperately feared damnation to hell, and therefore felt the need to provide for prayers for their soul after death. They hoped to shorten the period in purgatory before judgement, and to ensure favourable judgement to allow them to be admitted to heaven.

The medieval mind was less aware of the division of life and death (indeed far more accepting of the proximity of death), and less concerned by the distance between the living and the dead. The faithful departed and the saints were regarded as remarkably real and immediate; effigies and statues manifested that reality, not as idols but as a focus for intercession. Both the departed and the saints were remembered daily. But in the fourteenth century the commemoration of the Church Expectant (the faithful departed) was fixed on 2 November as All Souls' Day. This followed one day after the celebration of the Church Triumphant (All Saints' Day, 1 November).

The principal texts of the Mass of the Dead, like those in the Office of the Dead, were largely unchanging, but the prayers and readings were altered to accommodate varying circumstances (funerals, anniversaries of death, etc.). In its Latin form the Mass of the Dead remained substantially unaltered over the centuries. As in the Office not only *alleluia* but also *Gloria patri* were omitted.

The particular order below is taken from the *Missale Romanum* (1474). It would have been suitable for a commemoration of several departed; choices are given for the Epistle and Gospel in the Missal.

An Order of Mass for All the Faithful Departed

Introit	Antiphon *Requiem aeternam* Verse *Te decet hymnus*
Kyrie	one of the simplest of the chants
Collect	*Fidelium deus omnium conditor*
Epistle	*Fratres, ecce mysterium* (I Corinthians 15: 51–7)
Gradual	Respond *Requiem aeternam* Verse *In memoria*
Tract	*Absolve domine animas omnium*
	[in the Use of Salisbury: *De profundis*]
Sequence	*Dies irae, dies illa*
Gospel	*In illo tempore dixit Jesus . . . Amen amen dico vobis* (John 5: 25–9)
Offertory	Antiphon *Domine Jesu Christe* Verse *Hostias et preces*
Secret	*Hostias quaesumus domine*
Sursum corda and	
Preface of the dead	
Sanctus and	
Benedictus	
Canon	
Pater noster	
Pax	
Agnus dei	*Agnus dei qui tollis peccata mundi: dona eis requiem*
	Agnus dei qui tollis peccata mundi: dona eis requiem
	Agnus dei qui tollis peccata mundi: dona eis requiem sempiternam
Communion	Antiphon *Lux aeterna* Verse *Requiem aeternum*
Postcommunion	*Animabus quaesumus domine*
Dismissal	*Requiescant in pace* Response *Amen*

8.

Processions and Other Additional Observances

In addition to the main celebration of the daily round of Office and Mass there were a number of additional observances. Some, like processions, were limited to specific days; others, like memorials, the Marian antiphon, the Little Office of the Virgin, and the Lady Mass, were observed daily.

Processions, commemorations, memorials, suffrages, and the Marian antiphon commonly made use of a standard formula, consisting of:

Antiphon
Versicle and response
Collect

In some respects this formula represents a highly condensed Office in itself: the antiphon embodies all the psalmody, including antiphons and canticle, the versicle and response recalls that sung after chapter or hymn, and the collect provides a conclusion—exactly as in the Office.

PROCESSIONS

During a procession the worshipping community left the main area of the church used for the regular liturgy (i.e. the choir) and walked solemnly in a prescribed order (generally led at least by processional cross, candlebearers, and thurifer) to other parts of the church (and sometimes outside the church) before returning to the choir. Processions were not limited to the great collegiate and monastic churches, but took place in parish churches—albeit on a more modest scale.

Processions commonly occurred at three points in the liturgy: at the end of Lauds, before Mass, and at the end of Vespers. The most frequent were those before Mass. Local practices varied. Processions were found in monastic and secular foundations, but they declined in the Use of the Papal Chapel in Rome, where the Curia had little use for extended, ceremonial liturgy on a regular, day-to-day basis. Much attention has focused on the frequency of processions in the Use of Salisbury, but clearly this is representative of wider medieval practice in those places which escaped the influence of the liturgy of the Use of the Roman Curia.[1]

There were processions before the principal Mass (or before Terce which immediately preceded Mass) every Sunday and on double feasts (probably as many as a hundred or more in a year). There were special forms of the procession for some days, especially in Holy Week (see Chapter 9). Processions with litanies also took place on days of special prayer and petition (see 'Litanies', p. 136 f. below).

On some days processions occurred at the end of Lauds and Vespers. During Christmastide these took place on Christmas Day at Vespers and at Lauds and Vespers on the four days following (until Lauds of St Thomas of Canterbury). There were comparable processions during the Octave of Easter. In a number of monastic and secular Uses (including the Use of Salisbury) Vespers processions proliferated so that there was generally at least one in each week.

In the early Christian centuries in Rome there were processions before Mass. These were made through the city to the church where Mass was to be celebrated. Often the procession stopped at churches on the way (stations) to gather the congregation and to make intercession. The medieval form often reflected this in the use of stations but normally confined the procession to the church, or at least to the church and adjacent cloisters. The most striking exception at Salisbury, for instance, was the procession on a Rogation day (a form taken over from the early Church) which made its way from the cathedral to a church in the city for Mass. But on Palm Sunday, Ascension Day, Pentecost, and Corpus Christi the procession went around the outside of the cathedral. In a number of other Uses the Palm Sunday procession began outside the city wall and made its way to the cathedral for Mass (to take another English example, such was the case at Hereford).

In secular churches the Sunday procession included the sprinkling of altars with holy water. In monastic churches this act of purification

---

[1] The most accessible study of Western processions is found in T. W. Bailey, *The Processions of Sarum and the Western Church* (Toronto, 1971).

with holy water commonly moved through the domestic buildings as well as the church, so that the whole house was cleansed before Mass.

In its simplest form a procession moved out of the choir, stopped at a station, and then returned to the choir. At the very least an antiphon was sung while the procession left the choir; versicle and collect were usually sung at a station (altar, font, or rood); an antiphon was sung as the procession returned to the choir; and the ceremony ended with a versicle and collect.

The principle behind this can be seen in the Christmas Vespers processions. These not only formed a climax to the celebration of Second Vespers, they also served to meet the problem of successive feasts. For instance, on St Stephen's Day, Second Vespers coincides with First Vespers of St John; it is also a day within the Octave of Christmas and this had to be observed. One solution, given in the Hereford Breviary, was as follows:

1. Second Vespers of St Stephen as far as the Collect;
2. Procession to the altar of St John
   Respond: *Quatuor animalia* Verse: *Erat autem* and *Gloria patri* (borrowed from Matins of Evangelists)
   Sequence: *Clare sanctorum senatus apostolorum*;
3. At the altar of St John
   Antiphon: *Ecce ego Johannes* with *Magnificat*
   Collect: *Ecclesiam tuam*
   (a compressed form of the First Vespers of St John);
4. Procession back to the choir
   Antiphon: *Virgo hodie* ending in choir with
   Versicle: *Verbum caro*
   Collect: *Concede quaesumus*
   (a memorial of the Nativity).

Similar processions were made on Christmas Day (altar of St Stephen), St John (altar of Holy Innocents), and Holy Innocents (altar of St Thomas of Canterbury).

At Vespers in Easter Week the procession went to the font where the station was made, recalling the new life in the newly blessed water.

Before the Mass the Sunday procession at Salisbury left the choir by the north-east door, went round behind the high altar, down the south aisle to the west end of the nave, around the font, up the centre of the nave, made a station before the rood, and re-entered the choir at the door under the pulpitum. The procession ended with versicle and collect.[2]

By contrast, the Sunday procession at the cathedral priory of Durham seems to have left the choir by the north-east door, made its way to the north transept, then back up the ambulatory, round the back of the high altar and then to the south transept; here it left the church and went round the east, south, and west of the cloister before re-entering the cathedral at the south-west door, turning left for the west Galilee (in by the south door, out by the north), and finally making its way up the nave and back to the choir.[3] (See the plan of Durham, Fig. 2.1.)

On the Feast of the Purification candles were blessed and distributed to all for the procession, to signify Christ as 'the light to lighten the Gentiles' (hence the antiphon *Lumen ad revelationem*).

In greater churches and in extended processions more chants were required. Some of the ancient processions (e.g. Rogation) had a substantial repertory, and there were processional hymns. These were usually hymns with refrains (e.g. *Gloria laus et honor*, *Salve festa dies*), described as *prosa* in some sources. But in many instances antiphons, responds, versicles, and collects were borrowed (as shown in the example above). In some foundations polyphony was sung during processions, notably *conductus*.

Processional litanies are discussed below, under 'Litanies', pp. 136 f.

COMMEMORATIONS, MEMORIALS, AND SUFFRAGES

The conclusion to both Lauds and Vespers often included additional devotions termed commemorations, memorials, and suffrages. These were said after the collect of the Office. The basic format of all three corresponds to that outlined in the opening paragraphs above: antiphon, versicle, collect.

The distinction between commemoration, memorial, and suffrage is often difficult to discern, and their use varies between sources and Uses. Broadly all three were directed to a specific intention which was additional to the intention of the Office they followed.

---

[2] The Salisbury Sunday procession is described in N. Sandon (ed.), *The Use of Salisbury: i, The Ordinary of the Mass* (Newton Abbot, 1984), 4–8.

[3] A conjectural plan of the Durham procession is found after p. 355 in J. T. Fowler (ed.), *Rites of Durham* (Surtees Society, 107; 1902).

There were three basic categories:

1. Commemoration or memorial of a saint whose feast or octave coincided with another celebration which took precedence (also of a Sunday or season).
2. Commemoration or memorial to replace a Votive Office on occasions when the latter was not said communally in choir (notably the Blessed Virgin Mary). Such memorials were required on certain days, including All Saints and Holy Cross.
3. A sequence of memorials recited on a daily basis in a fixed order, and identified as ferial memorials or suffrages. (Such a series typically included memorials of the Holy Spirit, the patron saint or saints of the church, Holy Cross, Relics, All Saints, and for peace, but this might be varied according to the observance of the day.)

For the first category the example given above ('Processions', p. 129) at Second Vespers of St Stephen, is typical in structure (though normally without procession and second *Magnificat*). Similarly on the Feast of the Conception of the Blessed Virgin Mary (8 December) the memorial for Advent was said. These memorials were said at the end of Lauds and Vespers of the day.

Many breviaries include a collection of ferial memorials for daily use, regularly recited formulas for intentions that were always in the mind and worship of the community. In earlier times a number of these were offered as separate Offices, but with the proliferation of intentions such an extended series of recitations was impossible. In some Uses this series of suffrages was said at the end of Lauds and Vespers of the Virgin.

Ferial memorials (suffrages) were omitted on a number of feast-days, and no memorials were said in the Office of the Dead or in the Office on the last three days of Holy Week.

The Antiphon in Honour of the Blessed Virgin Mary

Of all the observances which follow the memorial order (antiphon, versicle, collect), the best known is the Marian antiphon sung after Compline of the day (or after Compline of the Virgin if that was also recited in choir). In some places it was sung in choir, in others in a Lady chapel or before the statue of the Virgin (to which there might be a procession), in others it was a private devotion. Some late medieval foundations treated it as a corporate ceremony separate from the Office, not necessarily sung in church. Others sang the Marian antiphon after Vespers (in some cases in addition to the ceremony after Compline) and other hours. (In the Tridentine Rite the Marian antiphon was sung before leaving choir after any Office.) The antiphon (like other memorials) was omitted during the last three days of Holy Week.

The use of a series of four seasonal Marian antiphons was established by the Franciscans in the thirteenth century and subsequently spread to Roman Use. Some writers have implied that these are independent compositions, but all four are found as *Magnificat* antiphons in at least some medieval sources (e.g. the Worcester Antiphoner includes *Ave regina* and *Salve regina*). A typical cycle (taken from the post-Tridentine Breviary) is as follows (versicles and collects varied according to date and place):

First Vespers of Advent to Second Vespers of Purification

Antiphon: *Alma redemptoris mater*
Versicle: *Angelus domini*
Collect: *Gratiam tuam quaesumus domine*
   [during Advent]

Versicle: *Post partum*
Collect: *Deus qui salutis aeternae*
   [from First Vespers of Christmas Day]

Compline of Purification to Compline of Wednesday in Holy Week

Antiphon: *Ave regina caelorum*
Versicle: *Dignare me laudare*
Collect: *Concede misericors deus*

Compline of Easter Day to None of the Saturday after Pentecost

Antiphon: *Regina caeli laetare*
Versicle: *Gaude et laetare*
Collect: *Deus qui per resurrectionem*

First Vespers of Trinity Sunday to None of the Saturday before Advent

Antiphon: *Salve regina misericordiae*
Versicle: *Ora pro nobis*
Collect: *Omnipotens sempiterne deus qui gloriosae*

A fifth antiphon, *Quam pulchra es*, was sung in late medieval Franciscan and Roman Uses between the Nativity of the Virgin (8 September) and the Saturday before Advent.

In England there was more flexibility. The Marian antiphon *Salve regina* was used throughout the year in some foundations; others made use of a varying number of different texts, including *Nesciens mater* and *Quam pulchra es*. But the extent of Marian devotion also resulted in the composition of other texts, and the polyphonic repertory of Marian antiphons found in collections like the late fifteenth-century Eton Choirbook includes a variety, both established and new. Customarily musicologists refer to Marian antiphons sung after an Office as Votive Antiphons.

The Little Office of the Virgin

The cult of the Virgin was so strong in the Middle Ages that between the twelfth and the sixteenth centuries most communities adopted the practice of reciting the Little Office of the Virgin on a daily basis. In some cases it was recited aloud in choir, in others (or at specific times of the year) it was said individually either in or out of choir. It is called the Little Office to distinguish it from the full form of the Commemorative Office of the Virgin (celebrated weekly, and discussed in the next section).

The Little Office included seasonal elements (e.g. readings and responds), but some of the principal texts were constant throughout the year (e.g. psalms and hymns). The Roman Breviary (among others) provided a rota of psalms for Matins. Unlike the Office of the Dead this is a full Office with all the hours. But the Offices of the Dead and of the Virgin have a single Nocturn at Matins in their daily form: monastic and secular Uses alike include only three lessons and three responds. (In both the Little Office and the Office of the Dead monasteries followed secular forms: this affected the structure of Matins, the number of psalms at Vespers, and the inclusion of *Nunc dimittis* at Compline.)

In the Roman Use, the Little Office of the Virgin was not said in choir between Christmas Eve and the Feast of the Circumcision, Epiphany Eve and the Octave of Epiphany, Maundy Thursday and the Saturday after Easter, Eve of Pentecost to Trinity Sunday, Feasts of the Virgin and their Octaves, or double feasts. Other variant Uses had similar restrictions.

Early in the Middle Ages the Little Office was followed by the Office of All Saints. In the later Middle Ages this was normally reduced to a memorial, most often in the ferial series discussed above. But the Roman Breviary included a Commemoration of All Saints after the Collect in each hour of the Little Office of the Virgin.

In some foundations a section of the community was detailed to recite the Lady Office in a Lady chapel, or else special singers (including boys) were engaged to undertake this task, together with the antiphon sung after Compline. Some of the medieval polyphonic settings of Marian texts were probably intended for such singers.

THE COMMEMORATIVE OFFICE AND MASS OF THE VIRGIN

Careful distinction has to be made between the Little Office of the Virgin, and the Commemorative Office of the Virgin. The Little Office was said in addition to the main Office of the day: the Commemorative Office displaced the Office of the day once a week, most often on Saturday. Again this illustrates the special place of the Virgin in medieval spirituality: if Sunday was the Lord's day, the day of resurrection, then Saturday was our Lady's day.

As with the Little Office, the Commemorative Office was omitted at certain times of the year; commonly between Christmas and the Octave of Epiphany, and in Lent. Only when a principal or double feast was celebrated on Saturday was the Commemorative Office transferred to another day in the week.

Like the Antiphons of the Virgin used after Compline, the Commemorative Office was usually seasonal. The Roman Breviary includes four sets of texts and chants for use:

1. In Advent.

2. From the Octave of the Epiphany to the Purification (namely between January 14 and February 2).

3. From the Purification until the Saturday before Ash Wednesday, and from the Octave of Corpus Christi until the Saturday before Advent.

4. In Eastertide.

Compline was little altered (as on other days), but the rest of the Office was characterized by Marian texts, many of which corresponded with those of the Feasts of the Virgin. The form of Matins varied: in some Uses there were only three lessons, but in others there were nine lessons (twelve in monastic Use).

The weekly Commemoration of the Virgin began with Vespers on Friday evening and normally ended with None on Saturday. (First Vespers of Sunday was celebrated on Saturday evening.) It encompassed not only the Office but also the Mass: the Mass of the Virgin Mary was celebrated as the Mass of the day.

In monastic liturgies the Commemorative Office of the Virgin generally followed the normal monastic structure, while the Little Office of the Virgin normally followed the secular order. Some foundations also observed Commemorative Offices of other saints (e.g. St Benedict, or a patron saint).[4]

VOTIVE MASS OF THE VIRGIN

Three daily Masses are regularly identified in the Ordinals and Customaries of most collegiate and monastic churches: the Morrow Mass, the Mass of the day, and Lady Mass.

The Mass of the day was that designated for the Sunday or feast (or its octave). The Morrow Mass was offered either for a secondary observance (i.e. a coincident or displaced feast), for a special intention, or as a Votive Mass (see next section). The third Mass, like the Little Office of the Virgin, was a daily celebration—the Lady Mass. It is found as a separate section in the Common of the Saints in the Missal. As with the Little Office it was basically unchanging, though with

---

[4] A recent study of additional devotions and observances in English monasteries has been written by Sally Roper. See her doctoral dissertation, 'Medieval English Benedictine Liturgy: Studies in the Formation, Structure and Content of the Monastic Votive Office c.950–1540' (University of Oxford, 1988).

seasonal texts. It may more often have been celebrated privately; but in some cases (as with the Little Office) it was offered by a part of the community or by a special group of singers and chaplains in a Lady chapel. This was certainly the case in some English foundations by the fifteenth century, and a specific repertory of polyphonic music can be identified.

OTHER VOTIVE MASSES

In addition to intercessions and devotions addressed to the Virgin throughout the year and not just on her feasts, other 'votive' intentions were observed, though less persistently. Some of these intentions were included in the regular cycle of suffrages in the Office (see pp. 130 f. above). Others were offered in Votive Masses.

The intentions of Votive Masses date back to at least the eighth century when they were codified by Alcuin in the Carolingian reforms. They provided a cycle of intentions for the daily celebration of the Mass when the calendar was less crowded by feasts. In the later Middle Ages they were suitable for the Morrow Mass and for times of special need or intercession.

Early cycles usually included Votive Masses for Holy Angels, Holy Cross, Holy Spirit, Holy Trinity, wisdom, charity, and penitence. A number were associated with particular days, notably the Trinity on Sunday and the Cross (predictably) on Friday. Other intentions were added locally and more widely adopted in the later Middle Ages.

LITANIES

Extended petitions to the Almighty were offered on specific days. These commonly took the form of a litany, an extended series of petitions with repeated responses. The most common was the Litany of the Saints, a series of short invocations of saints by name.

Traditionally Wednesday and Friday have been penitential days when such petition is appropriate, particularly in the season of Lent. The Use of Salisbury provided for processions on Wednesday and Friday in Lent: these included the sung litany as the procession re-entered the choir.

The Greater Litany was associated with 25 April, the old pagan day for blessing the growing crops. This (in spite of also being St Mark's day) was the day of Rogation. Lesser Rogation days were observed on Monday, Tuesday, and Wednesday immediately before Ascension. An ancient repertory of chants was sung on each of these days, with antiphons, penitential psalms and litany, respond and preces. If Mass were celebrated at another church (the station church) a litany was also sung as the procession returned. The same procession and chants were used on days of special need (e.g. drought, famine, tempest, war).

The processional litanies of Easter Eve are discussed in Chapter 9.

OTHER OBSERVANCES

The mimetic element embodied within some liturgical rituals, and especially in their ceremonial, was more overt in the observances of some medieval foundations.

Liturgical dramas

It is important to distinguish liturgical dramas from medieval mystery plays. Liturgical dramas were sung throughout and usually in Latin; they were conceived for performance in church within the liturgy (Matins, before Mass, or Vespers); they were acted by and for the community; they were not didactic tools to teach an illiterate congregation; they are closely related to processions and tropes.

Perhaps the best known of these mimetic ceremonies is also the earliest—the Easter sepulchre dialogue, *Quem quaeritis in sepulchro*, presented as a ritual drama. By the tenth century it was found in churches throughout Europe. In many respects it forms a natural conclusion to the ceremonies of Holy Week which include a number of imitative rituals—the blessing of palms and the procession on Palm Sunday; the Mass of the Lord's Supper, the burial of the Host, and the stripping of altars on Maundy Thursday; the ceremony at the cross on Good Friday; the kindling of new fire and the blessing of new water on Easter Eve. Here the three Marys come to the tomb on Easter morning and find the angel. What distinguishes it from the ceremonies of Holy Week is the direct dramatic quality of the presentation and of the dialogue. In the famous late tenth-century description in *Regularis*

Concordia (an English monastic customary compiled at Winchester) the monks representing the three Marys are instructed to appear as though they are searching for something. And though the texts are scriptural, couched in the manner of liturgical versicle and response (indeed borrowing liturgical chants), they are allocated to recognizable characters. Later versions of this dialogue are fully fledged plays with a number of scenes, and often entitled *Visitatio sepulchri*.

From the brief ceremony before the Mass (or at the end of Matins) the Easter drama burgeoned by the thirteenth century into a series of independent scenes; and other dramas proliferated not just at Eastertide but also at Christmas. Liturgical dramas are found throughout Europe, especially in monasteries: no less than ten are found in the late twelfth-century 'Fleury' playbook.

The Boy Bishop and the Feast of Fools

If the liturgical drama prospered most often in monasteries, the creation of a boy bishop and the celebration of the Feast of Fools proliferated in large secular churches.

Two feasts of children fall near Christmas: St Nicholas (6 December) and the massacre of the Holy Innocents (28 December). On one or other of these dates it was the practice to elect a boy from the community as bishop who presided for the day. There were special ceremonies for his institution, and he commonly preached a sermon: the rite can be found in the Use of Salisbury and elsewhere.

In the same spirit of 'exalting the humble and meek' the clerks in minor orders presided on the Feast of Fools (or the Feast of the Ass). This could become an extraordinarily blasphemous event held either on 1 January (Feast of the Circumcision and the last day of the Octave of Christmas) or 14 January. At Beauvais Cathedral in the thirteenth century, an ass was tied at the altar, everyone brayed instead of singing *amen* or *alleluia*, and old leather and sausage were burnt instead of incense. Such anti-liturgy was suppressed in the later thirteenth century, though the processional Prose of the Ass (*Orientis partibus*) survives as a hymn melody in use today.

9.

Holy Week and Easter

HOLY WEEK

Holy Week is the most solemn period of the liturgical year. It is also a week which recalls a series of well-documented events in the life of Christ, events that are central to the Christian religion: the entry into Jerusalem, the Last Supper, the Crucifixion, and the Resurrection. The liturgical preparation for Holy Week began long before: the suppression of *alleluia* from Septuagesima, the liturgy of Ash Wednesday with the imposition of ashes before Mass, the Lenten season with its penitential texts and observances, and the omission of *Gloria patri* from Invitatory psalm and responds from Passion Sunday. All this led to Palm Sunday, but most particularly to the deep solemnity of the *Triduum*: Maundy Thursday (*Cena Domini*), Good Friday (*Parasceve*), and Holy Saturday (*Sabbatum Sanctum*).

PALM SUNDAY

The distinctive feature of Palm Sunday was the extended procession before Mass. The contents and order of the procession varied (a comparison of the Uses of Rome and Salisbury can be found in Andrew Hughes's *Medieval Manuscripts for Mass and Office* (Toronto, 1982), 256). Nevertheless, the general structure can be perceived from this basic summary.

[Antiphon(s)]
Gospel: the narrative of Christ's entry into Jerusalem
Prayers
Blessing of palms
Distribution of palms with singing of antiphons
Procession with antiphons, hymn (in many Uses *Gloria laus*), and respond

In a number of places the procession began at another church or out-side the city walls; in most cases it at least went outside. At Salisbury the procession included four stations (north, south, and west of the church, then inside before the rood). The fact that the procession had to be adapted to local circumstances accounts for the variant forms and for the absence of detailed instructions over the direction of the procession in the Roman Missal. Many of the antiphons and responds corresponded but occurred at different points in the rite from Use to Use.

At Mass on Palm Sunday and on the Tuesday and Wednesday following, the Passion of Christ was sung as the Gospel (Matthew, Mark, Luke, in that order). Instead of a single deacon singing the Gospel it was customary for three deacons to take part in the Passion— one as narrator, one as Christ, and the other taking the words of Peter, Pilate, and the crowd (*turba*, a part also known as synagogue). Often the Passions had special chants given in the Missal or Gospel book, allocated to narrator (*media vox*), Christ (*bassa vox*), and synagogue (*alta vox*).

In other respects Mass on Palm Sunday corresponded with Mass on other Sundays in Lent.

THE *TRIDUUM*:
MAUNDY THURSDAY, GOOD FRIDAY, HOLY SATURDAY

The rites of the *Triduum* retain much of the liturgy of the early Church. Even in the reformed Roman Catholic orders introduced since the Second Vatican Council the structure and content are largely undisturbed even in the vernacular. They were little influenced by monasticism: during the *Triduum* at both Office and Mass the medieval monasteries normally followed the secular orders (e.g. at Matins, nine lessons and nine psalms, rather than twelve lessons, twelve psalms, and three canticles: see Chapter 6). Mass was not celebrated between Maundy Thursday and the Mass of the Easter Vigil.

The timetable of these three days was exceptionally crowded. At various times in the Middle Ages this led to omissions (i.e. of the midday hours) or elisions (e.g. of Vespers at the end of the principal liturgy on all three days) or to some curious timings (e.g. of the celebration of the Easter Vigil early on Saturday afternoon). It is impossible to generalize: Uses differed from place to place and from century to century.

THE OFFICE DURING THE *TRIDUUM*

The closest parallel to the Office during the *Triduum* is the Office of the Dead. From Matins of Maundy Thursday until None on Holy Saturday the Office was stripped to its bare essentials.

The introductory versicles (including Psalm 94, *Venite exsultemus* at Matins) were omitted: all the Offices began with the psalms. Although the psalms and canticles retained antiphons, *Gloria patri* was omitted.

At Matins there were no blessings before lessons and no endings to them. In the first nocturn on each day the lessons were taken from the Lamentations of Jeremiah; these had special tones provided. Twenty-four candles were lit at Matins: these were extinguished one by one at the beginning of each antiphon and respond: this continued at Lauds, and by the end of the last psalm the church was in darkness. Matins during the *Triduum* is often referred to as Tenebrae (from the antiphon *Tenebrae factae sunt*): and the readings from Jeremiah are sometimes known as the Tenebrae Lessons.

At the other Offices (including Lauds) chapter, hymn, respond, and versicle were omitted: the canticle followed the last psalm. (At Compline *Nunc dimittis* was sung as the last psalm before the repeat of the psalm-antiphon.) *Pater noster* was silent in some Uses, and there were special preces. The greeting *Dominus vobiscum* and the introduction to the collect *Oremus* were not said. Commemorations and memorials were not recited. Most Uses omitted the concluding *Benedicamus domino*.

To give an example, the order of Lauds on Maundy Thursday, from at least the thirteenth century onwards, was as follows:

Antiphon *Justificeris domine*	Psalm 50 *Miserere*
Antiphon *Dominus tamquam*	Psalm 89 *Domine refugium*
Antiphon *Contritum est cor meum*	Psalm 62 *Deus deus meus*
	[with Psalm 66]
Antiphon *Exhortatus es*	Canticle *Cantemus*
Antiphon *Oblatus est quia ipse*	Psalms 148–150 *Laudate*
Antiphon *Traditor autem dedit*	Canticle *Benedictus*
Kyrie with interpolated verses *Christus factus est*	

Pater noster, Preces, and *Miserere*, all in silence (or recited quietly by pairs of
   clerics or monks)
Collect *Respice quaesumus domine*

Additional observances (see Chapter 8) like the Little Office of the
Virgin and the Marian antiphon were omitted.

MASS AND SPECIAL CEREMONIES OF MAUNDY THURSDAY

During the Middle Ages there was only one Mass on Maundy
Thursday, and at churches where there was a bishop this was the Mass
of Chrism, at which the oils used during the year at the rites of
baptism, confirmation, and anointing of the sick were blessed.

A number of churches (monastic and secular) retained a ceremony
for the reception of penitents (together with a comparable ceremony
on Ash Wednesday for the ejection of sinners). In early times the
reception was followed by a Mass of Remission: in the Middle Ages
the reception preceded High Mass.

Mass of the day followed None (as was normal on weekdays in
Lent). It was festal and the chants of the Ordinary of the Mass were
solemn. In some Uses *Gloria patri* was sung at the Introit.

There were variable factors and special rites that might affect the
order of Mass.

1. If a bishop was present *Gloria in excelsis* was sung. In some Uses
the presence of the bishop also resulted in the inclusion of *Gloria patri*
at the Introit.

2. The Blessing of Chrism: this ceremony occurred only when a
bishop was present. The rite is therefore more commonly found in a
Pontifical than in a Missal. The procession of the oils took place after
the Offertory and Secret: oil of the sick, oil of catechumens (for
baptism), and chrism (confirmation) were brought to the altar. In the
Salisbury Use the chant *O redemptor sume carmen* was sung. The
blessing took place within the Prayer of Consecration (with special
texts).

3. Unless a bishop was present *Agnus dei* and the kiss of peace were
omitted.

4. Communion and Vespers: in secular (and some monastic) Uses
Mass and Vespers were often conflated. The length of the Mass begun

after None presumably meant that it ended after the time that Vespers was due to begin. The order was as follows: Communion antiphon; Vespers psalms and antiphons; *Magnificat* and antiphon; Postcommunion prayer (doubled as Vespers collect); *Benedicamus domino* (as end to both Mass and Vespers). In some Uses, Vespers, or all but the *Magnificat* and its antiphon, was said privately or quietly in pairs. When a bishop was present some Uses specified *Ite missa est* as the dismissal.

5. The deposition of the host: because there was no celebration of Mass between Maundy Thursday and Easter two hosts were consecrated at this Mass. One was consumed by the celebrant at Mass, the second was reserved, often in a special reliquary or sepulchre. Part of the buried host was to be consumed by the celebrant at communion on Good Friday (see below); the other part was to be raised with the cross before Matins on Easter Sunday—the risen Christ (see below). In some rites two additional hosts were consecrated and reserved, one for Good Friday and one for the resurrection ceremony before Easter Matins. The deposition of the host took place after the communion. In some places this was a simple ceremony undertaken during the singing of Vespers, but in due course it became a solemn procession with its own chants.

6. The stripping of altars: after the Mass, the altars were stripped of ornaments, candles, and cloths, and at least the high altar was washed with water and wine (a symbol of Christ's blood washing the world clean). Only the altar where the hosts were reserved remained unstripped and lit by candles. (In secular Uses the order was Mass and Vespers, meal, stripping of the altars, washing of feet; in monastic Uses the order was Mass, stripping of altars, washing of feet, Vespers, meal.) During the stripping of the altars the respond *Circumdederunt me* was sung. There was generally provision for other chants and a prayer, but this varied from place to place.

7. The washing of feet: before the Last Supper Christ washed the disciples' feet. This act was imitated in two rites of the medieval Church. At the first, as an act of humility, the feet of the poor were washed by the community. In some monasteries this was a daily rite. On Maundy Thursday it was more extensive and involved a larger number of the poor and the whole community. The rite was accompanied by chants; these varied according to place, and often there were options so that as many antiphons etc. were chosen as were needed for the ceremony.

The same element of choice was found in the second rite, Mandatum. The name derives from the antiphon *Mandatum novum*—I give you a new commandment: hence, the corruption 'Maundy'. This was a closer imitation of the Last Supper when designated priests washed the feet of the whole community as Christ washed the feet of his own community (the disciples). The Roman Missal is flexible with few rubrics for the ceremony. There was a sequence of optional antiphons with psalm verses, always ending with the chant with the refrain *Ubi caritas et amor*.

The Use of Salisbury was more precise (as were many others abroad). At the cathedral the ceremony took place in the chapter house. The rite began with the Gospel of the day and a sermon. Then, while antiphons were sung, two priests washed the feet of all present, one on each side of the chapter house. Preces, collect, and reading concluded the rite.

THE GOOD FRIDAY LITURGY

Unlike all other days of the year Mass was not celebrated on Good Friday and Holy Saturday. On Good Friday the principal service of the day took place after None. It consisted of a series of distinct observances, many of which were of very early origin. The three principal constituents were (in modern parlance) the Liturgy of the Word, the Veneration of the Cross, and the reception of Communion.

The Liturgy of the Word

The first part of the rite consisted of scriptural readings and intercessions.

The ministers entered and knelt prostrate before the altar. There were neither candles nor incense. Three readings followed with two tracts, and a collect:

Lesson: *In tribulatione sua* (Hosea 6: 1–6)
Tract: *Domine audivi auditum tuum*
Collect: *Deus a quo et Judas*
Lesson: *Dixit dominus ad Moysen* (Exodus 12: 1–11)
Tract: *Eripe me domine ab homine malo*
Passion: *Egressus est Jesus* (John 18 and 19: 1–42)

The Passion of St John was sung from the pulpitum to the special passion tone with three deacons as narrator, Christ, and synagogue— as on Palm Sunday (see above). The last four verses were sung by the narrator to the normal Gospel tone.

There followed the Solemn Prayers, nine intercessions each in the following form: bidding, silent prayer (kneeling), collect. Only in the penultimate intercession (for the Jews) did the medieval Missals direct that nobody was to kneel.

The Veneration of the Cross

Two priests carried the veiled cross into the middle of the choir. In some Uses (monastic and secular) they began *Improperia* (the reproaches) which the choir took up: *Popule meus* (O my people, what have I done to you?) was sung antiphonally between the two sides of the choir, with the refrain of the Trisagion (Greek: thrice holy) sung first by one side in Greek (*Hagios O theos*—Holy God), the other side answering in Latin (*Sanctus deus*). There were then verses shared antiphonally by two soloists on each side with the refrain *Popule meus* sung by the whole choir.

The cross was unveiled as the two priests sang *Ecce lignum crucis* (Behold the wood of the cross . . . come, let us adore). In the Roman Use *Ecce lignum* preceded *Popule meus*. All venerated the cross in turn (kneeling before it and kissing it) while the singing continued. The antiphon *Crucem tuam adoremus* was sung with Psalm 66 (*Deus misereatur nostri* without *Gloria patri*), then began the hymn *Crux fidelis*. In the manner of other processional hymns the refrain was sung by all at the beginning and after each verse (in some cases the whole refrain, in others alternately *Crux fidelis* and the second part *Dulce lignum*) while soloists sang the verses of *Pange lingua gloriosi proelium*.

In churches where lay people were present the cross was taken out of choir to a place in the nave where they could make the veneration.

The Communion

After the veneration of the cross the altar was prepared for the communion, and the hosts (or host—consecrated at Mass on Maundy Thursday) were brought in solemn procession from the place of deposition.

The rite began at *Pater noster*. *Agnus dei* and the kiss of peace were omitted. The priest received communion, but there was no Communion antiphon or Postcommunion prayer.

After the communion the remaining host (or part of it if only one was reserved on Maundy Thursday) was taken with the cross to the place of deposition, and the altar stripped. In Roman Use all this took place in silence, but Salisbury (among others) provided a series of responds and antiphons to be sung in procession and at the sepulchre. In some Uses the deposition of the cross took place immediately after the veneration.

In the Roman Use, Vespers was said privately after communion (and before the deposition). In other Uses, Vespers remained a separate Office as usual, but in many cases the whole Office (or else all but *Magnificat* and its antiphon and the collect) was recited privately or at least said without chant.

THE EASTER VIGIL

The practice of keeping a watching vigil through Saturday night in expectation of Sunday was well known in the early Church: it was recorded by the nun, Egeria, on her visit to Jerusalem in the fourth century. It was a precedent for the night Office of Matins, sometimes known as Vigils. The Easter Vigil echoes that early form, especially in the readings. But its impact lies in the use of rites to symbolize the new life of Easter—the kindling of new fire and the blessing of new water.

For three nights the lights of the church had been systematically extinguished during Matins and Lauds, anticipating the darkness of the death of Christ and the darkness of the tomb. Now the process was reversed. No one who has been to a modern Easter Vigil can fail to have been touched by the kindling of new fire outside the church, the blessing and lighting of the Paschal candle, the entry into church, the spread of light as the candles are lit one from another, the illumination of the whole church, and the climax of the singing of *Exsultet*.

The problem for the medieval Church was one of timing. A normal day was brim-full with liturgy: in Holy Week it spilled over. The result was that the Easter Vigil had to be celebrated before First Vespers of Easter—that is to say after None on Holy Saturday.

The Kindling of New Fire

The rite provided for the kindling of new fire and the blessing of the Paschal candle, but the form differed: by the later Middle Ages this did not always include a procession. In the older medieval Uses (represented by Salisbury and other English Uses, secular and monastic), the Vigil began outside or in the chapter house or a chapel of the main church. In other Uses (including Rome) the blessing took place in choir at the altar step and there was no need for a procession. With or without a procession the rite had a basic form.

The celebrant (bishop or abbot in great churches) kindled the fire in a brazier, blessed it, and blessed the studs of incense to be placed in the candle later. Each act was undertaken with a spoken prayer (of comparable content but variant text in the individual Uses). A single candle was lit. If there were a procession it now followed and the hymn *Inventor rutili* was sung.

In the second part of the rite the deacon took the Paschal candle (still unlit) to the pulpitum. Here he sang *Exsultet iam angelica turba*. This consisted of a resurrection prayer (*Exsultet*) in which the candle was blessed, dialogue (*Sursum corda*, as at Mass), and preface (*Vere quia dignum*). Prayer and preface had a special tone, often written out in full in the Missal. During the preface the five studs of incense were placed in the Paschal candle in the form of a cross (at *In huius igitur noctis*), the Paschal candle was lit (at *Qui licet divisus*) from the single candle brought from the new fire, then other candles were lit (at *O [vere] beata nox*). At Salisbury the whole church was lit at this point, in other Uses the illumination of the whole church took place after the blessing of new water.

The Old Testament Readings

After the *Exsultet* all sat in their usual places for Mass in choir and sanctuary. There followed a long series of readings (intoned without introduction) beginning with the Genesis creation narrative and including the account of the crossing of the Red Sea in Exodus. After each reading there was a collect, and after certain readings there was also a Tract. Before each collect in the Roman Use all knelt silently (as on Good Friday) and then stood for the collect itself. The number of readings varied: the Roman Missal included twelve lessons, each with a collect; many other sources included only four. All the series included the creation (Genesis 1 to 2: 2), the crossing of the Red Sea (Exodus 14: 24 to 15: 1), a reading from Isaiah (Isaiah 54: 17 to 55: 1–11 or Isaiah 4: 1–6), and a reading telling of Moses before his death (Deuteronomy 31: 22–30). The four Tracts were also consistent.

The order according to the Salisbury Missal was:

Lesson: *In principio* (Genesis 1 to 2: 2)
Collect: *Deus qui mirabiliter*
Lesson: *Factum est vigilia* (Exodus 14: 24 to 15: 1a)
Tract: *Cantemus domino* (Exodus 15: 1b–3)
Collect: *Deus cuius antiqua miracula*
Lesson: *Apprehendent septem mulieres* (Isaiah 4: 1–6)
Tract: *Vinea facta est dilecto*
Collect: *Deus qui nos ad celebrandum*
Lesson: *Scripsit Moyses canticum* (Deuteronomy 31: 22–30)
Tract: *Attende caelum et loquar* (Deuteronomy 32: 1–4)
Collect: *Deus qui ecclesiam*
Tract: *Sicut cervus desiderat ad fontes aquarum*

The Roman Missal (1474) included twelve lessons, with twelve collects and tracts.

The Blessing of New Water

The Tract *Sicut cervus* (from Psalm 41, 'Like as the hart desireth the water brooks') introduced the blessing of new water: the procession to the font, the blessing of the new water in the font, and (in some Uses) the baptism of an infant.

According to the Roman Missal, the Tract *Sicut cervus* was sung while a lighted candle was taken in procession to the font. After the collect *Omnipotens sempiterne deus*, the font was blessed, and the Litany followed. The church was lit and Mass began.

At Salisbury there were two prayers after *Sicut cervus* and then the sevenfold Litany. Only with the fivefold Litany did the procession with a candle to the font begin. (The Consuetudinary specifies that this is not the Paschal candle.) After the collect the font was blessed. Provision was made for the baptism of a child. The metrical Litany *Rex sanctorum* was sung as the procession returned to the choir and sanctuary.

The rite varied from place to place: the late medieval Roman Use is probably the simplest, that from Salisbury among the more complex.

The central blessing was common to all Uses. The blessing of the new water is comparable with the blessing of the Paschal candle (*Exsultet*). After the collect came the dialogue (*Sursum corda*) and a preface. The long blessing proceeded, intoned by the celebrant, who divided and blessed the water with his hand, dipping the lighted candle into it, and finally adding oil and chrism.

The Mass

The Mass followed without break. *Kyrie* was sung solemnly; *Gloria in excelsis* was intoned, and in most places the bells were rung in and out of church. After the Collect and Epistle, *Alleluia: Confitemini domino* was sung, followed by the Tract *Laudate dominum omnes gentes*. In the Roman Use *alleluia* was additionally intoned three times by the celebrant, each time at a higher pitch, and each time repeated by all. This is not specified at Salisbury, but it took place after the Tract at the monastery of St Mary's, York.

After the Gospel, Mass proceeded directly to the Secret, omitting both *Credo* and Offertory. Similarly *Agnus dei*, the kiss of peace, and the Communion were omitted.

Vespers at the End of the Mass

As on Maundy Thursday the communion (at which it was common for all the community to receive) was followed by the singing of an abbreviated Vespers, consisting of *Laudate dominum omnes gentes* (Psalm 146) with the antiphon *Alleluia*, and *Magnificat* with antiphon *Vespere autem*. The Postcommunion collect *Spiritus nobis domine* was intoned and the whole liturgy ended with *Ite missa est*.

EASTER DAY

The Easter season was one of joy and most texts have the suffix *alleluia*. There are Easter forms of many chants (often marked T.P.— *in tempore paschali*). On Easter Day and in the week following *alleluia* was often doubled or trebled.

Apart from the additions of *alleluia* and processions the usual forms of Office and Mass were restored on Easter Day, and the summer timetable began. (It lasted until the Feast of All Saints, 1 November.)

The Procession from the Sepulchre

One of the few additional rites of Easter was the raising of the cross and the host from the sepulchre where they were laid to rest at the end of the Good Friday liturgy. As ever the placing and precise order of this ceremony varied according to local custom. It either preceded Matins, or was incorporated into the end of Matins before *Te deum laudamus*, or else preceded Mass. The first occurrence was the most common. The procession itself might simply return to choir, or, having returned to choir to place the host on the high altar (or in a suitable aumbry or pyx), it might continue with the crucifix around the church as witness of the resurrection.

The texts and chants of the rite were equally variable, but predictable: among them *Dum transisset sabbatum, Sedit angelus, Christus resurgens, Surrexit dominus de sepulchro*.

If the raising of the cross and host took place before Matins, this did not preclude the singing of the Easter Sepulchre dialogue at the end of Matins or (more often) before the Mass, whether simply as sung versicle and response or as an acted drama (see Chapter 8, 'Other Observances').

The Form of Matins

Though the full form of Matins was observed in some foundations, it was more common for it to follow the same abbreviated form as on Christmas Day and Pentecost: three psalms with three antiphons, three lessons with three responds, [procession to the sepulchre or Easter Sepulchre drama], *Te deum laudamus*, versicle, collect, and so to the beginning of Lauds.

Morrow Mass and High Mass

Morrow Mass and High Mass took place as usual, the latter normally preceded by a festal procession, in some Uses including the Easter Sepulchre dialogue.

The Little Hours

There were variants in the secular Uses at the Little Hours. At Prime, Terce, Sext, and None the hymn, chapter, and respond were omitted; they were replaced by the Gradual *Haec dies* (as at Mass), sung without its verse. At Prime *Quicumque vult* was also omitted. *Haec dies* was followed by the versicle and response and the collect. This form persisted throughout the week after Easter.

The Form of Vespers

The secular form of Vespers on Easter Day and the week following incorporated elements of the Mass. Beginning with solemn *Kyrie* (as at Mass), there followed psalms under the antiphon *Alleluia*, Gradual (*Haec dies*) and Alleluia (both as at Mass), Versicle, *Magnificat*, Collect, *Benedicamus*, and then the procession. In other Uses the hymn might be replaced by the Sequence *Victimae paschali laudes*.

The Procession at Vespers

At the end of Vespers, after *Magnificat* and Collect, there was a procession with oil and chrism to the font. At Salisbury the procession left the choir singing the psalm *Laudate pueri* (Psalm 112) with antiphon *Alleluia*. The censing of the font followed, and there was a versicle and response and a collect. The procession then proceeded singing Psalm 113 *In exitu Israel* with antiphon *Alleluia*, halting at the cross on the west side of the choir screen: again a versicle and response and a collect were sung. Finally the procession re-entered the choir singing a Marian antiphon with versicle and collect. In other Uses the procession included antiphons rather than whole psalms; but in either case the form was basically that of a series of commemorations or memorials (see Chapter 8, 'Processions', and 'Commemorations, Memorials, and Suffrages').

THE SEASON OF EASTER

The Octave of Easter

The unusual form of the Little Hours and of Vespers persisted throughout the week, as did the procession to the cross at Lauds (from

Monday) and the procession to the font at Vespers (from Easter Day). At First Vespers and at Lauds on the Sunday after Easter there was a procession to the cross (not to the font), but thereafter the processions at these Offices ceased. At the other hours the normal forms were restored on this Sunday.

The Use of Salisbury required the Paschal candle to be lit daily at the principal services during the Octave of Easter, but not at the Little Hours.

Eastertide and Pentecost

The Paschal candle was lit, at least at Mass, on Sundays and feast-days until Ascension Day. On Ascension Day it was lit at all the principal services. Eastertide was observed until the end of the Octave of Pentecost in most churches, and in some cases the Paschal candle was not put away until then. The processions at Rogationtide (25 April, and Monday to Wednesday before Ascension Day) are discussed in Chapter 8. There was a Vigil comparable with that at Easter on the eve of Pentecost, and again the font was blessed as at the Easter Vigil. Matins normally followed the short form with a single nocturn, as on Christmas Day and Easter Day.

PART III.

After the Reformation

IO.

The Tridentine Reform

REFORMATION AND COUNTER-REFORMATION

The religious and political upheaval that took place in northern Europe in the sixteenth century was obviously the most extreme event since the schism of the Eastern and Western Churches. The liturgical consequences of the Reformation were far-reaching. In the new Protestant era the old order was ousted: monastic foundations were dissolved, marking the end of a distinct Christian culture as well as an individual style of liturgy; the Latin liturgy was abandoned; new vernacular liturgies were formed which emphasized scriptural reading and song, intelligibility and theological clarity, admission of sin, and search for salvation. In place of regional variants there now emerged independent denominations with their own patterns of worship. The old dependence on rite and ceremony, Mass and Office, Calendar and feasts, continuous formalized prayer and devotion, gave way to services which consisted of readings, exegesis in the form of a sermon, and vernacular psalms or hymns.

Luther made use of existing hymn texts and melodies, and adapted them to vernacular worship. The pattern of Lutheran worship echoed medieval forms, especially in the Fore-Mass. But no authoritative orders were established, and no standardized liturgical books were widely circulated, except in Scandinavia. The situation in more radical Protestant Churches (e.g. Calvinists, Anabaptists) was more extreme: neither forms nor texts were retained—all depended on the scriptures. By contrast, the more moderate Church of England retained the principal features of the Latin daily Office and of the Mass, and this liturgy is examined in Chapter 11.

THE TRIDENTINE RITE

The shock waves of this defiance of ecclesiastical authority based on the continuity of Apostolic succession have persisted for centuries. But the contemporary response of the Roman Church was to consolidate, revalue, and reassert itself with new authority. This work was begun by the Council of Trent, a meeting of Roman Catholic bishops that convened for twenty-five sessions between 1545 and 1563. It was continued, mostly in Rome, during the ensuing years.

The theological defence and consolidation of Catholic dogma and doctrine, the spiritual mission of Ignatius Loyola's new Order of Jesuits, and the devotional fervour of Philip Neri and the Oratorians are far more striking consequences of the Council of Trent and the Counter-Reformation of the Roman Catholic Church than the liturgical reforms. Nevertheless the revision of the Calendar, the Breviary, the Missal, and the chant were vital. For what was re-established in the sixteenth century persisted, largely unaltered, throughout the Roman Catholic Church until the recent Second Vatican Council.

The spread of printing enabled the Roman Catholic Church to assert its authority without local variants, and with a new expectation of uniformity of practice. Pope Pius V set up a commission to revise the liturgical books. The *Breviarum Romanum* was issued in 1568, the *Missale Romanum* followed in 1570. These were intended for use throughout the Roman Catholic Church. Only those places which could claim a Breviary or Missal more than two hundred years old (including the Ambrosian and the monastic Uses) were exempt, and many who might have claimed exemption chose to take the easier (and cheaper) course and follow the Roman Rite. It quashed all younger Breviaries, including the radical compilation made for Pope Paul III by the Spanish Cardinal Quiñones (1535).

The stability of the liturgy was further enhanced in 1588 by the establishment of the Congregation of Sacred Rites, the body in the Curia which scrutinized and authorized all change at an international level. (The liturgical division of this was renamed the Congregation for Divine Worship in 1969.)

The Calendar

By far the most radical consequence of Tridentine reform was the revision of the Calendar. The proliferation of the medieval Calendar had resulted in the disruption of the recitation of the weekly ferial psalter. In an attempt to restore this pivotal feature of the daily Office the new Calendar suppressed many feasts and their octaves, leaving over 200 free days in each year for the recitation of the weekly psalter. (Simple feasts used ferial psalms.)

In the ensuing centuries this new position was itself eroded: 149 double and semi-double feasts (1568) expanded to 164 (1602), 176 (1631), and 275 (1882).

The Tridentine Breviary of 1568 not only suppressed some feasts and octaves but also reclassified those that were left. Five classes were established; to this was added the class of 'greater double' in 1602.

Tridentine Classification of Feasts

Rank of Feast		Number
Duplex i classis	Double of the first class	19
Duplex ii classis	Double of the second class	17 (18 in 1602)
Duplex maius	Greater double [from 1602]	(16 in 1602)
Duplex	Double	53 (43 in 1602)
Semiduplex	Semi-double	60 (68 in 1602)
Simplex	Simple	The remainder

There remained complex rules for the celebration of feasts, and in particular the precedence to be observed when two feasts fell on the same day (e.g. Ascension and Sts Philip and James) or when a feast fell on a Sunday. All classes of double feast falling on a Sunday took precedence over the Sunday observance (a rule observed until 1911). With the expansion in the number of feasts during the centuries after 1602 the Sanctorale came once again to be dominant.

The Office

The revision of the Calendar clearly had significant consequences for the recitation of the daily Office. The re-establishment of the hours was made clearer by the suppression of the additional observances that had become customary. Supplementary Offices (e.g. of the Dead), extended ferial memorials, devotional observances (*Trina Oratio* and Gradual Psalms), and weekly Commemorative Offices (e.g. patron saint) were discontinued. Out too went the medieval rhymed Offices (never a part of the Roman Curia's Breviary). However, the Little Office of the Virgin remained as an optional private devotion, as did the option of reciting a Commemorative Office of the Virgin each Saturday (except at specified times).

Within the Office the most significant changes were made to Prime. The conclusion was shortened: on feast-days it ended with the collect recited immediately after the respond. The heavy load of Sunday psalmody was redistributed over the week (see the Tables of Psalmody in Appendix 2.4.).

The Tridentine Breviary omitted the processions after Vespers at Christmas and Easter—practices abandoned long before in Rome.

At the end of the sixteenth century the texts of the patristic and hagiographical lessons used at Matins were revised, and in 1631 Pope Urban VIII sanctioned the rewriting of medieval, stressed hymn texts in classical metre.

Private, Corporate, and Public Recitation of the Office

The Tridentine Breviary followed on from its medieval Roman predecessor. It was a portable printed book (often in four compact volumes) containing all the texts of the Office. Music was less commonly included, and for the most part the recitation of the Office must have been spoken. Corporate recitation remained the expected norm, but the completeness and portability of the Breviary meant that it could be recited privately by a priest either in or out of church. Though such practice was never officially sanctioned at the time it must have been widespread, especially in parishes.

In the secular Roman Church, musical celebration of the daily Office was increasingly rare. It continued of course in monasteries, and was found in France in cathedral and collegiate churches, at least until the Revolution (1789). Furthermore, in spite of pressure in the seventeenth century to come into line with Rome, France was an important centre for local, liturgical revision. (The tide was turned

in the nineteenth century when a stronger Papacy could assert its
authority even in France!)

These Gallican revisions can be observed from the last two decades
of the seventeenth century in local diocesan forms of the daily Office.
There were not only local details, but quite radical revisions of the
content. Scriptural texts were introduced to replace other antiphons,
readings, and responds; the bulk of the Office was reduced; and the
Calendar was simplified. But even in France it is clear that a sung
Office attended by the people was generally limited to Sundays and
greater feasts. The same was true elsewhere; and of all the Offices,
Vespers became most important.

In the seventeenth and eighteenth centuries, at sung Vespers in a
great cathedral or city church (as at Mass, discussed below) there was a
public liturgy often involving three distinct groups: first, the priests
and servers whose role was primarily ceremonial; second, the choir
who dominated what was recited; third, the people, passive and
devotional. This is a very different concept from the corporate Office
of a medieval community. The priests and servers were primarily a
visual presence. Though a duty priest (*hebdomadarius*) was needed to
chant the versicles and chapter, the canons had little active part in the
Office. The most striking moment was the ceremonial censing of the
altar at the *Magnificat*. Far more evident was the choir, no longer the body
of the community *in situ* in the choir, but now a select group of
professional singers and musicians often placed in a gallery or on
platforms. Finally, the people, passive as before, but in the new spacious
Renaissance churches often able to view and hear more of what went on.

The music at these celebrations was no longer dominated by the
chant but by polyphony. Even the most modest of the city churches of
Rome and Venice could boast a solo singer or two and an organist,
often hiring extras for the biggest feasts. The large churches and court
chapels had a musical establishment large enough to subdivide into as
many as three or four choirs with their separate organists and, in some
cases, instrumentalists.

Vespers on Sundays and Feasts

Most of the spectacular Vespers music from Palestrina to Handel in
Rome, or from Gabrieli to Vivaldi in Venice (let alone other centres),

was intended either for Sunday Vespers, Vespers of Our Lady, of the Apostles, Corpus Christi, or a dedication feast. The most common and consistent were the first three: they could, after all, serve for the majority of celebrations in the year. The choral items were most often those that were common: psalms, hymn, canticle. Proper items might have been chanted, replaced by suitable motets (often solo voices), or else by organ music. Monteverdi's famous Vespers of Our Lady (1610, a show-piece for a composer looking for a change of post) bears this out.

On lesser days and in smaller churches Vespers might have been performed by alternating chant verses with other music: chant and *falsobordone* (basically a harmonized form of the chant) in the psalms; chant and choral polyphony in the hymn and *Magnificat*, or chant and organ, or possibly a mixture of organ and choral polyphony.

Though composers (e.g. Victoria) wrote collections of complete cycles of polyphonic hymn verses for the whole year, the Office repertory was dominated by settings of *Magnificat* and selected psalms.

Vespers on Sundays and Double Feasts

SUNDAY VESPERS	VESPERS OF OUR LADY VESPERS OF VIRGINS AND OTHER HOLY WOMEN	FIRST VESPERS OF APOSTLES AND EVANGELISTS; VESPERS OF MARTYRS AND CONFESSORS
Deus in adiutorium	*Deus in adiutorium*	*Deus in adiutorium*
Gloria patri	*Gloria patri*	*Gloria patri*
Alleluia	*Alleluia*	*Alleluia*
Psalms with ferial or proper antiphons	Psalms with common or proper antiphons	Psalms with common or proper antiphons
109 *Dixit dominus*	109 *Dixit dominus*	109 *Dixit dominus*
110 *Confitebor*	112 *Laudate pueri*	110 *Confitebor*
111 *Beatus vir*	121 *Laetatus sum*	111 *Beatus vir*
112 *Laudate pueri*	126 *Nisi dominus*	112 *Laudate pueri*
113 *In exitu Israel*	147 *Lauda Jerusalem*	116 *Laudate dominum*
Chapter	Chapter	Chapter
Hymn (of the year *Lucis creator*)	Hymn (BVM *Ave maris stella*)	Hymn (Apostles *Exsultet orbis*)
Versicle	Versicle	Versicle

Antiphon	Antiphon	Antiphon
Magnificat	*Magnificat*	*Magnificat*
Collect	Collect	Collect
Benedicamus	*Benedicamus*	*Benedicamus*

FIRST AND SECOND VESPERS OF DEDICATION	SECOND VESPERS OF APOSTLES AND EVANGELISTS
Psalms	Psalms
109 *Dixit dominus*	109 *Dixit dominus*
110 *Confitebor*	112 *Laudate pueri*
111 *Beatus vir*	115 *Credidi*
112 *Laudate pueri*	125 *In convertendo*
147 *Lauda Jerusalem*	138 *Domine probasti*

It is plain from these lists that the repertory of psalms on many days of the year was closely related. As well as the eleven psalms listed above, three others appear (Psalm 127 at Corpus Christi, and Psalms 129 and 131 at Christmas), giving a grand total of fourteen psalms for Vespers on all double feasts and Sundays of the year. In practice not all the psalms in a celebration were necessarily sung polyphonically.

Two points emerge from this: first, a repertory of fourteen psalms and a *Magnificat* can provide a nucleus for a festal polyphonic repertory; second, the frequent repetition of a small group of festal psalms gives the Tridentine Office the quality of the daily devotional hours of Our Lady, the Dead, and All Saints recited in medieval times, in marked contrast to the complete *cursus* of the ferial cycle.

THE MASS

The Tridentine Mass is in essence a centrally authorized, stable form of the medieval Mass, closely related to the first printed Roman Missal (1474). It remained substantially unaltered until 1964.

In compiling the Missal of 1570, the revisers sought to eliminate later medieval accretions. As with the Breviary, the simplification of the Calendar was significant. Later medieval texts were excised, notably the tropes (e.g. in the *Kyrie*) and the large repertories of Sequences. Only four Sequences remained: *Victimae paschali laudes*

(Easter), *Veni sancte spiritus* (Pentecost), *Lauda Sion* (Corpus Christi), and *Dies irae* (Mass of the Dead).

High Mass (*Missa Solemniter*)

As with the Tridentine Office the celebration of sung Mass was polarized. In the Middle Ages the celebrant's action in the sanctuary was complemented by the participation of the remainder of the community in choir with their chants. But with the use of professional choirs performing from galleries or platforms the choral part of the liturgy was often delegated to a body of musicians. The remaining canons or priests and the people were passive: silent devotion articulated by ceremonial and by music (with an occasional prompting bell) marked the norm.

From the sixteenth century, as in the celebration of Vespers, the music for High Mass now focused on the Ordinary rather than the Proper. The emergence of cyclic polyphonic Masses, especially in the fifteenth century, led to the musically unified Ordinary (in spite of its disparate texts) as the norm thereafter. Most polyphonic Masses build their unity from musical concepts and materials—motive, melody, or model. But this kind of unity is found in plainsong Masses too. As with Vespers three sets of Ordinary chants served for much of the year: Sundays (*Missa Orbis factor*), feasts of the Virgin (*Missa Cum jubilo*) and feasts of Apostles (*Missa Cunctipotens genitor*). Throughout the sixteenth and seventeenth centuries it is possible to find examples of groups of organ masses set by a single composer to use with these three sets of chants (e.g. Girolamo Cavazzoni, Andrea Gabrieli, Merulo, Frescobaldi).

Some settings of the Ordinary respond to the Tridentine decrees on intelligibility of text in sacred music, but more interesting is the musical response to the ceremonial needs of the Mass. Few composers of the later sixteenth century set all three petitions of *Agnus dei*: Victoria (Collegium Germanicum, Rome) and Lassus (Munich court) generally settled for one, Palestrina (St Peter's, Rome) for two. Frescobaldi (St Peter's, Rome) omitted *Benedictus*, presumably to allow for an elevation motet or instrumental toccata. And in the later seventeenth and eighteenth centuries the long settings of *Benedictus* or organ elevations (especially in France and Austria) suggested music to accompany the silent canon and to act as a focus for the moment of greatest devotion of those present—the elevation of the consecrated host.

Whereas the chanted Propers had provided music for the moments of action and movement in the early and medieval Mass, the polyphonic Ordinary of the Renaissance and Baroque provided a cyclic continuum as a largely non-synchronous accompaniment to the ceremonial at the altar. But what of the Tridentine Proper? Of the five proper antiphons it was the Offertory which attracted most attention: Palestrina, for example, published a whole volume of them. Though the remainder of the Propers may have been chanted, some were replaced, especially during the seventeenth century, by motets with suitable devotional texts (e.g. *O sacrum convivium, O salutaris hostia*), or by organ or instrumental music (especially in Venice). Mozart's Church Sonatas (Salzburg) provide a late example. Examples of complete sets of proper antiphons (such as Byrd's great cycle of *Gradualia*) are exceptional.

Other Forms of Worship

The spiritual fervour of the Counter-Reformation period, fired by the Jesuits, Oratorians, and a host of lay Confraternities, led to new devotional trends and liturgical forms. If the Virgin Mary had been at the centre of medieval popular devotion, the Blessed Sacrament took over at the Counter-Reformation. This may be observed in three specific ways.

First, the feast of Corpus Christi grew in stature and popularity. Though a late feast (formally established in 1264) it was not excised from the Calendar but accorded a rank comparable only with Easter and Pentecost by the inclusion of a Sequence. In seventeenth-century Rome it was one of the busiest times for musicians who were drawn in by every church for the celebration of Vespers and Mass of Corpus Christi. Organs, singers, and players were hired; platforms built; music specially written. Musicians also had a part in the Corpus Christi procession. Although festal processions tended to disappear from the liturgy (except on Palm Sunday), the Corpus Christi procession became a highlight of the year, as a fervent popular devotion.

At the end of Vespers at Corpus Christi it had been customary to give the blessing with the Blessed Sacrament placed in a monstrance (an ornamental case, literally for 'showing'). To this blessing were added antiphons, hymns, responds, and prayers to form a separate ritual. Taken as a whole, the rite is known as Benediction. It was normally appended to an Office (commonly Vespers), but also served as a devotional liturgy in its own right. Many musical settings of such texts as *Adoro te devote, Ave verum corpus, O sacrum convivium, O salutaris hostias,* and *Tantum ergo* have been composed for Benediction.

Benediction was incorporated in the Forty Hours Devotion. This practice derived in principle from the watching over the Host in Holy Week (the forty hours from Maundy Thursday night until the Easter Vigil), but in its popular form it emerged in Milan in the earlier sixteenth century at a time of national crisis. The Blessed Sacrament was exposed for adoration for forty hours; it included Benediction, Processions, Litanies, and Votive Masses of the Blessed Sacrament and of Peace. A constant presence was kept in the church by a rota of the faithful.

The extrapolation of liturgical forms for devotional purposes was not new to the post-Tridentine period, and even extended in Rome to Lenten devotions using the Office of Compline (for which special polychoral music was composed).

THE LITURGICAL ACHIEVEMENT OF THE TRIDENTINE REFORM

Current liturgical thinking is generally critical of the Tridentine era (effectively the four hundred years from the 1560s to the 1960s). Nevertheless the Tridentine liturgy provided the basis for consolidation after the schism of the Reformation, for spiritual growth and devotional fervour among the laity, and for mission to every continent in the world.

The great achievement of a unified, authorized, stable order for the liturgy is at once its strength and its weakness. The decision to centralize the Calendar, for instance, rebounded since saints that would have been local or regional became international, with consequent crowding, and the ousting of the ferial *cursus* once again.

The recitation of the Office as corporate worship declined, and public celebration was restricted to Mass and Vespers on Sundays and feasts. These were often polarized celebrations, the liturgical whole divided and apportioned to clergy and professional musicians.

Nevertheless it provided the bedrock for fervent popular devotion and great musical opportunity to professional composers.

In effect it preserved and codified the medieval liturgical heritage in readiness for the scholarly revaluations that began in the nineteenth century. Even the idiosyncratic editions of chant represented by the Gradual of *Editio Medicaea* (1614–15) or the localized French editions of chants in the later seventeenth and eighteenth centuries are important. They represent the first attempts at collating and editing variant manuscript readings derived (originally) from an oral tradition. They (and others like them) are important as sources for historical reconstruction, and also as precursors of the great movement of editing chant begun in France in the nineteenth century and largely based at Solesmes.

The authority and inflexibility of Roman control of the Tridentine liturgy were not total. The liturgical diversity and individuality already noted in France can be found in varying degrees throughout the Roman Catholic Church. Individual foundations and patrons still influenced both the style and content of the liturgy, even if the order was more fixed.

The Reformed Liturgy of the Church of England (1549–1662)

Unlike the continental Protestant Churches, the Church of England held on to some of the most important features of the daily Office and the Mass, albeit in the vernacular. And whereas the public recitation of the Office declined sharply in the Roman Church it persisted in the Church of England, sung in choral foundations of cathedrals and colleges, recited by parson and clerk in parish churches. Roman Catholic laity favoured new devotions, but the staple public prayer of the English was Mattins and Evensong, and it remained so until the 1960s.

The English Reformation was achieved in stages: the break from papal authority (Act of Supremacy 1534), the redistribution of land and wealth (dissolution of the monasteries and other corporate foundations, 1536–48), and the reform of the liturgy (Act of Uniformity 1549). Had the English Reformation been rooted in a theological crisis (as abroad) rather than in a domestic issue (King Henry VIII's need for a new wife to bear him a male heir) the liturgical consequences might have been more radical. In the event the transition was gradual, and the formation of the Book of Common Prayer took place over a number of years.

The chronology underlines the steady progress towards a vernacular liturgy:

1534 Marshall's Primer in English
1537 Publication of Matthews' Bible in English (revised and reissued in 1539 as the Great Bible); Archbishop of York orders Epistle and Gospel to be read in English;
Lessons ordered to be read in English after *Te deum* and *Magnificat*

1538 Recitation of Creed, Lord's Prayer, and Ten Commandments in English
1544 Publication of Cranmer's English Litany (for the French war) for use in procession
1545 Publication of the King's Primer with English texts for the Offices
1548 The Order of the Communion
1549 The first Book of Common Prayer
1552 The second Book of Common Prayer

The changes that were introduced progressively over fifteen years have been followed by a period of remarkable stability. The basic form and order of the 1552 Prayer Book has persisted with comparatively small revisions as the principal liturgical book of the Church of England to this day, though it has now been largely superseded in practice by the alternative services authorized for use since 1965. Its use was suspended only for the periods of Marian reaction (1553–8) and the Puritan Commonwealth (1645–60).

Although the introduction of a vernacular liturgy took so long to be implemented fully, the underlying trend of liturgical reformation had been achieved much earlier. Archbishop Cranmer, who was the architect of the reform, had completed a draft of a new prayer book by about 1538. The text was still largely in Latin. It shows Cranmer's assimilation of three main influences: the medieval Use of Salisbury, the practices of continental Protestants (especially Luther and Bucer), and the revised Breviary commissioned by Pope Paul III and undertaken by Cardinal Quiñones (published 1535).

Cranmer's formation of a new liturgy would have been quite as radical had it remained in Latin. Even in the early drafts the forms of Morning and Evening Prayer had changed, and there was a new approach to the recitation of the psalter and the reading (in English) of scripture. By 1549 he had arrived at the classic Anglican pattern of two lessons and two canticles at Mattins and Evensong. The Order of Holy Communion still retained the same sequence as the medieval Mass. Forms of the proper texts for Introit, Offertory, and Communion were included, though Gradual, Alleluia, and Sequence were omitted along with the celebrant's private prayers.

The hardening of theological influence from the Genevan Church, and ongoing revaluation of liturgical formation, resulted in continuing change, and the 1549 Prayer Book can only be regarded as an interim measure. The second Book of Common Prayer (1552) might well have been equally transitory, but historical rather than liturgical events have resulted in its exceptional permanence. Though it has been subject to regular scrutiny there has been only minor revision, most significantly in 1662 after the Restoration. It is therefore this second Prayer Book that is considered in detail.[1]

The Book of Common Prayer

The Book of Common Prayer is a unique compilation. It is a book of modest proportions—physically smaller than either medieval Breviary or Missal, scarcely larger than a Book of Hours—yet it contains provision for the whole liturgy. Its contents absorb not only Breviary and Missal but also Processional, Manual (with the rites of baptism, marriage, churching of women, commination, visitation of the sick, and burial), and Pontifical (confirmation and ordination). Its preface subsumes both Ordinal and Customary. There is no need for Choir Psalter, Antiphonal, or Gradual: the psalms are appended to the Book in numerical order, and all that is required to supplement the Book of Common Prayer is the Bible.

This conciseness is the result of abbreviation, and above all by the excision of the greater part of the Proper. Much of this was achieved in the compilation of the 1549 book, but it was furthered in the 1552 version.

Versions of the Book of Common Prayer

Between 1549 and 1662 the Book of Common Prayer was subject to change. From recent modern experience this should not surprise us: more exceptional is the stability of the Book between 1662 and 1965. The most important changes came in 1552 but there were further significant amendments, especially in 1559, 1561, and 1604.

Apart from the addition of the introductory material in 1552, the order of Mattins and Evensong remained largely unchanged, except

---

[1] There are important studies of the history and liturgy of the Book of Common Prayer by Procter and Frere, Brightman, and Cuming. All are listed in section 5.8 of the Select Bibliography.

for the position of the Apostles' Creed (oddly placed between *Kyrie* and Lord's Prayer in 1549).

The Order of Holy Communion changed substantially in 1552, but retained its basic form thereafter, though important rubrics were added in 1662.

The 1559 Book saw the insertion of some additional prayers after the Collects at Mattins and Evensong, and the introduction of the Grace at the end of Mattins, Evensong, and Litany. The Elizabethan Act of Uniformity was (and continues to be) printed at the beginning of the Book together with a revised and extended Preface. In 1561 the Calendar and Lectionary were significantly amended and revised.

1662 was the last revision. Here for the first time the Lord's Prayer was directed to be said by all on all occasions (the old practice of priestly recitation with the people responding 'But deliver us from evil' persisted in some instances, even in 1552). The doxology was added to the Lord's Prayer at the second recitation in Mattins, Evensong, and Holy Communion. More additional prayers were provided (e.g. the Prayer for All Sorts and Conditions of Men, and the General Thanksgiving). There were two additions to the Calendar.

Revisions in scriptural texts are not discussed here, nor are the 'parish' services (baptism, confirmation, marriage, etc.), nor the ordination services (first printed in 1550); however, the three distinct forms of the Burial Service are outlined below.

No student of the formation of the Book of Common Prayer can ignore Brightman's *The English Rite* (London, 1915), which sets out the sources and texts of the versions of the Book in parallel columns, along with a historical introduction and copious annotation.

The Calendar

The medieval Calendar was drastically pruned in 1549: though the Temporale was little altered, the Sanctorale was reduced from hundreds to just twenty-one feasts, so-called red-letter days (printed in italics in modern prayer books).

In addition to Sundays (including Easter, Whit, and Trinity) the Prayer Book of 1549 and thereafter lists these feasts:

Feasts of Our Lord: Christmas, Circumcision, Epiphany, Ascension.
Feasts of St Mary: Purification and Annunciation.

Feasts of Apostles (ten feasts in all), and feasts of St Paul, St Barnabas, St Mark, St John Baptist, St Michael and all Angels, St Luke, All Saints, St Stephen, Holy Innocents.

Monday and Tuesday after Easter Day and after Whit Sunday.

Three other observances were added in 1552: St George, St Laurence, and St Clement, together with Lammas Day in August. A further fifty-nine holy days were restored in 1561, and a reference to the first of the Greek Advent Antiphons, *O sapientia* in December. The additions of 1552 and 1561 are all black-letter days (in Roman type in modern prayer books) and are without proper lessons, collects, Epistles, or Gospels.

To all intents and purposes, the daily services of Mattins and Evensong are fixed ferial Offices within which the psalms are recited monthly, the Old Testament is read annually, and the New Testament twice in a year (once at Mattins, once at Evensong). The psalter is apportioned by day of the month; the main *cursus* of readings is printed in the Calendar.

The Psalter

The whole psalter is recited in numerical order. It is divided into sixty portions to be recited at Mattins and Evensong on each day of the month. In months with thirty-one days the portions for the thirtieth day are said again. There are no antiphons, but 'Glory be to the Father' is recited at the end of each psalm (or section of Psalm 119). There are no psalms in the Order of Holy Communion.

The numerical sequence applied to the medieval Offices of Matins and Vespers was adopted throughout this *cursus*: the ancient association of certain psalms with certain hours is lost. Proper psalms were provided only for the four principal feasts of Our Lord (Christmas Day, Easter Day, Ascension Day, Whit Sunday). In 1662, proper psalms were added for Ash Wednesday and Good Friday.

The distribution of the Psalter in the Book of Common Prayer is listed in Appendix 2.6.

THE OFFICE

In fusing elements from the medieval orders of Matins, Lauds, and Prime for the new service of Morning Prayer (Mattins), and from

Vespers and Compline for the new service of Evening Prayer (Evensong), Cranmer derived an identical form for both. Precedents can be observed in the correlation of Lauds and Vespers or Prime and Compline, but here the form is entirely new.

Mattins and Evensong

In the 1552 Prayer Book Cranmer introduced an opening section of preparation, rather than beginning directly with 'O Lord open thou our lips'.

A Summary of the Order of Mattins and Evensong (1552)

(Key: Minister, ALL PRESENT, *Dialogue between minister and people.*)

Sentence
Invitation
CONFESSION
Absolution
OUR FATHER

Opening versicles
PSALMS
Old Testament Reading
CANTICLE
New Testament Reading
CANTICLE

APOSTLES' CREED
Greeting
Kyrie eleison
LORD'S PRAYER
Preces
Collects
Optional additional prayers

The genesis of these services from the medieval models can be summarized by presenting them individually. In their larger design they echo the forms of Lauds and Vespers; in their detail they are a skilful compilation from a group of Latin Offices, as can be observed here.

A Comparison of Mattins and Evensong (1549)
with Secular Lauds and Vespers

MATTINS AND EVENSONG (1549)	SECULAR LAUDS AND VESPERS
Lord's Prayer	Pater noster
Opening versicles	*Opening versicle*
PSALMS	PSALMS WITH ANTIPHONS
Old Testament Reading	Sentence from Scripture
CANTICLE	[*Respond*] and HYMN
New Testament Reading	VERSICLE AND RESPONSE
CANTICLE	CANTICLE WITH ANTIPHON
APOSTLES' CREED	
Greeting	
Kyrie eleison	*Kyrie eleison* (weekdays)
LORD'S PRAYER	*Pater noster* (weekdays)
Preces	*Preces* (weekdays)
	Greeting
Collect of the day	Collect of the day
Two further Collects	Memorials and Suffrages
(Optional additional prayers)	

The Order of Mattins (1552)

ORDER (1552)	MEDIEVAL PRECEDENT (SECULAR UNLESS OTHERWISE STATED)
Scriptural Sentence	Though confession and absolution
Invitation	are part of Prime (after the preces),
Confession	the most likely source for this
Absolution	section is the English Order for
	Holy Communion
Lord's Prayer	*Pater noster*, privately before Matins and Prime
O Lord open thou our lips	*Domine labia mea*, Matins
O God make speed to save us	*Deus in adiutorium* ⎫
Glory be to the Father	*Gloria patri* ⎬ all Offices
Praise ye the Lord	*Alleluia/Laus tibi* ⎭
Venite (Psalm 95 [94])	Invitatory psalm (Psalm 94 [95]), Matins
Psalms (monthly cycle)	Psalms (weekly cycle or proper), all Offices

Old Testament Lesson (annual cycle)	Reading divided into three portions (annual cycle or proper), Matins
We praise thee, O God	*Te deum*, after ninth lesson, Matins
(O all ye works of the Lord in Lent)	(*Benedicite*, lesser canticle with psalms, Lauds on Sundays and feasts)
New Testament Lesson (annual cycle)	Gospel after *Te deum*, Matins (monastic Use)
	Capitulum before canticle, Lauds
Blessed be the Lord God	*Benedictus*, canticle, Lauds
[Athanasian Creed on certain days; by 1662 instead of Apostles' Creed]	*Quicumque vult*, after psalms, Prime
Apostles' Creed	Prime, after *Pater noster*
The Lord be with you	*Dominus vobiscum*, greeting before all prayers
Lord have mercy upon us	*Kyrie eleison*, Lauds (weekdays) and Prime
Lord's Prayer	*Pater noster*, Lauds (weekdays) and Prime
O Lord show thy mercy, etc.	*Fiat misericordia* etc., preces, Lauds (weekdays), selected and re-ordered;
Give peace in our time	*Da pacem*, antiphon in memorial for peace, within suffrages after collect, Lauds
O God make clean our hearts	*Cor mundum*, preces, Prime
Collect of the day or week (proper)	Collect of the day or week (proper)
O God who art the author of peace, collect for peace	*Deus auctor pacis*, collect, memorial for peace, Lauds
O Lord our heavenly father, collect for grace	*Domine sancte pater*, collect, Prime

The Order of Evensong (1552)

ORDER (1552)	MEDIEVAL PRECEDENT (SECULAR UNLESS OTHERWISE STATED)
Scriptural Sentence	Though Confession and Absolution
Invitation	are part of Compline (after the

ORDER (1552)	MEDIEVAL PRECEDENT
Invitation	preces), the most likely source for
Confession	this section is the English Order
Absolution	for Holy Communion.
Lord's Prayer	*Pater noster*, privately before Vespers and Compline
O Lord open thou our lips	*Domine labia mea*, Matins
O God make speed to save us	*Deus in adiutorium* ⎤
Glory be to the Father	*Gloria patri* ⎬ all Offices
Praise ye the Lord	*Alleluia/Laus tibi* ⎦
Psalms (monthly cycle)	Psalms (weekly cycle or proper), all Offices
Old Testament Lesson (annual cycle)	Reading divided into three portions (annual cycle or proper), Matins
	Capitulum before canticle, Vespers
My soul doth magnify	*Magnificat*, canticle, Vespers
New Testament Lesson (annual cycle)	Capitulum before canticle, Compline
Lord now lettest thou	*Nunc dimittis*, canticle, Compline
Apostles' Creed	Prime, after *Pater noster*
The Lord be with you	*Dominus vobiscum*, greeting before all prayers
Lord have mercy upon us	*Kyrie eleison*, Vespers (weekdays) and Compline
Lord's Prayer	*Pater noster*, Vespers (weekdays) and Compline
O Lord show thy mercy, etc.	*Fiat misericordia* etc., preces, Vespers (weekdays), selected and re-ordered;
Give peace in our time	*Da pacem*, antiphon in memorial for peace, within suffrages after collect, Vespers
O God make clean our hearts	*Cor mundum*, preces, Prime
Collect of the day or week (proper)	Collect of the day or week (proper)
O God from whom all holy desires, collect for peace	*Deus a quo sancta desideria*, collect, memorial for peace, Vespers
Lighten our darkness, collect for aid against perils	*Illumina quaesumus*, collect, Compline

The English Offices are individual in their form, and yet highly dependent on medieval sources in shape and content. They include much of the old Memorial for Peace used at Vespers and Lauds, but exclude all other antiphons as well as omitting hymns (with their versicles) and responds. Some analyses of the Offices point out that the English preces correspond with the late medieval Bidding of Bedes, a vernacular form of prayer included at Mass in the Salisbury Use at the Offertory. However, it is pertinent that the texts are found among the Latin ferial preces used at Lauds and Vespers.

Proper Elements in the Offices

Very little of the Office is varied by day, season, or feast. The absence of antiphons, hymns, and responds leaves a pared-down liturgy that is almost all common and unchanging. Exceptionally, Easter Anthems (from the Epistles of St Paul) replace *Venite* (Psalm 95) at Mattins on Easter Day. In the Books of 1549 and 1552 the recitation of psalms was disturbed on only four feast-days (see above). Though in 1549 and 1552 some provision was made for special lessons on certain holy days, the full scheme of proper lessons for Sundays and thirty-six other holy days appeared only in 1559 (subsequently amended in Elizabeth's reign and 1662). Four alternatives were provided for the Canticles: at Mattins, *Benedicite* and Psalm 100 (*Jubilate*); at Evensong, Psalm 98 (*Cantate domino*) and Psalm 67 (*Deus misereatur*). The collects are taken from the *cursus* provided for Holy Communion.

Additions and Alterations to the Offices

The appendage of the introductory rite to both Offices in 1552 probably reflects the need to include a confession on days when Holy Communion was not celebrated. Some of the five prayers included after the collects in the 1662 Prayer Book had been used in the reign of Elizabeth I (after the Litany) but now make their first appearance at this point. Also new to the 1662 Book is the rubric after the third collect: 'In quires and places where they sing, here followeth the anthem.' How this relates to musical practice is discussed below.

The Litany

The Prayer Book directs that the Litany is to be recited after Mattins on Sunday, Wednesday, and Friday, and as directed by the ordinary (in most cases the diocesan bishop). Though prepared especially for the *causa necessitatis* of the French War in 1544, Cranmer drafted a version that was generally adaptable and durable. This was originally a condensed form of the processional Litany. But though Cranmer's primary source was the Litany in the Sarum Processional there are materials drawn from *Commendatio animae* in the Manual and from the Solemn Prayers of the Good Friday Liturgy, as well as phrases taken over from Luther's Litany (printed in Marshall's Primer, 1534). Subsequent changes in the Litany were confined to the concluding prayers.

Quite exceptionally the Litany was issued with music: a plainchant setting and a polyphonic version for five voices. No other vernacular order was published with music.

THE ORDER OF HOLY COMMUNION (1552)

Although a good deal of (mostly experimental) music was written for the Order of the Communion (1548) and the form in the first Book of Common Prayer (1549), neither lasted much more than a year. Historically the transition is very important, but in studying the Order of Holy Communion in detail it seems important to examine the rite printed in the second Book of Common Prayer (1552), which remains unaltered as the authorized order to this day, and to which modern forms are but alternatives.

The order and manner of celebrating Holy Communion were the most sensitive and contentious issues facing the compilers of the Book of Common Prayer. Here the theological and doctrinal differences embraced within the membership of the Church of England were most evident. The majority accepted the real presence of Christ in the consecrated bread and wine. However, the vocal and influential Puritan faction (close in outlook to the Genevan Church) regarded the liturgy as a memorial meal, the Lord's Supper, rather than as a sacrament of Holy Communion. For them there was no question of real presence: this was a shared holy meal, remembering the Last Supper ('Do this in remembrance of me').

Most of the serious problems were textual. They related not just to the nature of the consecration, but to the whole liturgy. The medieval perception of the sacrifice of Christ and the sacrifice offered by the priest was under attack: the new emphasis was that of the salvation of sinners. (Both approaches contrast with the modern stress on 'euchar-ist', i.e. thanksgiving.) The radical element had a deep mistrust of any word or action that implied adoration or the offering of a sacrifice, and the practice of kneeling to receive communion (indeed of kneeling at all) was hotly debated throughout the period.

These issues have implications for the style of the liturgy, and especially the extent (or absence) of ornaments, vestments, and cere-monial. A difficult paragraph in the Elizabethan Act of Uniformity (1559) printed in subsequent Prayer Books prescribes use (i.e. cere-monial) to be 'as was . . . in the second year of the reign of King Edward the Sixth' (1548–9); it has remained highly contentious. Furthermore, the small number of rubrics regarding the manner of celebration (admittedly expanded in 1662) leaves open many details.

As with the Office, the Order of Holy Communion is fixed, unchanged by feast, and therefore predominantly ordinary. The *cursus* of collects, Epistles, and Gospels provides for all Sundays of the year and for thirty-six other holy days. (This tallies with the provision of proper lessons for the Office.) No provision is made for the celebration of Holy Communion for any special intentions. Though the collect for Advent Sunday and the collect for Ash Wednesday are prescribed throughout the seasons of Advent and Lent respectively, there is no instruction to omit 'Glory be to God on high' (*Gloria in excelsis*) as in the medieval rite.

This is a rite directed for the use of priest and people: references to deacons and clerks are almost entirely suppressed. It is also a rite to be heard and seen. The silently recited, private prayers of the celebrant are not included, and 'the table, at the Communion-time having a fair white linen cloth upon it, shall stand in the body of the church, or in the chancel, where morning and evening prayer are appointed to be said'.

The priest is instructed to recite the Lord's Prayer and the Collect for Purity alone, by way of preparation, when he reaches the north side of the altar, 'the people kneeling'. 'Turning to the people' he says the Ten Commandments; after each commandment the people recite the petition 'Lord have mercy upon us . . .'. Still facing the people the priest recites a Collect for the king and the Collect for the day. The Epistle and Gospel follow. The people are required to stand for the Gospel, but the responses to the announcement and conclusion of the Gospel are not included (though they are commonly said). One of the few provisions for singing is made for the Nicene Creed which follows ('the people still standing'). After this come the notices and the sermon (or else an authorized printed homily).

The priest returns 'to the Lord's Table' and recites from the specified repertory of Offertory Sentences. Unlike the old Offertory Antiphons, the sentences come not from the Psalms but from the New Testament. The alms are collected and brought to the priest, who then prepares the bread and wine. The priest recites the Prayer for the Church Militant: this extended prayer follows the usual order of intentions in intercessions, a sequence found in the vernacular Bidding of Bedes and in the intercessions incorporated in the Canon of the Mass.

The priest is then charged with reading at least one of the three Exhortations to prepare the minds of the people. There follows the Invitation to confession, the Confession (for which all are required to kneel), and the Absolution. A further group of New Testament extracts (the 'Comfortable Words') concludes this section.

Having reached the point equivalent to the beginning of the Canon of the Mass, the priest begins 'Lift up your hearts' (*Sursum corda*) with a short preface concluding with 'Holy, holy' (*Sanctus*). There are only five proper prefaces (Christmas, Easter, Ascension, Whit Sunday, and Trinity). *Benedictus qui venit* is not included in the 1552 Book. The priest kneels to say the Prayer of Humble Access, a splendid Cranmerian piece dearly loved to this day. Then standing he recites the Prayer of Consecration. Thereafter all receive communion, kneeling. *Agnus dei* is not said, and the Lord's Prayer which precedes communion in the medieval and Roman Rites is said as part of the thanksgiving immediately after communion.

The Lord's Prayer is said by all present, and the priest then recites a Prayer of Thanksgiving. This is followed by general thanksgiving in the saying or singing of 'Glory be to God on high'. The placing of *Gloria in excelsis* at the end of the Communion Service is in marked contrast to the medieval Rites, but returned it to a position it held as a hymn at the end of a service (though an Office) in the early Church.

The Holy Communion ends with the blessing 'The peace of God . . .'.

The Order of Holy Communion (1552)

(Key: Celebrant or assisting minister, ALL PRESENT (*BCP*) or CHOIR (*Missal*), *Dialogue between celebrant or minister and people/choir.*)

BOOK OF COMMON PRAYER (1552)	MEDIEVAL MISSAL
Lord's Prayer	Prayers of preparation ending with
Collect for Purity	Pater noster
	INTROIT
The Ten Commandments	KYRIE
	GLORIA IN EXCELSIS
Collects for the King and	Collect(s)
of the day	
Epistle	Epistle
	GRADUAL
	ALLELUIA (and SEQUENCE)
Gospel	Gospel
CREED	CREDO
Notices	
Sermon	
Offertory Sentences	OFFERTORY
	Secret
Prayer for the Church	[substance in first part of Canon]
Exhortation	
Invitation	
CONFESSION	
Absolution	
Comfortable Words	
Lift up your hearts	*Sursum corda*
Preface	Preface
SANCTUS	SANCTUS and BENEDICTUS
Prayer of Humble Access	
Prayer of Consecration	Canon of the Mass (silent)
	Pater noster
	Pax domini
	AGNUS DEI
	Rite of peace

Book of Common Prayer (1552)	Medieval Missal
(COMMUNION OF ALL PRESENT)	(Communion of priest)
	COMMUNION
LORD'S PRAYER	
Prayer of Oblation or	Postcommunion prayer
Thanksgiving	
GLORIA IN EXCELSIS	
Blessing	*Ite missa est*

A comparison of the two orders shows how radical is the new form in the Book of Common Prayer. However, not all is as new as it may seem: the Prayer for the Church and the Prayer of Oblation are both derived from the medieval Canon of the Mass. Furthermore, though the Order of Holy Communion is directed to the people and presented to them in a clear and rational manner, its recitation is dominated by the priest. Suitable as this may be in a parish church, it is far less appropriate for cathedral and collegiate foundations where in the medieval rite the whole community had a more active part in the chanting of Proper and Ordinary.

The frequency and character of celebrating Holy Communion in cathedral, collegiate, and parish churches varied. Indeed the practice distorted the unity of concept apparent in the 1552 Order. The evidence is summarized in three rubrics which are included at the very end of the Order. The first makes provision for the Order when there is no communion; the second requires priests and deacons in cathedrals, collegiate churches, and colleges to receive communion 'every Sunday at the least'; and the third charges that 'every parishioner shall communicate at the least three times in the year, of which Easter to be one' (a requirement broadly taken over from the Use of Salisbury).

The single Order of Holy Communion came to be regarded as two separate units, quite coincidentally regaining the original pattern of two adjacent services in the early Church. The normal Sunday time-table of services in parishes was:

Mattins
Litany
Ante-Communion

Ante-communion followed the Order of Holy Communion until the Prayer of the Church Militant; the service then concluded with a collect (chosen from those provided) and the blessing.

In cathedrals and collegiate churches with a choral foundation the pattern was:

Mattins (sung)
Litany (sung)
Ante-Communion (sung)
Communion (said)

The musical evidence alone confirms this: Elizabethan and Jacobean composers provided Mattins Canticles, Responses to the Commandments and Creed, and Evensong Canticles. They did not set *Sanctus* or *Gloria in excelsis*. After the Restoration (1660) even the Ante-Communion music disappears.

THE BURIAL SERVICE

The significance of the Office and Mass of the Dead in the medieval Rite is sufficient reason to examine the Burial Service of the Book of Common Prayer here. But there are two further reasons: first, it is the only service to change its form radically in each of the three principal versions of the Book; second, even in the 1662 form it retains important echoes of the medieval rite and continues to identify material to be sung by priest and clerks.

The three forms of the service may be summarily compared.

The Forms of the Burial Service

1549	1552	1662
Procession	Procession	Procession
Burial	Burial	
Psalms		Psalms
Lesson	Lesson	Lesson
		Procession
		Burial
Lord's Prayer	Lord's Prayer	Lord's Prayer
Preces		
Collect	Collect	Collect
Communion	Collect	Collect

1549 is most directly related to the medieval order. The rite includes what amounts to an Office followed by Holy Communion, though both come after rather than before the burial. Nevertheless the rubric allows for the 'Office' section (and implicitly the Communion) to be said before burial. The 1552 form is a simple outdoor service, but still retaining a very abbreviated outline of an Office. 1662 is a curious mixture in which the Office (with different psalms from 1549) is effectively interrupted by the procession from the church to the grave and the burial.

The texts that may be sung by priest and clerks in all three orders are the same, and the majority have their origins in the Use of Salisbury. Indeed they show the kind of borrowing of antiphons and responds that is typical of the processional repertory as a whole.

Prayer Book Text	Source in Use of Salisbury
1. Procession from churchyard gate	
I am the resurrection	*Ego sum resurrectio* (Antiphon to *Benedictus*, Lauds of the Dead)
I know that my Redeemer	*Credo quod redemptor* (Respond, Vigils of the Dead)
We brought nothing	(I Timothy 6: 7 and Job 1: 21; no liturgical precedent)
2. Preparation at the grave	
Man that is born	*Homo natus de muliere* (Job 14: 1–2; Fifth Lesson, Vigils of the Dead)
In the midst of life	*Media vita in morte sumus* (Respond at Compline, Third Sunday in Lent)
3. After committal	
I heard a voice	*Audivi vocem* (Antiphon to *Magnificat*, Vespers of the Dead)

Nowhere else in the Book of Common Prayer do medieval Propers survive in this way—in the manner of sung antiphons to accompany a procession and ritual actions.

The Influence of the 1549 Book

The history of the Book of Common Prayer is such that though the specific orders of the 1549 version were in use for so short a period, the influence of its ethos and ritual style has persisted far longer. Reference to the 1549 Book has been encouraged by the paragraph on ornaments and ceremonies incorporated in the Elizabethan Act of Uniformity (1559). This has inevitably proved a contentious section in a denomination which embraces such wide traditions of theological outlook and liturgical practice. But it has proved a reference point for those who wish to stress the continuity of the Church of England with a liturgy extending from the pre-Reformation Use, and for those who perceive worship as an act that demands ceremony and ritual in the service of the Almighty. Along with other ambivalent or imprecise provisions, it has enabled a more elaborate practice than is implied in the 1552 Book and its successors, a practice which is therefore often undocumented.

From the sixteenth century there has been constant and inevitable tension between the extreme wings of the Church of England. At certain times and in individual places one or other wing has gained ascendancy. The polarity was strongest in the seventeenth century with the sudden swing from the dominance of the 'high church' party led by Archbishop Laud in the reign of Charles I to the other extreme of 'puritan' Protestantism (here extending beyond the Church of England to influential non-conformists) during the Commonwealth. In this case the result was the suspension of the Book of Common Prayer, and with it the stripping of altars, dismantling of ornament (including stained glass), vestment (including surplices), and ceremonial, the suppression of choirs, dismantling of organs, and prohibition of church music in general.

If the Commonwealth represented an exceptional period, the wide spread of religious outlook has always been part of the Church of England, and it continues to affect the presentation of the liturgy in different cathedrals, collegiate foundations, and parish churches. Between the extremes there is the larger body of middle ground (which prevailed in the stabilization of the 1662 Book), a body coloured at any time by current influences and trends but avoiding extremes of theology and liturgical practice.

MUSIC AND THE BOOK OF COMMON PRAYER

The establishment of the Book of Common Prayer in 1549 not only instituted new liturgical orders; for its forms and vernacular language also rendered instantly obsolete the chant of the medieval Church and the burgeoning repertory of Latin polyphony. This is not the place to bewail the loss but rather to underline the consequences.

The Book of Common Prayer has always been published without music. This reflects the new circumstances of the Church. The dissolution of all religious houses and most collegiate foundations as well as smaller communities (e.g. chantries and religious hospitals) created a new balance. Corporate foundations able to sustain a sung liturgy were reduced in less than fifteen years from many hundreds to less than fifty: the Chapel Royal, the cathedrals, the colleges in Oxford, Cambridge, Eton, and Winchester, and no more than five other places. The new Book was intended for parish churches, their people (especially on Sundays), and their priests (often assisted by no more than a parish clerk).

Given the dismantling of liturgical communities and the overnight obsolescence of a musical heritage that had evolved over the preceding millennium, it is remarkable that in England rather than anywhere else in Europe the corporate singing of a daily Office has continued in choral foundations.

Provision for singing the services of the 1549 Prayer Book was made in John Marbeck's *Book of Common Prayer Noted* (1550).[2] (Though the only printed book of its kind, it represents what must have been a common practice of adaptation.) It was rendered obsolete shortly afterwards by the requirements of the 1552 Book, but its methods give some indication of how the musical needs of the vernacular liturgy were met. Further evidence comes from the corpus of music that survives from the period *c.* 1550–1640.

A series of emerging practices can be discerned:

(a) adaptation of the medieval chant (especially the repeated formulas of the tones) to the verncular (e.g. the Litany, Marbeck), and composition of new melodies in the idiom of simple chant (e.g. Marbeck)—albeit more rhythmic in idiom;

[2] A facsimile of Marbeck's settings is to be found in J. E. Hunt (ed.), *Cranmer's First Litany, 1544, and Merbecke's Book of Common Prayer Noted, 1550* (London, 1939).

(b) use of functional polyphony based on and decorating the chant (this was a long-established practice, often improvised in the Middle Ages, and continued thereafter; see the polyphonic form of the Litany, and Tallis's preces and festal psalms);

(c) free polyphonic compositions derived from the principle of (b) and resulting in the 'short' style used for many English canticles (largely syllabic, and found in the early vernacular repertory of the Wanley Partbooks, but also in the music of Tallis, Byrd, Gibbons, and their contemporaries);

(d) compositions alternating (accompanied) solo sections and choral sections, the so-called 'verse' style, similar in principle to the alternation of soloists and choir in responsorial chant, and also to *alternatim* practice (alternate use of chant and polyphony based on the chant);

(e) free compositions alternating a larger group of soloists with the choir ('great' services), comparable with both the use of larger numbers of soloists on great feasts in the medieval Uses, and the elaborate polyphony for festal occasions in the late fifteenth and early sixteenth centuries. Such music was not necessarily accompanied, and must have been limited to only a few large and able choirs.

On the face of it the 1552 Book of Common Prayer makes little provision for music, let alone for the use of music to distinguish feast and feria. In practice choral foundations sang the liturgy, and this practice is codified in the Elizabethan Injunctions issued in 1559. The injunctions permit the use of 'a modest and distinct song' that may be 'plainly understood as if it were read without singing'. The implication is that the music of the daily Office derived mostly from (a), (b) and (c) listed above, and—on the evidence of what survives—increasingly on (c) in the singing of canticles. The absence of surviving music for the psalms suggests that these were sung from the psalter to the old plainsong tones (metrical psalms were not sung during the Office).

The few liturgical psalm settings that do survive are for the four festal cycles provided by the Book of Common Prayer (listed in Appendix 2.6). They show that musical style distinguished liturgical observance in the later sixteenth and earlier seventeenth century. A number of the early seventeenth-century festal preces and psalms (e.g. those of William Smith) derive from Durham Cathedral, indicating their 'high church' associations. And it is not too fanciful to see a hierarchy of canticle settings: (*c*) 'short' settings, often with alternation between the two sides of the choir, for ordinary days; (*d*) 'verse' settings with one or two soloists, for the equivalent of the old Feasts of Nine Lessons; and (*e*) 'great' services with as many as eight choral parts and as many soloists for principal feasts.

At most these sets of canticles consisted of *Venite*, *Te Deum*, *Benedictus* (or *Jubilate*), Responses to the Commandments, Creed, *Magnificat*, and *Nunc dimittis*. As indicated above in the discussion of the Order of Holy Communion, even in those cathedrals and colleges where there was a celebration of the Communion each Sunday and on feasts, this was said rather than sung after the Creed.

The ritual distinctions implied by the types of musical setting of services became more prominent during the reign of James I and especially Charles I. For the first time in England larger organs with two divisions (Chair and Great) were built. Some foundations bought wind instruments and engaged special players on feast-days. Though there was nothing on the scale of the continental celebrations with instruments and several choirs (see Chapter 10), the Laudian movement stands out as the most significant period of ritual and ceremonial in the Church of England until the Oxford Movement in the nineteenth century.

Additional Music: The Anthem and the Metrical Psalm

The Elizabethan Injunctions allowed additional choral music before or after Mattins and Evensong 'for the comforting of such that delight in music'. In choral foundations this provided for the anthem. Though formal provision for the anthem was not included until the Book of 1662, it is plain that this confirms earlier practice rather than establishing a new precedent. The practice of singing an anthem (or antiphon) at the end of the Office dates back to the memorials and votive antiphons of the medieval liturgy (see Chapter 8). During the first half of the sixteenth century votive antiphons in honour of the Blessed Virgin Mary shared popularity with antiphons in honour of our Lord (so-called Jesus Antiphons). Injunctions prescribed as early as 1548 by the Visitors to Lincoln Cathedral required that such an antiphon (anthem) be sung in English, and followed by 'the collect for the preservation of the King's Majesty'. Unlike the earlier votive antiphon rite (antiphon, versicle and response, collect), the Reformation anthem was an independent item, and the majority drew on the Bible or the Prayer Book for their texts. As with the continental motet, the Psalms were a ready source.

Psalms of a different kind were also included within the terms of the Elizabethan Injunctions. For the beginning and end of divine service were the points at which the increasingly popular metrical psalms were sung in parish churches. In spite of the existence in printed books of musical settings of metrical canticles, Lord's Prayer, and Athanasian Creed, it seems that the Office was said; singing of metrical psalms took place before and after the Office, and in unison. The four-part settings, often found printed alongside versions for voice and lute, belong to domestic music-making in the home. Even in cathedrals a metrical psalm was often sung at the end of the Mattins when those in choir processed to the nave for the sermon. It was common in Elizabeth's reign and thereafter for the version of the metrical psalter (with melodies, and expanded from the collections of Sternhold and Hopkins) to be bound as an appendage to the Book of Common Prayer and published as a single volume. It was the only widely circulated form of music used in English churches, and it remained exceedingly popular until the end of the seventeenth century.

PART IV.

Using Liturgical Sources

12.

Establishing the Order of a Latin Liturgical Celebration

All the information included in this book serves to provide an introduction to the framework and pattern of formal Western liturgy. But at every turn there have to be caveats—local practice, seasonal variation, variation over a period of time. The same information can also be used as a base to establish the order of a specific liturgy in an identified foundation at a particular period of time. Of course this is a highly complex and specialized procedure, and it is only possible to give practical pointers here.

There are four layers to the process of reconstruction: text, music, ritual, and ceremonial. Each requires an independent line of enquiry, but each also involves comparable difficulties. Almost all the problems in the Latin liturgy derive from the fact that so few services are presented in a complete form. This is true of almost all the liturgical books (see Chapters 4 and 13).

ESTABLISHING A NORM

Before attempting to reconstruct a celebration it is important to establish a norm. This is not only a norm for the Use as a whole (as opposed to local variation), but also for the order of that particular liturgical service.

In some cases (e.g. the Ordinal of St Mary's Abbey, York, *c.*1400) this may be relatively straightforward: the opening section of the Ordinal (as at St Mary's) may describe each of the principal services in detail. In other instances there may be some general rubrics presented as a separate section of a liturgical book (e.g. the *Magna rubrica* found in later medieval Breviaries). More often the liturgical books as a whole assume a knowledge of the norm, or else establish it piecemeal in a number of different places.

There are three places to examine when attempting to reconstruct the norm:

1. (a) The Ferial Psalter in the Breviary normally includes the ferial Office, though not necessarily complete.
   (b) The Ordo Missae in the Missal gives the full text of the priest's part of the Mass.
2. The first week of Advent is often the first part of a liturgical book and frequently includes detailed instructions, though seasonal details (e.g. the omission of *Gloria in excelsis*) may result in a deflection from the norm.
3. The first week after the Octave of the Epiphany is the first non-seasonal week *per annum* and may also include details of the norm.

The detailed outlines of the liturgical orders in the chapters above should provide a starting point.

Establishing Variants from the Norm

Most of the variants from the norm are presented in detail. It is important to be aware of other factors that may affect the order.

1. Seasonal variants are the most common. Always establish in which season the reconstructed order falls. This may affect text, music, ritual, and ceremonial. The most obvious examples come from the penitential season beginning after Septuagesima: a series of changes to the norm effected on Septuagesima, Ash Wednesday, Passion Sunday, Palm Sunday, and Maundy Thursday.
2. Seasonal variants are most significant on Sundays and ferias. How they affect a feast-day may vary. Often feasts that may fall in or out of Eastertide have variants. How a feast is observed in the penitential seasons of Advent and after Septuagesima may also vary from the norm. Feasts of the Temporale are dealt with individually.
3. The observance of a feast of the Sanctorale may be described on the first occurrence of a feast of that class or type (either in the year or in the season), or more likely in the Common of Saints (Commune Sanctorum).

Once again, the discussion of the Church Calendar and of individual orders in the preceding chapters should provide useful guidelines.

Using the Books

The main books of the liturgy are discussed in Chapter 4. Though facsimiles or printed editions may be available, it is often necessary to use manuscripts or early printed books. Earlier sources are particularly difficult to use. They are densely written with frequent abbreviations and contractions of the Latin. Those who are unused to dealing with manuscripts may be well advised to use a printed source or edition of similar type for their initial investigations. A number of these are introduced in Chapter 13.

For the principal services *Liber Usualis* may be a workable starting point, but be aware of its limitations (see Chapter 4). For the Mass a useful model may be Nick Sandon's series of publications of the Use of Salisbury: even when working on other Uses these may serve as an indicator of the complexities.

Establishing a Liturgical Order: Text

Armed with a knowledge of the norm for the year, with an awareness of seasonal and festal variants, it is possible to make a start on textual reconstruction for a specific day. In most cases that is the easiest part of reconstruction.

The Day

Establish the rank of the day from the Calendar or the title of the day in Breviary or Missal. Establish its place in the annual liturgical calendar, so that it is clear in which season it falls and which observances fall on either side of it. Be sure when the day begins (Matins on feria, Vespers on the night before on Sundays and feast-days) and ends (after Compline on Sunday or feria, after None on feast-days unless there is Second Vespers). This is discussed in more detail in Chapter 3 'The Extent of the Liturgical Day'.

The Office

The texts are most easily found in the Breviary. If an Ordinal is available this may provide a list of incipits. Incipits are used frequently in liturgical books. They need to be used with care: they may well be ambiguous (e.g. psalms beginning *Confitemini domino*). They may indicate only the first of a well-known series of texts (e.g. *Deus in adiutorium*).

The comparative stability of Prime, Terce, Sext, None, and Compline means that most of what is discussed here is related to Matins, Lauds, and Vespers. However, the reconstruction of the daily Office of the Virgin (*Servitium Beatae Mariae Virginis*) or the Office of the Dead (*Officium defunctorum*) needs to relate to the specific provisions for that Office in the Breviary and Ordinal.

Ferial texts should be established ('Establishing a Norm', 1–3 above), allowing for seasonal variants (e.g. suppression or addition of *alleluia*, omission of *Gloria patri* or *Te deum*).

On feast-days psalms may be ferial or proper. Where they are proper the sequence may be listed in the appropriate place in the Sanctorale, or else given in the Commune Sanctorum. Antiphons may be listed either complete or as a series of incipits, but again they may be borrowed from a common series. Sometimes a single antiphon or psalm incipit may indicate the first of a frequently used series. The same is true of chapters, responds, hymns, versicles, and collects. Where there are First and Second Vespers some material may be used at both services. Lessons at Matins are clearer to follow: they may not be given in full but only with beginning and ending. It is important to clarify if and how they were announced and concluded.

On Sundays, chapters, responds, hymns, and versicles may be seasonal (including *per annum*), and some items may be selected from a series *ad libitum* (e.g. chapters). The text of Matins lessons *per annum* may be presented in two separate series after the Octave of Corpus Christi (or after the Octave of Pentecost in sources before the fourteenth century): the first series identified by book (*Historia* . . . etc.) gives the first six (or eight) lessons; the second series identified by Sunday gives the last three (or four) together with the antiphons for *Benedictus* and *Magnificat*.

The end of Lauds and Vespers may be difficult to establish; in particular whether there are proper or ferial memorials and whether *Benedicamus* is sung once or twice. The Ordinal or special rubrics may help. Some Breviaries have a separate list of memorials (some of which may be described as suffrages).

At the end of Matins the final respond may be doubled on certain feasts (e.g. double feasts in twelfth and thirteenth centuries), or in certain seasons (e.g. the penitential seasons when *Te deum* is omitted in secular Use), or displaced by *Te deum*. Again care is needed to establish the exact practice.

The Mass

The order of the Mass is more stable from Use to Use and from day to day. Nevertheless the Morrow Mass may have an intention other than that of the day. Information needs to be gathered as before from Missal and Ordinal.

The Ordinary of the Mass is found in Ordo Missae, together with the proper prefaces in the Canon. The Proper of the Mass is found in Temporale, Sanctorale, or Commune Sanctorum. Masses for special intentions often form a separate section of the Missal. It is important to establish whether *Gloria in excelsis* and *Credo* are sung, whether *Kyrie* is troped, and whether there is a Sequence (usually found in a separate section of the Missal and Gradual). Some Masses (e.g. ferial) have *Benedicamus domino* rather than *Ite missa est*. Other seasonal variants also need to be taken into account.

Care should be taken in establishing how the Introit was usually performed. The antiphon may be repeated after the verse(s) as well as after *Gloria patri*, depending on Use or rank of the day. It is equally important to establish the practice of performing the Gradual and the Alleluia with regard to repetition of all or part of the refrain: the *alleluia* repetition is often shortened if a Sequence follows.

ESTABLISHING A LITURGICAL ORDER: MUSIC

The principal sources of choir chants are Antiphonals (for the Office) and Graduals (for the Mass). Officiants' chants may be found in Breviary and Missal, but sometimes these are less easy to find.

Ferial (Regular) Chants for the Office

There are standard chants for the opening of each Office, for chapters, lessons, versicles, and collects within a Use. These chants may be included in the Ferial Psalter (e.g. of a Noted Breviary), in the Tonary of a Breviary, or in the Ordinal. There may be solemn forms for feasts. Different lessons have different chant formulas: the Old Testament tone differs from the tone for Epistles. (Samples of the Roman forms of these tones and how to use them may be found in *Liber Usualis*.)

There are psalm tones in each of the eight modes, together with *Tonus Peregrinus*. There are variant forms of the tones (e.g. different endings). Psalm and canticle tones have ferial and solemn forms. The psalm or canticle tone may well be identified after an antiphon, either by incipit or, more often, by ending (in printed books this may be written over the vowels *e, u, o, u, a, e*, for *saeculorum Amen*, the end of *Gloria patri*). There are special tones for the Invitatory Psalm 94 at Matins: they may be given separately. The Tonary is a useful source of information on tones and their matching to antiphons.

It is often difficult to establish when the intonation of the psalm tone is repeated at the beginning of every verse. It is generally sung only at the beginning of the first verse of each psalm (or portion of psalm after *Gloria patri*), but in every verse of a canticle or psalm sung to a solemn tone.

Proper antiphons may be listed by incipit even in an Antiphonal. This means that they are likely to be found elsewhere in the book. Start by looking at the first Sunday of a season, or in Commune Sanctorum.

Some hymns, especially those used throughout the year, have seasonal melodies.

The choice of *Benedicamus* melody may relate to the *Kyrie* melody at Mass; there may be a rubric on this matter.

The Mass

As with the Office there are special tones for versicles and responses, Epistle (or comparable reading), Gospel, Preface and collects. They may be found in a Missal or in an Ordinal. (Roman examples can be found in *Liber Usualis*. Salisbury tones are given in Sandon's editions and in Frere's *Use of Sarum*.)

It may be difficult to establish which chants should be used for the Ordinary of the Mass. In the Kyriale they tend to be grouped by movement rather than by rank or season of observance. The *Kyrie* may be identified by the appropriate trope text (even if the text of the trope is not sung); the intonation to *Gloria in excelsis* and *Ite* or

Benedicamus may be written out in the Missal. Later Roman Graduals (including the relevant section of *Liber Usualis*) group chants as related sets by rank and season, and this may be of assistance since they confirm earlier practice. Sandon's edition of the Salisbury Mass Ordinary also provides a guide to the seasonal, festal, and ferial use of these chants.

The Proper is generally written out in full. Details regarding the performance of Introit, Gradual, and Alleluia are mentioned in the preceding section above, and in Chapter 7.

Establishing a Liturgical Order: Ritual

Even with all the text and music compiled, there is a long way to go before every detail of a liturgical celebration has been completed. Though text and music are part of the rite, this still leaves the allocation of duties to be considered.

The principal source is the Customary, though the Ordinal and rubrics of Breviary and Missal may also include some relevant information. Once again caution has to be exercised, especially when books intended for general use are consulted. For instance, a portable Breviary following the Use of the Roman Curia (and therefore suitable for individual private recitation) may imply in its lack of direction that there is no distinction of officiants. But many foundations using a similar liturgical order may allocate parts of the Office with precision in their books.

Within the daily Office celebrated in community there is a series of normal patterns (already mentioned in Chapter 2). First the two sides of the choir will take turn for duties week by week. Within the duty side there will be a hebdomadary priest (duty priest for the week) responsible for the beginning of the Office and the prayers (including the *Kyrie*, *Pater noster*, and preces). The remaining duties are choral or solo. Choral duties (i.e. beginnings of antiphons, psalms, hymns, and canticles) belong to the rulers of the choir or cantor(s) depending on the rank of the day. Solos (e.g. lessons, chapters, versicles, beginnings of responds and verses within them, and *Benedicamus*) are allocated by seniority (e.g. one or more boys, one or more of the clerks of the second form, one or more of the senior clergy in the back row of stalls), and most often sung from the lectern at the choir step. Certain

items (e.g. the beginning of *Te deum*) are most often allocated to the
senior person present. As a rule the more important the rank of the day
the more cantors, rulers, and soloists there are, and the more senior
they are. (On the nature of the community and the layout of the
medieval choir in church, see Chapter 2.)

These duties are allocated in a similar fashion in modern Benedictine
monasteries and the corporate nature of the celebration is readily
apparent.

At Mass similar distinctions can be made. Here again there is the
ritual allocation of the choral and solo chants (the latter confined to
Gradual and Alleluia), distinguished by the place at which they are
performed (see Chapters 3 and 8), the number of cantors, rulers, and
soloists, and their status in choir. In the sanctuary the celebrant is
responsible for the majority of the officiants' texts, whether sung, just
audible, or silent, but the assisting subdeacon sings the Epistle and the
deacon the Gospel. It is also customary for the deacon to begin the
confession and, in some Uses, to sing *Ite missa est* (or *Benedicamus*).

ESTABLISHING A LITURGICAL ORDER: CEREMONIAL

The final stage of reconstruction is probably the most difficult and the
most elusive: the movements, gestures, actions, ornaments, and
vestments of the liturgy are often elaborate, complex, and remote
from modern experience. (It is no surprise that broadcast liturgical
reconstructions have appeared on radio rather than on television.)
Ceremonial action is assumed throughout the liturgy. Here too there
are norms (taken for granted in many liturgical books) and variants
(more often described).

It is far beyond the scope of this study to explore ceremonial. It is
difficult to describe succinctly or accurately. Anyone translating from
a Customary will find that a great deal of interpretation has to be
applied to descriptions of movements and gestures in particular.
Moreover, any detailed ceremonial is conditioned by the building in
which the liturgy is conducted. The Salisbury customary is particularly
helpful in allowing for circumstances outside the cathedral church of
Salisbury; and the *Ceremoniale Romanum* (1516) and the Tridentine
Ceremoniale Episcoporum (1602) are intended as normative guides for
cathedral and collegiate churches following Roman practice.

Ceremony affects the situation as well as the manner in liturgical observance. Anyone seeking to reconstruct ceremonial has to understand the layout and architecture of the choir and sanctuary; the furniture, vessels, and ornaments, their placing and decoration; the scheme of liturgical colours (including questions of veils in Lent and Passiontide); the range and use of dress and vestments for choir and ministers. Only then is it possible to tackle the issues of positions, posture, movement, and gesture.

The complexity of the matter can be grasped by examining Fortescue and O'Connell's classic study, *The Ceremonies of the Roman Rite Described* (London, 1943)—a book devoted to ceremonial observance in the last fifty years of the Tridentine Rite.

FILLING GAPS IN THE ORDER

Few local liturgies can be reconstructed complete and with absolute certainty. More often there is a gap in the information at some level. It is important to take care when drawing on sources from other foundations for additional material or information. Mixing Uses can be particularly perilous. It would be dangerous to use a Roman book to complete a Salisbury rite in spite of their common secular ancestry. It would, however, be reasonable to use material from (for instance) the Benedictine Cathedral Priory at Durham to fill out the reconstruction of a liturgy for Canterbury Cathedral Priory: there were links between the two foundations in the late eleventh and twelfth centuries.

Even when books come from the same foundation there may be problems if they were compiled at different periods. For instance, the texts reproduced in the modern edition of the thirteenth-century Salisbury Missal and the contemporary facsimiles in the Salisbury Gradual exclude the feast of Corpus Christi, and it is only mentioned in the Customary. Yet it was observed from 1264 and can be found in later manuscripts and early printed sources. A number of the texts and chants can also be found in other parts of the earlier books. Establishing the observance at the time of its adoption is therefore possible if tendentious.

More problematic is the question of the use of polyphony. Most liturgical sources until the sixteenth century assume the use of chant rather than polyphony. The evidence for polyphony frequently derives from accounts, statutes, or records of individual appointments. The polyphony that does survive is scattered and often fragmentary. There remains the further question of improvised polyphony. Because of modern emphasis on polyphony in musical history it may be tempting to overestimate its use in medieval liturgy and to build reconstructions around surviving polyphony. In most foundations polyphony must have been the exception rather than the rule, and it is important to begin with the chant.

13.

The Ordering of Selected Medieval Sources

The descriptions of the Office, Mass, and other liturgical observances in Chapters 6 to 9 are inevitably general. The guidance given in Chapter 12 on establishing a specific liturgical celebration is equally open—intended to prepare the reader for problems, rather than following through identified, detailed solutions. What follows here is more specific. It is intended to introduce the reader to the organization of a number of surviving medieval sources. The individual sections of this chapter should be useful for anyone attempting to establish the order of a liturgy, or simply as an introduction to the ordering of a source.

These selected sources have been chosen for their accessibility, not as manuscripts or *incunabula*, but as texts reproduced in editions or facsimiles, and printed in the last hundred years or so. They should be available in most well-established reference libraries in the English-speaking world. All of them (among others) have been available and consulted while writing this guide.

Most of the sources are English in origin. They have the advantage of English introductions, commentaries, and (in some instances) indices. Such deliberate selectiveness should not be seen as narrowly insular. All belong to the mainstream of the Western (i.e. Roman) Rite, and as such they are representative of the kind of local variants found in secular and monastic Uses. Comparable, if not identical, divergences can be found in the Uses of individual dioceses and monasteries throughout Europe.

The late medieval Use of the Roman (Papal) Curia accounts for the other sources introduced here. Since this Use was so influential in the formation of the Tridentine Breviary and Missal it is appropriate to refer to it: but in the pre-Tridentine era it was only one of many local Uses within the Roman Rite.

Each manuscript source has a specific place and date of origin, as such it is unique. And though the printed sources circulated and were used more widely, they too normally reflect the specific practice of the 'mother' church. Some attempt is made here to place each book, or group of books, in the context of its liturgical milieu, though this is no more than rudimentary. Most of this information is taken from David Knowles and Neville Hadcock, *Medieval Religious Houses: England and Wales* (London, 1953, rev. 1971).

There are two main groups of sources, secular and monastic. The extent of reference to the Use of Salisbury is an indication of the study and editorial endeavour it has enjoyed. The need to group together individual manuscripts from a variety of Benedictine houses is a reminder of the extent of the destruction, loss, and diffusion of monastic book collections.

The sources introduced here are as follows:

1. *Secular Uses*
The Use of Salisbury
   Breviary, Missal, Consuetudinary and Customary, Ordinal, Tonary, Directory, Antiphonal, Gradual, Processional
The Use of Hereford
   Breviary, Missal
The Use of York
   Breviary, Missal, Processional
The Use of the Roman Curia
   Breviary, Missal

2. *Monastic Uses (Benedictine)*
   Breviary (Hyde Abbey, Winchester), Missal (Westminster Abbey), Ordinal (St Mary's Abbey, York), Customary (Cathedral Priory, Norwich), Ordinal (Barking Abbey (nuns)), Antiphonal (Cathedral Priory, Worcester), 'Rites of Durham' (Cathedral Priory, Durham)

THE USE OF SALISBURY

By the Reformation, the diocesan Use of Salisbury was commonly regarded as the normative English secular Use. The influence of Salisbury spread rapidly to other dioceses. The first wave of influence was constitutional: the Statutes were adapted or adopted by a number of other secular cathedrals in the thirteenth and fourteenth centuries.

Liturgical influence followed; in the later Middle Ages, the Use was gradually adopted by a number of other dioceses throughout England, Wales, and Ireland. By the mid-fifteenth century, these included the secular cathedrals (and dioceses) of Chichester, Exeter, Lichfield, Lincoln, London, Wells, a number of other dioceses with a monastic cathedral (though not the cathedral priory), as well as Augustinian houses and many secular collegiate churches. At the Reformation (according to the Preface to the Book of Common Prayer) only the local Uses of Bangor, Hereford, Lincoln, and York were current; and even in these dioceses Salisbury Use had been adopted or at least had made headway.

The Use was inevitably adapted to meet specific local needs, but its particular repertory of variant texts and chants is discernible. By the early sixteenth century most of the principal books were available in published editions, printed for the most part at presses in France.

The Use of Salisbury is traditionally associated with the Norman bishop, St Osmund, who established the see in the old fortified city (Old Sarum, 1075). However, the earliest surviving sources were compiled during the episcopacy of Richard Poore (1214–37). Poore transferred the see to Salisbury (1218) founding the new church which he built near the river (1220), and consecrating a temporary high altar (1225). The chapter moved to the new site in 1227. The constitution, customs, and liturgical order of the collegiate foundation were probably codified at this time. It was a substantial institution with endowments for over fifty canons. In the early fifteenth century, in addition to the canons, there were thirty-six or more vicars (priests, deacons, subdeacons), as well as clerks and up to fourteen choristers.

Breviary

Printed source: *Breviarum ad usum insignis ecclesiae Sarisburiensis* (Paris, 1531).
Modern edition: F. Procter and C. Wordsworth (eds.), *Breviarum ad usum insignis ecclesiae Sarisburiensis* (3 vols., Cambridge, 1879–86; repr. Farnborough, 1970).

The Breviary of 1531 represents the Use of Salisbury in its last years. The modern edition takes account of (but does not collate) other Breviaries of the Salisbury Use printed in the periods 1475–1544 and 1555–7. The third volume provides a comprehensive table of contents, introduction, and indices.

Section	Edition (columns)
1. Calendar	i. 3–14
2. Temporale	i. i–mccccxlix
including Little Hours of Blessed	
Virgin Mary in Advent	i. xxxii–xxxix
Preces (Compline, Lauds)	i. xii–xv, liv–lv
Lady Office for Advent	i. lxxii–lxxx
3. Psalter	
Beginning of the Offices	ii. 1–4
Psalter and Litany	ii. 5–268
Offices of the Dead and Blessed Virgin Mary	ii. 271–314
Commemorations etc.	ii. 315–54
4. Common of Saints	
Common in Eastertide	ii. 355–63
Common in other seasons	ii. 364–459
Blessings	ii. 459–62
Table of classification of feasts	ii. 462–75
Ordo Missae	ii. 479–500
Commemorative and Common Masses (including Mass of the Dead)	ii. 501–54
5. Sanctorale	
St Andrew	iii. 29–30
Thereafter, each month of the year is separately numbered	iii. *passim*

Missal

Two versions of the Salisbury Missal have been edited, one based on early manuscripts, the other on the printed Missals. In both there are a number of items (e.g. prayers before and after Mass) which are not listed here. These account for the gaps in the lists of pages and columns.

(a) Earlier Manuscript Missal

Principal sources: Manchester, Rylands Library, MS L. 24, Noted Missal ('Crawford Missal'), 13th century. Paris, Bibliothèque de l'Arsenal, MS 135, Noted Missal and Noted Breviary, 13th century.

Modern edition: J. W. Legg (ed.), *The Sarum Missal Edited from Three Early Manuscripts* (Oxford, 1916; repr. 1969).

The 'Crawford Missal' includes the contemporary inscription 'Memoriale Henrici de Ciscesteria canonici Exon. prec. lx.s.': Henry of Chichester was Precentor of the collegiate church at Crediton, Devon, from which he resigned in 1264.

SECTION	EDITION (PAGES)
1. Calendar	xxi–xxxii
2. Kyriale	1–9
Blessing of Salt and Water	10–12
3. Temporale	13–201
4. Ordo Missae	216–29
5. Sanctorale	232–353
6. Commune Sanctorum	354–83
7. Votive Masses and Masses for Special Intentions etc.	384–460
including Mass of the Blessed Virgin	387–91
and Mass of the Dead	431–45
8. Sequences	461–95

Appendices include Calendars from other sources (including Paris), together with additional Kyries and Sequences not found in the Manchester source.

(b) Later Printed Missal

Original sources: Missals published between 1487 and 1557.
Printed edition: F. H. Dickinson (ed.), *Missale Sarum* (4 soft-bound issues, Burntisland, 1861–83)

SECTION	EDITION (COLUMNS)
1. Calendar	17**–28**
2. Preparation for Mass	29**–36**
Sunday Procession	35**–42**
3. Temporale	1–560
4. Ordo Missae	577–638
5. Sanctorale	
(St Andrew to St Linus)	657–984
6. Commune Sanctorum	657*–734*
7. Votive Masses and Masses for Special Intentions	735*–928*
including Masses of the Blessed Virgin Mary	759*–782*
and Mass of the Dead	859*–883*
8. Kyries (with Tropes)	928*–934*

Consuetudinary and Customary

Principal sources: Trowbridge, Wiltshire County Record Office, D1/1/1, *Vetus Registrum Ecclesie Sarum* (or Register of St Osmund), first section, 13th century (written for the cathedral). Oxford, Corpus Christi College, MS 44, Customary etc., late 14th century (from Llanthony Priory, Gloucester [Augustinian]).

Modern edition: W. H. Frere (ed.), *The Use of Sarum*, i (2 vols., Cambridge, 1898; repr. Farnborough, 1969).

The Consuetudinary and Customary are printed as parallel texts in Frere's edition. Frere consulted a number of manuscripts for both texts in addition to the Salisbury and Oxford sources noted here. The Consuetudinary represents Salisbury practice until about the end of the fourteenth century; the Customary then displaced it (just as the New Ordinal replaced the Old at this time), and represents practice thereafter. Each includes descriptions of the principal duties of the cathedral officers—Dean, Precentor, Chancellor, and Treasurer—and those in their charge, but also describes the ordering of the choir and special ceremonies. Frere provides a comprehensive glossarial index, and this, together with the lists of contents, makes it unnecessary to provide further guide here. There is a musical appendix of tones and chants found in the sources.

Ordinal

Manuscript source: British Library, MS Harley 1001, Ordinal etc., early 14th century (used at St Giles Risby, near Bury St Edmunds, Suffolk).

Modern edition: W. H. Frere (ed.), *The Use of Sarum*, ii (2 vols., Cambridge, 1901; repr. Farnborough, 1969).

There are two forms of the Ordinal in the Use of Salisbury: the Old Ordinal and the New. The first reference to the New Ordinal occurs *c.*1390. Frere considers the Old Ordinal to have been conceived alongside the Consuetudinary and to date from the second half of the thirteenth century. The Salisbury Ordinal separates instructions for the Office from the Mass. Some of the text overlaps with the Consuetudinary and Customary.

(a) The Old Ordinal

SECTION	EDITION (PAGES)
The Office	1–147
1. Temporale	1–102
2. Sanctorale	102–38
St Andrew to St Saturninus	
3. Commune Sanctorum	139–45
4. Office of the Dead	146–7
The Mass	148–207
5. Temporale	148–76
6. Sanctorale	177–89
7. Commune Sanctorum	190–1
8. Votive Masses (including Lady Mass)	192–3
9. Miscellaneous items and additions	194–207

(b) *The New Ordinal*

Frere edited only the opening of the New Ordinal (*Use of Sarum*, ii, 208–33, using Oxford, Corpus Christi College, MS 44, fourteenth century, and London, British Library, MS Harley 2911, fifteenth century). This extract supplements the rubrics for Advent found in Procter and Wordsworth's edition of the Salisbury Breviary (see above). But for the most part the New Ordinal is otherwise close to the rubrics found in the printed Breviary and Missal.

Tonary

Manuscript source: Oxford, Corpus Christi College, MS 44, Customary etc., late 14th century (from Llanthony Priory, Gloucester [Augustinian]).
Modern edition: W. H. Frere (ed.), *The Use of Sarum*, ii (2 vols., Cambridge, 1901; repr. Farnborough, 1969).

The Tonary (Tonale) is organized in eight sections, one for each mode (1–8 plus *Tonus Peregrinus*). Within each section there is a series of subsections:

(1) variant melodic characteristics of the mode;
(2) psalm and canticle tones;
(3) *neuma* to be appended to the last antiphon of a group of psalms at Vespers, Matins, and Lauds;
(4) *Gloria patri* for use in Responds at Matins;

(5) psalm tones for use in the Introit at Mass, together with appended Alleluia in Eastertide.

Directory

Printed source: Clement Maydeston, revised W. Clerke, *Ordinale Sarum sive Directorium Sacerdotum* (London, 1497).

Modern edition: W. Cooke and C. Wordsworth (eds.), *Directorium Sacerdotum* (2 vols., Henry Bradshaw Society, 20, 22; 1901–2).

The Directory (also identified as Pie, Pica, Pye, or even Ordinal) was intended to clarify the sophisticated rules of festal and ferial observance. The earliest Salisbury examples date from the end of the fourteenth century (e.g. Oxford, Corpus Christi College, MS 44, see 'Consuetudinary and Customary' and 'Tonary'). Maydeston (*c.* 1390–1456), a member of the Bridgettine Order at Sion (Richmond, Surrey), compiled a comprehensive Directory which was printed posthumously by Caxton (1487). This was subsequently revised by William Clerke, a chaplain of King's College, Cambridge, and published by Pynson (1497).

The problems of reconciling seasons and feasts were outlined in Chapter 3, as was the complication of the movable date of Easter which affected the rest of the Calendar. The Directory provides a comprehensive day-by-day listing of every observance, seasonal and festal, with limited details of individual items.

The Directory is divided into seven separate sections, one for each of the possible dates on which Sunday can fall after the feast of the Epiphany. These seven dates are identified by the Sunday letter (A–G).

Within each section there are six subsections. The first five subsections provide for the period after Epiphany to the end of July. Each allows for one of the five Sundays on which Easter can fall according to the moon. The sixth subsection deals with the period from the end of July to Epiphany in the following year.

Taken overall the tables allow for each of the thirty-five days on which Easter Day can fall. Leap-years had two Sunday letters (e.g. AB) and the second letter applied after 28 February.

Column 1 Section of Directory
   2 Date of Sunday after Octave of Epiphany (or Septuagesima [s] when no Sunday after Octave of Epiphany)
   3 Date of Easter Day

I	2	3	I	2	3
A(1)	January 15	March 26	E(1)	January 19 s	March 23
(2)	January 15	April 2	(2)	January 19	March 30
(3)	January 15	April 9	(3)	January 19	April 6
(4)	January 15	April 16	(4)	January 19	April 13
(5)	January 15	April 23	(5)	January 19	April 20
B(1)	January 16	March 27	F(1)	January 20 s	March 24
(2)	January 16	April 3	(2)	January 20	March 31
(3)	January 16	April 10	(3)	January 20	April 7
(4)	January 16	April 17	(4)	January 20	April 14
(5)	January 16	April 24	(5)	January 20	April 21
C(1)	January 17	March 28	G(1)	January 14	March 25
(2)	January 17	April 4	(2)	January 14	April 1
(3)	January 17	April 11	(3)	January 14	April 8
(4)	January 17	April 18	(4)	January 14	April 15
(5)	January 17	April 25	(5)	January 14	April 22
D(1)	January 18	March 29			
(2)	January 18	April 5			
(3)	January 18	April 12			
(4)	January 18	April 19			
(5)	January 18	April 26			

Antiphonal

(a) Manuscript Source

Principal source: Cambridge, University Library MS Mm. 2. g, Antiphonal, second quarter of 13th century (probably used at the Augustinian priory, Barnwell, Cambridgeshire).

Additional sources: Salisbury, Cathedral Library, MS 152, Noted Breviary, later 15th century (associated with St Mary's, Arlingham, Gloucestershire). Oxford, Bodleian Library, MS Bodley 948, Noted Breviary, c.1400 (St Andrew Undershaft—alias St Mary Axe, Leadenhall St., London). *Antiphonale Sarisburiense* (2 vols., winter and summer, Paris, 1519–20) (see (*b*) below).

Modern facsimile: W. H. Frere (ed.), *Antiphonale Sarisburiense* (in portfolios, London, 1901–24; repr. in 6 vols., Farnborough, 1966).

The title of the facsimile edition implies comprehensiveness and consistency: this is misleading. It is in fact a compilation of several sources and even so lacks chants (and texts) to some of the Office (e.g.

most hymns); there is also no Calendar or Psalter. As presented it is both problematic and instructive.

The principal source—the so-called Barnwell Antiphonal—is not from Salisbury itself but from an Augustinian monastery which had adopted the Use (probably Barnwell Priory, Cambs.). It has particular problems. Some parts of the manuscript have been lost; other observances that might be expected are omitted (e.g. Dedication); and there are two Offices that are specifically Augustinian. Such a situation is typical: a liturgical manuscript, even of so widespread a Use as Salisbury, is often particular to an individual church or foundation. The source also reflects its date of compilation: probably copied in the second quarter of the thirteenth century, it lacks feasts that were introduced after that time (e.g. Corpus Christi, Transfiguration), though these observances are found in later sources. Frere selected the Barnwell Antiphonal as the earliest available, and 'normalized' it by supplying what was lacking from other sources; but he provided only those items that could have been expected in a Salisbury manuscript of the mid-thirteenth century. He also omitted the section of the source which included the hymns. In later sources these are integrated into the main body of an Antiphonal.

The sources are identified as A (Arlingham), B (Barnwell), L (St Andrew Undershaft, London), and P (printed Antiphonal). The volume numbers refer to the 1966 reprint, but the numbering of plates is identical with the original facsimile edition. The sequence of the list follows the liturgical order of the principal source: supplementary material is interpolated into that order.

Section	Sources (folios, except B, pages)	Facsimile (plate nos.)
I. Temporale		
Advent Sunday to Vespers	A. 2–49^{v}	ii. 1–96
Hymn, Sunday after Octave of Epiphany supplemented (and partially duplicated) by:		
Advent Sunday to third week of Advent	L. 1, 1^{v}, 6^{v}, 7, 12, 15^{v}, 17^{v}–20	vi. a–m

Advent Sunday psalm-antiphons (with psalms)	L. 177, 178–80	vi. B–G
Octave of Epiphany	L. 55, 55^v	vi. n, o
End of Vespers, Sunday after Octave of Epiphany to Compline Respond, First Sunday in Lent	B. 101–50	ii. 101–50
End of Compline Respond, First Sunday in Lent to Memorials to the BVM during weeks after Octave of Corpus Christi (*Hist. Reg.*)	B. 151–304	iii. 151–304
Conclusion of Memorials (as above), then Matins for *Hist. Sap.* (i.e. August) to Vespers, Sunday before Advent	B. 305–42	iv. 305–42
Feast of Dedication	L. 166^v–171^v	vi. p–z, A

2. Sanctorale

St Andrew (30 November) to Second Nocturn of Matins, Sts Peter and Paul (29 June)	B. 345–444	iv. 345–444
End of Matins, Sts Peter and Paul to First Nocturn of Matins, St Martin (11 November)	B. 445–588	v. 445–588
Second Nocturn of Matins, St Martin to Second Nocturn of Matins, St Cecilia (22 November)	B. 589–608	vi. 589–608
Second Nocturn of Matins, St Cecilia to St Saturninus (29 November)	L. 336^v–40	vi. R–Z

3. Commune Sanctorum

First Vespers to Hymn at Lauds, Common of Apostles	L. 215–19^v	vi. H–Q
Last psalm-antiphon at Lauds, Common of Apostles to Common of Virgins	B. 633–68	vi. 633–68
Vespers, Compline, and part of Matins of the Daily Office of the Blessed Virgin Mary	P. xcvii^v–xcix	vi. α–δ

(b) Printed Source

Original source: *Antiphonale Sarisburiense* (2 vols., winter and summer, Paris, 1519–20). There is no modern edition, but as a more suitable companion to the sixteenth-century Breviary described above the printed Antiphonal is listed briefly here. Each section has its own sequence of pagination:

SECTION	SOURCE (FOLIOS)
1. Temporale (winter)	
Advent to Pentecost	i. 4–268
2. Calendar	i. 6 leaves
3. Psalter (with hymns, and including Offices of	
Blessed Virgin Mary)	i. i–cxcii
4. Commune Sanctorum (including Antiphons of	
Blessed Virgin Mary)	i. i–l
5. Sanctorale (winter)	
St Andrew to Sts Gervase and Protase	i. i–lxxvii
6. Temporale (summer)	
Trinity and Dedication	ii. ii–lxxi
7–9 as for 2–4	ii, as i above
10. Sanctorale (summer)	
St Dunstan to St Saturninus with added collects for	
late feasts (fo. clxxix)	ii. i–clxxix

Gradual

Principal source: London, British Library, MS Add. 12194, Gradual, early 13th century.

Additional sources: London, British Library, MS Add. 17001, Gradual, late 14th century. London, British Library, MS Lansdowne 462, Gradual, mid-15th century. Oxford, Bodleian Library, MS Rawlinson Liturg. d. 3, Gradual, early 13th century.

Modern facsimile: W. H. Frere (ed.), *Graduale Sarisburiense* (London, 1894).

As with the Salisbury Antiphonal Frere opted for an early but imperfectly surviving source, and supplemented it with additional materials. There is again an extensive introduction and index with references to a very wide range of sources, including those of other Uses, monastic and secular, English and continental.

As an early source the Gradual includes instructions for processions and Sequences, together with some complete items for processions which were not to be found in a contemporary Antiphonal. In its original state the manuscript included a section of Sequences, but this is incomplete and not reproduced in facsimile. The Gradual presented here is a suitable companion to Legg's edition of the Missal—see Missal (*a*) above. No edition or facsimile has been made of the printed Gradual, but a number of copies of various early printed editions survive, mostly in major libraries.

Though the plates are numbered or lettered successively, this conceals lacunae (in the main source) or non-successive selections (from the additional sources). The losses are noted by Frere in his introduction (p. xxxv), but may be usefully summarized in a clearer and simpler form here. The numbers of the plates are shown. Where a leaf is missing it is shown as [−1].

British Library, MS Add. 12194: List of Lacunae

[−1] 1–14 [−1] 15–18 [−1] 19–116 [−1] 117–36 [−1] 137–40 [−1] 141–66 [−1] 167–76 [−2] 177–80 [−2] 181–8 [−1] 189–94 [−1] 195–6 [−1] 197–202 [−1] 203–36

The contents of *Graduale Sarisburiense* are listed below. The main text is divided into principal sections. Supplementary materials are listed, showing where they are found in the facsimiles and where they belong in relation to the main text. In some cases the supplementary material overlaps in part. The first and last identifiable materials (not necessarily complete items, but marked by a capital letter) are noted for the supplementary plates. The sources are denoted by letter, A: Add. 12194, B: Add. 17001, C: Lansdowne 462, D: Rawlinson Liturg. d. 3.

SECTION	SOURCE	FACSIMILE (PLATE NOS.)
1. Temporale		
Gradual, Advent Sunday to		
Dedication	A	1–176
supplemented by		
Advent Sunday, before Offertory	B	A–D (before pl. 1)
Christmas Dawn Mass to Day Mass,		
Alleluia	B	E–Hi (after pl. 14)
Sunday after Christmas to Epiphany,		
Gradual	B	Hii–J (after pl. 18)

SECTION	SOURCE	FACSIMILE (PLATE NOS.)
Easter Introit	B	Ki (before pl. 117)
Sunday after Ascension, Alleluia to Pentecost, Alleluia	B	Kii–M (after pl. 136)
Friday after Pentecost, Alleluia, to Trinity Sunday, Communion	D	a–c (after pl. 140)
Trinity 21, Communion to Trinity 24, Alleluia	D	d–f (after pl. 166)
2. Sanctorale		
Conversion of St Paul to St Linus supplemented by	A	177–201
Vigil of St Andrew to Conversion of St Paul, Gradual	D	g–h (before pl. 177)
Purification, Processional antiphons to Tract	D	i–k (after pl. 180)
St John the Baptist, Gradual verse to Sts Peter and Paul, Introit	D	l–o (after pl. 188)
Seven Holy Brothers, Gradual verse to St Mary Magdalen, Alleluia	D	p (additional to pls. 190–1)
St Laurence, Offertory to Assumption, Gradual	D	q–s (after pl. 194)
St Sabina, Communion to St Michael, Introit	D	t–v (after pl. 196)
3. Commune Sanctorum		
Vigil of Apostles to Commemoration of the Cross supplemented by	A	202–36
Vigil of Apostles, Offertory to Apostles, Communion	D	w–z (after pl. 202)
4. Ordinary of the Mass	C	1*–19*

Processional

Principal sources: *Processionalibus . . . ad usum insignis preclare ecclesie Sarisburi-ensis* (London, 1502). *Processionale . . . ad usum . . . Sarisburiensis* (Rouen, 1508). Salisbury, Cathedral Library, MS 148, mid-15th century (from the cathedral).

Modern facsimile and editions: [G. R. Rastall (ed.)], *Processionale ad usum Sarum* (Clarabricken, 1980). W. G. Henderson (ed.), *Processionale ad usum insignis praeclarae ecclesiae Sarum* (Leeds, 1882; repr. Farnborough, 1969). C. Wordsworth (ed.), *Ceremonies and Processions of the Cathedral Church of Salisbury* (Cambridge, 1901).

The medieval processions at Salisbury are well known, and provide the cornerstone of Terence Bailey's *The Processions of Sarum and the Western Church* (Toronto, 1971). But Salisbury's delight in processions was shared by churches throughout the West: only in the Papal Curia and in places elsewhere that adopted its Use were they infrequent. The early Graduals include details of processions (see 'Gradual' above), but in the fifteenth and sixteenth centuries details and texts are generally found in separate Processionals.

The facsimile edition provides a clear text preceded by a list of contents and an index of texts set to chant. Henderson edits the 1508 text without music (together with additions and collations from editions printed between 1517 and 1554). Wordsworth's older edition (also without music) is useful as an earlier source intended for Salisbury Cathedral itself. The manuscript includes a number of local items not found in the printed editions: orders for the admission of members of the cathedral foundation, the Bidding of Bedes, relics of the cathedral church, and processions to other churches in the city.

SECTION	1502 AND FACSIMILE (FOLIOS)	EDITION OF 1508 (PAGES)	EDITION OF MS 148★ (PAGES)
1. Calendar	—·	—	3–14
Blessing of Salt and Water	1^v–4^v	1–5	18–20
Order of Sunday Procession	5	5	21
Bidding of Bedes	—	—	22–32
Relics of the Church of Salisbury	—	—	33–43
2. Temporale (Advent Sunday to Dedication)	5–130	6–135	47–97
3. Sanctorale (St Andrew to St Katharine)	130–58^v	135–62	98–103
4. Commune Sanctorum	158^v–162	162–4	—
5. Miscellaneous processions for special needs etc.	162–7	164–70	117–26

SECTION	1502 AND FACSIMILE (FOLIOS)	EDITION OF 1508 (PAGES)	EDITION OF MS 148* (PAGES)
6. Antiphons of the Blessed Virgin			
Mary	167–9ᵛ	170–2	—
Prosae for Sanctorale	—	172–3	—
Seven Penitential Psalms	170–3	173–4	—

* Only selected items from MS 148 are given here.

THE USE OF HEREFORD

Alongside the Use of Salisbury the two secular Uses which persisted in medieval England were those of Hereford and York. Neither was as widespread as that of Salisbury, but both survived until the Reformation. Some of the principal liturgical books from Hereford were printed in the early sixteenth century.

Hereford lies adjacent to the Welsh border, and was a smaller foundation than Salisbury: thirty-three canons, twenty-seven vicars and chantry chaplains (1396), and a further group (about a dozen) of clerks and boy choristers. As well as the medieval church (the core of the building dates from 1079–1110) the college of vicars has survived, but not the processional cloister or chapter house. Among its treasures, the medieval cathedral library with its chained books is duly world famous.

Breviary

Principal source: *Breviarum secundum usum Herfordensis* (2 vols., winter and summer, Rouen, 1505).

Additional sources: Hereford Cathedral Library, MS P. 9. vi, Noted Breviary, second half of 13th century. Worcester Cathedral Library, MS Q. 86, Psalter, 13th century, with added Breviary, 14th century.

Modern edition: W. H. Frere and L. E. G. Brown (eds.), *The Hereford Breviary* (3 vols., Henry Bradshaw Society, 26, 40, 46; 1904–15).

Frere's substantial introduction to the third volume of the edition is particularly important as a comparative essay distinguishing the English Uses of Hereford, Salisbury, and York. This volume also contains extensive comparative lists of the contents of the three Uses. The edition as a whole collates variants of the sources of the Hereford Breviary, and the third volume includes the texts (at least in part) of the Tonary (found in the Noted Breviary), Ordinal (London, British Library, Harleian MS 2983), and the Collectar (Oxford, Balliol College, MS 321). Texts which correspond to the Use of Salisbury are not given in full; they can obviously be found in the edition of the Salisbury Breviary.

The printed breviary (1505) is bound as follows in the near complete copy surviving in Worcester Cathedral Library:

SECTION	EDITION (PAGES)
1. Calendar	i. xiii–xxiv
2. Psalter and	i. 1–29
Commune Sanctorum	i. 30–86
3. Temporale (winter section: Advent to Pentecost)	i. 89–397
4. Sanctorale (winter: St Andrew to Sts Gervase and Protase	ii. 51–197, and ii. 49–50
5. Offices of Dedication, Blessed Virgin Mary, and Dead, etc.	ii. 1–48
6. Temporale (summer: Trinity Sunday onwards)	i. 398–478
7. Sanctorale (summer: St Dunstan to St Saturninus, with Commemoration of St Ethelbert)	ii. 166–422

Internal evidence shows that it was the printer's intention that sections 1 and 2 should be bound after sections 3 and 4. The section of the Sanctorale from St Dunstan (19 May) to Sts Gervase and Protase (19 June) appears in both the winter and summer volumes (to allow for the variable date of Easter). The Eastertide texts of Commune Sanctorum are separated (ii. 142–53).

Missal

Principal source: *Missal[e] ad usum famose et percelebris ecclesie Helfordensis* (Rouen, 1502).

Additional source: Oxford, University College, MS 78A, Missal, 14th century (from St Dubricius, Whitchurch, Gwent)

Modern edition: W. G. Henderson (ed.), *Missale ad usum percelebris ecclesiae Herfordensis* (Leeds, 1874; repr. Farnborough, 1969).

Henderson's editing is not outstanding. Nevertheless he provides a text sufficiently workable to establish the order of Mass at Hereford. The edition follows the order of the printed Missal:

SOURCE	EDITION (PAGES)
1. Calendar	xxi–xxxii
Rubrics, *Kyrie* tropes,	xxxiii–xliii
Blessing of Water before Mass, etc.	xliv–xlvii
2. Temporale (Advent to Holy Saturday)	1–114
3. Ordo Missae	114–41
4. Temporale (Easter Day to week before Advent, with Dedication	141–215
5. Sanctorale	219–364
6. Commune Sanctorum, with Votive Masses, Mass of the Dead, etc.	365–457

No Processional survives from Hereford. However, the occurrence and contents of processions can be established from information in the Ordinal (see the edition of the Breviary, vol. iii, pp. 68–81) and Missal (*passim*).

THE USE OF YORK

The Use of York was prevalent in the North of England, and persisted until the Reformation in spite of the encroachment of the Use of Salisbury. Breviary, Missal, and Processional were printed in the late fifteenth and early sixteenth centuries, as was the Manual. A manuscript Pontifical also survives. All five books are available in editions published by the Surtees Society.

    The Saxon foundation of York Minster was a secular cathedral throughout the Middle Ages, the seat of the Archbishop of York. The present church is a compilation of English Gothic built mostly in the thirteenth and fourteenth centuries. As the largest of the English medieval cathedrals its vast windows (a number still retaining their medieval glass), bold stone mouldings, and rich sculptural detail are indicative of the wealth of the foundation. Unlike Hereford and Salisbury it retains its early fifteenth-century choir screen. In the later Middle Ages the cathedral foundation consisted of some thirty-six prebends, thirty-six vicars, about twelve choristers, and twenty-three or more chantry priests. In addition to the Latin liturgical books listed below, some of the York Use appeared in an early printed translation: *The Lay Folk's Mass Book and Offices in English according to the Use of York*, ed. T. F. Simmons (Early English Text Society, OS 71, 1879).

Breviary

Principal source: *Breviarum secundum usum ecclesie Eboracensis* (Venice, 1493). Modern edition: S. W. Lawley (ed.), *Breviarum ad usum insignis ecclesie Eboracensis* (2 vols., Surtees Society, 71, 75; 1880–2).

SECTION	EDITION (COLUMNS)
1. Temporale	i. 1–652
2. Offices of Dedication, Blessed Virgin Mary, St William of York, All Saints	i. 652–706
3. *Rubrica de Dominicis* [simple directory]	i. 705–26
4. Calendar	i. pp. 1–15
Blessings at Matins	pp. 16–18 (between cols. 726 and 727)
5. Psalter	i. 727–944
6. Commune Sanctorum	ii. 1–82
7. Sanctorale	ii. 83–730

Appendices 1–4 contain materials not found in 1493, but in at least one of the later editions (ii. 731–84). Appendix 5 contains the Office of St Richard Hampole, culled from MS sources (ii. 785–820).

Missal

Principal source: *Missale secundum usum insignis ecclesie Eboracensis* (Rouen, [1509]). Modern edition: W. G. Henderson (ed.), *Missale ad usum insignis ecclesiae Eboracensis* (2 vols., Surtees Society, 59, 60; 1874).

Henderson's edition is a collation of both manuscript and printed sources dating from the twelfth to the sixteenth centuries. As such it has to be treated with caution. The Calendar draws on Breviary sources as well. A detailed list of contents (of both volumes) is found at the beginning of volume ii.

Source	Edition (pages)
1. Calendar	i. xxix–xlv
Regula (order of Mass on Advent Sunday)	i. xlvi–xlvii
2. Temporale (Advent to Saturday after Pentecost)	i. 1–162
3. Ordo Missae (Preparation, Ordo, Canon)	i. 163–212
4. Temporale (Trinity to week before Advent, with Dedication)	i. 213–59
5. Sanctorale	ii. 1–132
6. Commune Sanctorum, with commemorative, and special Masses, Masses for the Dead, etc.	ii. 133–96

Additional materials follow, including sequences of the Common, additional later feasts and observances, some found only in the manuscript sources (ii. 197–236).

Processional

Principal source: *Processionalibus . . . ad usum celebris ecclesie Eboracensis* (Rouen, 1530). Later edition, London, 1555.

Manuscript source: Oxford, Bodleian Library, MS E Museo 126 (3612), late 15th century (from St Oswald's Parish Church, Methley, Yorkshire) not used in the edition; see below.

Modern edition: W. G. Henderson *Manuale et Processionale ad usum insignis ecclesiae Eboracensis* (Surtees Society, 63; 1874).

Henderson did not know the manuscript source. It is an unprepossessing example of late medieval book production, but it shows important local differences and adaptations which reflect the dedication of the church and the physical characteristics at Methley. Judging by the deletions of the procession of St Thomas of Canterbury, it was in use until the 1540s. The manuscript Processional combines Temporale and Sanctorale in a single sequence. An introduction, partial edition (with music), and collation with Henderson has been undertaken by Jane Kuhlmann Frogley (unpublished M.Litt thesis, University of Oxford, 1988). Only the details of Henderson's edition are given here.

Section	Edition (pages)
1. Temporale (Advent Sunday to Sunday before Advent)	133–94

Henderson appends additional material from a manuscript Manual (pp. 205–7), all for Saints.

THE USE OF THE ROMAN (PAPAL) CURIA

The historical importance of the liturgical practice of the Papal Court is stressed at a number of points in the text of this book. From the thirteenth century onwards the Use of the Curia came increasingly to be regarded and observed as the Use of Rome. And in the liturgical reforms which followed the Council of Trent in the second half of the sixteenth century, this Use was the model for the authoritative texts of the Tridentine Breviary and Missal which persisted with only minor revisions until the twentieth century (see Chapter 10 above).

Breviary

No critical edition of the Breviary has been made. Nevertheless many substantial public, university, and ecclesiastical libraries have copies of the Roman Breviary printed before the reformed version (i.e. Tridentine Breviary) of 1568. Care needs to be taken that Breviaries printed between 1535 and the 1560s are not those following the order devised by Cardinal Quiñones: this Breviary was never approved by the Roman Church, but may be catalogued misleadingly as a Roman Breviary. Copies of *Breviarum Romanum* (the Tridentine Breviary) printed between 1568 and 1911 (the year of Pius X's revisions to the Breviary) can often be obtained in second-hand bookshops; though they differ in some respects from earlier Breviaries, the substance and order is much the same.

The source summarized here is a Breviary printed in Venice in 1522/3.

Printed source: *Breviarum romanum completissimum* . . . (Venice, 1522 [1523]).

This edition of the Breviary is numbered by openings rather than by page or folio. This system is followed here, with the indication *l* or *r* after a number to identify left- or right-hand side of the opening.

SECTION	OPENING
1. Calendar	[iv]r–[x]l
Tables, rubrics, prayers etc.	[x]r–[xxvii]l
End of hours etc.	[xxvii]l
General rubrics and index of psalms	[xxvii]r–[xxviii]r
2. Psalter	
Psalms	1r–55l
Hymns	55l–61r
3. Temporale	62r–222r
4. Sanctorale	224l–521r
St Saturninus to St Peter of Alexandria	
5. Commune Sanctorum	522r–546l
Dedication	546l–548r
Blessed Virgin Mary	548r–554r
Dead	554r–556r
Orders for sick, dying, and burial	556r–562l
Blessings	562l–565l

There is a series of additional Offices added after the colophon (565l), mostly intended for specific religious Orders (565r–637l).

Though this Breviary is bound in a single volume, Roman Breviaries were commonly produced in four volumes (for portability). Each contains Psalter, Commune Sanctorum, Temporale, and Sanctorale. Because of the shifting of seasons according to Easter the Sanctorale sections of each volume overlap. A typical scheme for Temporale and Sanctorale is as follows:

Pars hiemalis (winter)
    Temporale: Advent to Saturday after Ash Wednesday
    Sanctorale: St Andrew (30 November) to St Gregory (12 March)
Pars verna (spring)
    Temporale: First Sunday of Lent to Octave of Pentecost
    Sanctorale: St Romuald (7 February) to St Julian (19 June)
Pars aestiva (summer)
    Temporale: Trinity Sunday to 16th Sunday after Pentecost
    Sanctorale: St Venantius (18 May) to Sts Lawrence and Justinian (5 September)
Pars autumnalis (autumn)
    Temporale: 4th week in August to last Sunday after Pentecost
    Sanctorale: St Joseph Calasanctus (27 August) to St Bibiana (2 December)

Missal

Printed source: *Missale completum secundum consuetudinem romane curie . . .*
(Milan, 1474).
Modern edition: R. Lippe (ed.), *Missale Romanum, Mediolani, 1474* (2 vols.,
Henry Bradshaw Society, 17, 33; 1899–1907).

The main text of Lippe's edition of the 1474 Missal is printed in the
first volume. In the second volume there are notes and the text is
collated with sixteen further editions of the Missal published between
1481 and 1561, together with a partial comparison with the Tridentine
Missal (using editions of 1574 and 1894). There are comprehensive
indices in volume ii.

SECTION	SOURCE (FOLIOS)	EDITION (VOL. I, PAGES)
1. Calendar	[pp.] i–xii	xiii–xxiv
Blessing of Water	[pp.] xiii–xiv	xxv–xxvii
2. Temporale (first part)		
Advent Sunday to Holy Saturday (Easter Vigil)	$1-75^v$	1–195
Rubrics	75^v-76	196–7
3. Ordo Missae	$76-85^v$	198–211
4. Temporale (continued)		
Easter Day to last Sunday after Pentecost	85^v-116^v	212–99
5. Sanctorale		
St Andrew to St Catherine	$118-48^v$	300–402
6. Commune Sanctorum	$150-164^v$	403–46
Dedication	164^v-165	447–8
7. Masses for Special Intentions	165–79	449–94
including Blessed Virgin Mary	166^v-168	454–8
and the Dead	175^v-179	483–94
Blessings	179–81	495–7, 500–2

One leaf from the copy of the 1474 Missal is lacking (fo. 149 to the end of the
Sanctorale and the beginning of the Commune Sanctorum); the missing text
is supplied from the edition of 1481.

The Mass of the Transfiguration (6 August) is supplied from the Missal of
1485 (i. 498–9); other additional Blessings, Masses etc. from Missals after
1474 are also included in an appendix (ii. 301–85).

MONASTIC USES

No comprehensive set of liturgical books survives from a single English monastic house. Nevertheless, the existence of individual manuscripts from a series of different houses makes it possible to piece together much of the necessary evidence, and to gain some idea of variant customs.

The Breviary of Hyde Abbey, Winchester

Manuscript sources: Oxford, Bodleian Library, MS Rawlinson Liturg. e. 1*
  and MS Gough Liturg. 8, *c.* 1300.
Modern edition: J. B. L. Tolhurst (ed.), *The Monastic Breviary of Hyde Abbey,*
  Winchester (6 vols., Henry Bradshaw Society, 69, 70, 71, 76, 78, 80; 1932–
  42).

Taken together these two manuscripts, copied in about 1300, comprise one of about seven substantially complete English monastic Breviaries extant. Tolhurst's edition is particularly useful for the extensive liturgical introduction to the monastic Office which forms the sixth volume. The edition is not paginated but follows the order and foliation of the sources.

The Saxon Newminster established by Edward, son of Alfred the Great, became a Benedictine monastery in 965, one of three monastic foundations close to the Royal Palace in Winchester. With the Norman rebuilding of the cathedral priory (Old Minster), Newminster moved from the crowded site to Hyde Meadow beyond the city wall in 1110. From then on it was known as the abbey of Hyde. The abbey was a substantial foundation: according to Henry VIII's *Valor Ecclesiasticus* (1535) its net annual income was £865, more than Pershore, Selby, or Sherborne—of whose churches more survives. There were forty monks in the twelfth century, but after the Black Death the number averaged about thirty until the Dissolution.

The Breviary is laid out in the following manner:

SECTION	SOURCE (FOLIOS)	EDITION (VOLUME)
1. Temporale	*Rawlinson* MS	
Advent to Holy Saturday	1–98^{v}	i

Easter to week before Advent	99–168	ii
Dedication and Corpus Christi	168–78	ii
2. Sanctorale		
January to June	189–280	iii
July to December	280ᵛ–409ᵛ	iv
3. Commune Sanctorum with Offices of Blessed Virgin Mary and Relics	410–49	v
Suffrages, Chapter Office	449–51	v
4. Commonly used texts (*Psalmi familiaries*, texts for Little Hours, Compline, and Matins	451–3ᵛ	v
	Gough MS	
5. Calendar	4–9ᵛ	v
6. Psalter with canticles for Lauds	10–65ᵛ	—
7. Litany, Office of the Dead	66–70ᵛ	v

The Missal of Westminster Abbey

Original source: London, Westminster Abbey Library, MS 37, third quarter of 14th century.
Modern edition: J. W. Legg (ed.), *Missale ad usum Ecclesie Westmonasteriensis* (3 vols., Henry Bradshaw Society, 1, 5, 12; 1891–6).

This is a sumptuous manuscript rich in gold leaf, decoration, and illumination. It was presented by Nicholas Lytlington, Abbot of Westminster between 1362 and 1386, and is presumed to have been written at that time. It includes, and may have been used at, the coronation service.

The abbey of Westminster needs little introduction. There was a church on the site from at least 618, but the Benedictine foundation dates from 959. It was King Edward the Confessor who established it as the royal church, and his rebuilt abbey was consecrated in 1065. The monastic community expanded to eighty (late eleventh century) and then to about 100 (early thirteenth century). Having fallen to twenty-eight (late fourteenth century, a time of plague) it averaged about forty to fifty monks in the fifteenth century. Before its suppression in 1540 it was the richest monastery in England, with a net annual income of £2,470 (1535). Much of the present building was erected between 1245 and about 1400.

Legg's edition presents the complete text of the Missal in the first two volumes. The third volume is both appendix and commentary. It deals with three further manuscripts believed to derive from Westminster Abbey: the first dominated by a large collection of blessings (Oxford, Bodleian Library, MS Rawlinson C. 425, early fourteenth century); the second consisting of Litany, Office of the Dead, Commemorative Offices, commemorations, additional prayers at the Office, and including Compline (Oxford, Bodleian Library, MS Rawlinson Liturg. g. 10, c.1400); the third a Psalter (London, British Library, MS Royal 2. A. xxii, late twelfth century with later additions). Selected texts are printed from all three.

The second part of volume iii is a comparative liturgical introduction, still useful in spite of its age, with tables that compare selected features with other Uses (English and foreign). The extensive notes which follow are also comparative, and include (among many others) comparisons with another Benedictine Missal available in a modern edition (*The Missal of St Augustine's, Canterbury*, ed. M. Rule, Cambridge University Press, 1896). The concluding section is a comprehensive list of liturgical forms presented in a single alphabetical index.

The Missal is presented in the following order:

SECTION	SOURCE (FOLIOS)	EDITION (COLUMNS)
		vol. i
1. Calendar	3–8ᵛ	pp. v–xvi
Blessing of salt and water before Mass	9	1–4
2. Temporale		
Advent to last week before Advent, with Dedication	10–145	5–478
3. Ordo Missae		*vol. ii*
Preparation for Mass	145ᵛ–148	481–9
The Mass	148–62ᵛ	489–526
4. Special blessings	162ᵛ–205	527–672
5. Coronation rites	206–23ᵛ	673–733
Royal burial	224	734–5

6. Sanctorale	225–88	736–1028
7. Commune Sanctorum	289–311^v	1029–110
Votive Masses, Commemorative Masses, Masses for special intentions, and for the Dead	312–31^v	1110–86
8. Professions of monks, nuns, etc.	333–42^v	1187–216

The Ordinal of St Mary's Abbey, York

Manuscript source: Cambridge, St John's College, MS 102 D. 27, *c*.1400.
Modern edition: The Abbess of Stanbrook [L. McLachlan] and J. B. L. Tolhurst (eds.), *The Ordinale and Customary of the Abbey of Saint Mary York* (3 vols., Henry Bradshaw Society, 73, 75, 84; 1936–51).

Though incomplete (there are no instructions for the Sanctorale) this source provides one of the most detailed accounts of the conduct of life and liturgy in an English Benedictine house in about 1400 (the approximate date of copying). From internal evidence the editors reconstructed an *horarium* (vol. iii, pp. vii–xi). Some of the liturgical details appear to reveal affinity with monasteries in the south (notably Muchelney), others come closer to secular Use (the Mass seems especially close to the local Use of York), yet others appear to be individual to St Mary's.

St Mary's Abbey was established by the Normans as part of the movement to rekindle monasticism in northern England in the last quarter of the eleventh century. It was from St Mary's in 1132 that thirteen brothers left to forge a more rigorous monastic life as Cistercians in the hostile moorland at Fountains near Ripon. Nevertheless St Mary's survived the exodus. The Norman church was replaced (1271–95), and it was for this new building that the Ordinal was subsequently written. Little remains of the abbey, but an outline ground plan is given in the edition (vol. iii, after the index). It was a rich monastery (net annual income £1,650 in 1535), comparable to houses like Gloucester, Peterborough, and Tewkesbury, and had a community of a little over fifty at the dissolution.

A good deal of the text is not concerned with liturgy directly (in that sense it is also a Customary). The ordering of the source is as follows:

SECTION	EDITION (PAGES)

Introduction, including comments on singing (e.g. the
psalms) and practical information about the conduct of
the Office. ... i. 1–17

Tonary. The musical text is not reproduced in the
edition. ... i. 17–20

Advent Sunday. Much of the information in this section
is relevant not just to this Sunday but throughout the
year; indeed variants for other days are noted. Sadly,
the description of First Vespers is lost, but there is a
detailed account of the liturgical day thereafter.

Compline and Compline of the Blessed Virgin Mary	i. 24–9
Matins	i. 33–44
Lauds	i. 44–6
Matins and Lauds of the Blessed Virgin Mary	i. 46–9
Prime and Prime of the Blessed Virgin Mary	i. 49–53
Lady Mass (here called *Missa familiaris*)	i. 56–8
Mass of the Dead	i. 68–9
Morrow Mass	i. 69–74
Processions before Mass	i. 87–95
Terce and Terce of the Blessed Virgin Mary	i. 95–7
High Mass, with separate consideration of the conduct of priest, deacon, subdeacon, thurifer, taperers, and choir	i. 97–135
Sext and Sext of the Blessed Virgin Mary	i. 135–6
None and None of the Blessed Virgin Mary	i. 155
Second Vespers (in summary only)	i. 156

The first week of Advent	i. 159–63
The Office of the Dead, on weekdays	i. 163–6

Ordinal for Temporale (with details of customs as
necessary)

Second Sunday in Advent to Sunday before Advent	i. 166 to iii. 367

Interspersed in the liturgical description are sections concerned with
conduct and practice outside the church (i.e. *Mandatum* ceremony and
Collatio (i. 21–4), dormitory (i. 29), great silence (i. 31), chapter (i. 74),
and meals (i. 142, and 156)), some of which include liturgical elements.
There is also an outline of the allocation of duties in choir (the *tabula*: i.
58–67).

Though there is no Ordinal for the Sanctorale many details of
customs can be gleaned from the present text. The manuscript also

contains a quantity of chant, especially for the run-of-the-mill daily items (e.g. tones for versicles and responses recited frequently). These are not reproduced in the printed edition. There is an index of subjects, seasons, and feasts, but no index of texts.

Another manuscript (Oxford, Bodleian Library, MS Bodley 39, written before 1350) includes an incomplete Customary from St Mary's York, but only that part dealing with the duties of officers, therefore the liturgical information included is fragmented. The text is included in *The Chronicle of St Mary's Abbey, York*, ed. H. H. E. Craster and M. E. Thornton (Surtees Society, 148; 1933.)

The Customary of the Cathedral Priory, Norwich

Manuscript source: Cambridge, Corpus Christi College, MS 465, third quarter of 13th century.

Modern edition: J. B. L. Tolhurst (ed.), *The Customary of the Cathedral Priory Church of Norwich* (Henry Bradshaw Society, 82; 1948).

Tolhurst dates the Calendar at the beginning of the manuscript to about 1280, but attributes the main text of the Customary to around 1260. Annotations and additions were made between about 1280 and 1380, implying that the text was still current at the time of copying of the Ordinal of St Mary's, York. The editor gives an account of the daily routine at the cathedral priory (pp. xxiii–xxvii) and a tabular *horarium* with annotations (pp. xxviii–xxxvi).

All the monastic foundations represented by the sources selected here are distinct, but Norwich is particular as one of the seven major Benedictine cathedral priories established in medieval England and promoted by the Normans. Here the prior was superior of the monastic community while the diocesan bishop (whether monk or secular cleric) was titular abbot. The presence of a diocesan bishop affected the conduct of the liturgy, but the principal observances were much the same as other monasteries.

The size of the monastic community was originally about sixty, and seems to have held up to fifty during the fourteenth century in spite of the Black Death, though it fell below forty in the sixteenth century. The basic structure of the church remains that founded by Bishop Hugh Losinga in 1096 and largely completed in the twelfth century: the present fabric within the cathedral may be different, but the space is the same as that occupied by the Benedictine monks.

The Norwich Customary is both more comprehensive than the Ordinal of St Mary's, York and more succinct. It contains both Temporale and Sanctorale (integrated within an ongoing sequence), but there is far less detail regarding both the content and conduct of the liturgy. The book is not very easy to use, and the principal features may usefully be noted:

Section (or specified information)	Source (folios)	Edition (pages)
1. Calendar	3–8^v	1–12
2. Integrated Temporale and Sanctorale	9–129^v	13–195
First and second weeks in Advent	9–10^v	13–16
Feasts from 6 to 21 December	10^v–16	16–23
Third and fourth weeks in Advent	16–17^v	24–6
Christmas Eve to Octave of Epiphany	17^v–33^v	26–49
Feasts from 14 January to 8 March	33^v–42^v	49–63
Ash Wednesday and Lent	42^v–49	63–72
Feasts from 12 March to 4 April	49–51	72–5
Palm Sunday to Second Sunday after Easter	51–72	76–103
Feasts from 14 April to 1 May	72–4	103–6
Rogationtide and Ascensiontide	74–8^v	106–12
Feasts from 3–26 May	78^v–82	112–18
Eve of Pentecost to Octave of Trinity	82–90	118–29
After the Octave of Trinity to end of week next before Advent	90–1, 91^v–93	130–1, 132–4
Feasts from 2–19 June	91–91^v	131–2
Feasts from 22 June to 30 November	93–131	135–98
Sunday before Advent	129^v	195
3. Miscellaneous		
Readings at meals and Collatio	131–2	198–9
Mandatum ceremonies	132–3	200–1
Prefaces at Mass and use of *Credo*	133–4	201–2

Office of Blessed Virgin Mary	134–6ᵛ	202–6
Processions at Office and before Mass	136ᵛ–142	206–12
Practical instructions relating to seasons and feasts	142–52	212–24
Blessings at Matins	152ᵛ–153ᵛ	224–6
4. Commune Sanctorum (Ordinal)	153ᵛ–159	226–35
5. Addenda Office in Holy Week and during Octave of Dedication	new 1–1ᵛ	236–8

In the edition there is an index of subjects, seasons, and feasts, but no index of texts.

The Ordinal of Barking Abbey (Nuns)

Manuscript source: Oxford, University College, MS 169, 1404.
Modern edition: J. B. L. Tolhurst (ed.), (with notes by L. McLachlan), *The Ordinale and Customary of the Benedictine Nuns of Barking Abbey* (2 vols., Henry Bradshaw Society, 65, 66; 1927–8).

The manuscript was presented to the abbey by Sibille Fenton (abbess, 1394–1419) in 1404. It is an important account of the way in which the liturgy was conducted in a convent of nuns, distinguishing those parts conducted by the community itself from those undertaken by the clerics who served them. Most of the details are concerned with conduct in choir (i.e. what concerns the nuns), and there is less information (especially in the Mass) about liturgical practice in the presbytery. The manuscript itself (fo. 219, edition p. 359) distinguishes the use of the Benedictine order of the Office, the first version of Jerome's Latin psalter (superseded by his second translation—the so-called 'Gallican' psalter—almost everywhere else by this time) and the Use of St Paul's, London (the local diocese) at Mass.

The remains of the monastic buildings are fragmentary, though a conjectural plan is printed in the survey of the Royal Commission on Historical Monuments (England, Essex, volume ii). The community was established in 975, but the church to which the Ordinal relates was built mostly in the later twelfth century. Of the houses of nuns it was second only to Shaftesbury in endowments. The convent survived until 1539 when there were over thirty nuns.

By comparison with the York and Norwich sources the Barking Ordinal is straightforward in layout, but the edition has no index of subjects, seasons, feasts, or texts.

SECTION	SOURCE (FOLIOS)	EDITION (PAGES)
Calendar	1–5^v	i. 1–10
(January to October)		
(November and December)	missing	i. 11–12 [reconstructed]
Temporale	7–100^v	i. 14–164
Sanctorale	101–208^v	ii. 165–346

The Antiphonal of the Cathedral Priory, Worcester

Manuscript source: Worcester Cathedral Library, MS F. 160, c.1230.

Modern facsimile: [L. McLachlan (ed.),] *Antiphonaire monastique, XIIIe siècle, Codex F. 160 de la Bibliothèque de la Cathédrale de Worcester*, (Paléographie Musicale, ser. i, vol. xii; Tournai, 1922).

The Worcester Antiphonal is perhaps the best-known medieval English monastic source. It is the most complete English source of monastic choral chant to have survived, and dates from the earlier part of the thirteenth century. The whole manuscript consists of more than an Antiphonal for the Office (there is a partial Gradual among other sections), but only the Antiphonal section is partly reproduced in the facsimile, some of it reordered. The contents are in some respects distinct, and scholars (including Dame Laurentia McLachlan) have argued that they represent an insular tradition antedating the influx of continental influence, monks, and liturgical books in the tenth and eleventh centuries. There is also evidence of later chant composition at Worcester: some groups of unique chants are written in modal sequences. The Antiphonal was copied at Worcester in about 1230.

Worcester's Anglo-Saxon character persisted after the Conquest, but the new church (begun 1084) was built in the massive Norman Romanesque style, and that in turn was largely displaced in the fourteenth-century rebuilding. The community expanded in the eleventh century from twelve to fifty monks during the abbacy of St Wulfstan (1062–95), and—in spite of a dip to thirty-seven in the late fourteenth

century (a feature in all communities at a time of virulent plague)—
remained at about forty-five during the fifteenth century and until the
dissolution. Like Norwich it was a cathedral priory and it is possible
that many of its customs were comparable if not identical.

Dame Laurentia's introduction to the facsimile edition is very full.
In addition to a comprehensive commentary on the manuscript, the
contents reproduced, and their context, there is also a transcription of
the Calendar (pp. 29–40) and a Tonary (pp. 126–54). Individual items
are indexed by type (pp. 156–80). Perhaps most useful for someone
approaching the source for the first time is the table of contents (pp. 14–
23) which lists all the observances with page references to the facsimile
together with a summary of choral chants included. (Rubrics commonly prescribe other chants to be used on each day in the Office.)

It is important to reiterate that the facsimile is not a complete
reproduction of the source, and that there is a certain amount of
reordering.

Section	Source (folio)	Facsimile (pages)
1. Calendar	147–8	1–3
2. Temporale		
Advent Sunday, Matins, end of fifth respond, to Trinity 25	2–95^v	4–191
Invitatory	96–9^v	192–9
3. Processional (Temporale)		
Advent to Rogationtide	100–15^v	200–31
4. Sanctorale		
St Andrew to St Clement (including *Magnificat* antiphons for the Blessed Virgin Mary *per annum*)	182–270 (245–245^v)	232–410 (360–1)
5. Commune Sanctorum	270–82^v	410–35
6. Office of the Dead	282^v–284^v	435–9
Magnificat tones	285^v–286	441–2
7. Hymnal	164^v–169^v	1★–11★
Chapters	170	12★

The facsimile omits all later additions (fos. 116–46^v), and also the
psalter (fos. 149 ff.) canticles (fos. 162 f.), litanies (fo. 163^v), *commendatio animae* (fo. 164), and collects (fos. 170^v ff.) from the original
Antiphonal, as well as the whole Gradual section (fos. 287 ff.).

Rites of Durham

Principal sources: Durham Cathedral Library, MS C. III. 23 (roll) *c.*1600.
  Durham University Library, MS Cosin B.II.11, *c.*1620.

Modern edition: J. T. Fowler (ed.), *Rites of Durham* (Surtees Society, 107;
  1902). This replaces an earlier version, also published by the Surtees
  Society in 1844.

By way of conclusion it may be of interest to refer to a group of
manuscripts that are not liturgical at all, but which include descriptions of
the cathedral priory at Durham, its life and liturgical customs just
before the dissolution. According to the inscription in the Cosin
manuscript, the 'rites of Durham' were first written down in 1593,
over fifty years after the dissolution of the monastery. In spite of the
time-lapse, the text (in English) is full of detail which conjures up
vivid images of the priory, and especially the interior of the church. It
also includes summary accounts of some of the ceremonies and
processions. The descriptions are interspersed with lists of monuments
and their inscriptions, but by sifting through it is possible to gain an
impression of English Benedictine life in the first half of the sixteenth
century.

Durham is the most imposing of the English cathedral priories, a
strong mass based on a Norman core, standing on the rocky promon-
tory above the River Wear and guarded by the bishop's castle. Much
of the monastic building has survived, as have the castle (now University
College) and surrounding medieval streets above the market place
(many of the houses are now part of the university). Valued in the
sixteenth century at a level comparable with Gloucester, Winchester,
and Worcester, the community included around seventy monks at the
high points (late thirteenth and mid-fifteenth centuries), but forty-five
to fifty seems to have been a norm. At the dissolution the number had
fallen to twenty-seven. The community maintained a Lady Chapel
with a choir of boys in the later Middle Ages: both this foundation
(which sang in the western galilee chapel) and the many organs are
described in *Rites of Durham*.

Appendices

APPENDIX 1

Important Features of the Liturgical Calendar

1.1 THE CYCLE OF THE TEMPORALE IN THE MEDIEVAL AND TRIDENTINE RITES

The list gives the main features of the Temporale, including the feasts of saints in the week of Christmas generally found in the Temporale section of liturgical books. Those in capitals were observed as principal feasts (or solemn days in Holy Week). The Latin title of a saint's day is in the genitive and assumes an unwritten phrase such as 'In festo . . .' (On the feast of . . .).

Season or Feast	Typical Latin Title	Period or Date
Advent	Adventus	Four Sundays before Christmas
CHRISTMAS	IN NATIVITATE DOMINI	25 December
Feasts within the Octave of Christmas:		
St Stephen, first Martyr	S. Stephani protomartyris	26 December
St John, Apostle and Evangelist	S. Joannis apostoli et evangelistae	27 December
Holy Innocents	Sanctorum Innocentium	28 December
St Thomas of Canterbury, Bishop and Martyr	S. Thomae episcopi et martyris	29 December
	Sexta die post nativitatem	30 December
St Silvester, Pope and Confessor	S. Silvestri papae et confessoris	31 December
Circumcision	In circumcisione domini	1 January
Octaves of Christmas week feasts		2–4 January

Season or Feast	Typical Latin Title	Period or Date
EPIPHANY	IN EPIPHANIA DOMINI	6 January
Sunday within the Octave of Epiphany	Dominica infra octavam epiphaniae	Omitted if the Octave falls on Sunday
Sundays after the Octave of Epiphany	Dominicae post octavam epiphaniae	Variable: None if Easter falls between 22 and 24 March; never more than five.
Septuagesima	Dominica in septuagesima	Nine weeks before Easter; seven weeks before Passiontide. The beginning of the penitential season
Quinquagesima	Dominica in quinquagesima	Eight weeks before Easter
Sexagesima	Dominica in sexagesima	Seven weeks before Easter
Ash Wednesday	Feria quarta cinerum	The beginning of Lent
Lent	Tempus quadragesimae	
Passion Sunday	Dominica passionis	The fifth Sunday of Lent, the beginning of Passiontide
Holy Week:	Major hebdomada:	Week before Easter
PALM SUNDAY	DOMINICA IN RAMIS PALMARUM	
MAUNDY THURSDAY	FERIA V IN CENA DOMINI	
GOOD FRIDAY	FERIA VI IN PARASCEVE	
HOLY SATURDAY	SABBATUM SANCTUM	
EASTER DAY	DOMINICA RESURRECTIONIS	Eastertide begins
Octave of Easter	Dominica in albis	First Sunday after Easter
Sundays after Easter	Dominicae post pascha	Second to fifth Sundays after Easter
ASCENSION DAY	IN ASCENSIONE DOMINI	Thursday; forty days after Easter
Sunday after Ascension	Dominica infra octavam ascensionis	Last Sunday in Eastertide

Season or Feast	Typical Latin Title	Period or Date
PENTECOST (WHITSUN)	DOMINICA PENTECOSTES	Fifty days (seven weeks) after Easter
TRINITY SUNDAY [from 1334]	DOMINICA TRINITATIS	Sunday after Pentecost
CORPUS CHRISTI [from 1264]	CORPUS CHRISTI	Thursday following
Sunday within the Octave of Corpus Christi	Dominica infra octavam corporis Christi	Second Sunday after Pentecost
Sundays after Octave of Corpus Christi	Dominicae post octavam corporis Christi	Variable: twenty-one when Easter falls on 24 or 25 April; twenty-six if it falls between 22 and 26 March

Some Calendars count from Trinity rather than from Pentecost. Therefore the fifth Sunday after Pentecost is the fourth Sunday after Trinity; but the fourth Sunday after the *Octave* of Pentecost is also the fourth Sunday after Trinity.

The Sundays in the periods after the Octave of Epiphany and after the Octave of Corpus Christi are often referred to as *per annum* (Sundays of the Year).

1.2 MAJOR FEASTS OF THE SANCTORALE IN THE MEDIEVAL AND TRIDENTINE RITES

Scarcely any calendars of saints are identical, and it is impossible to reflect the variety. Nevertheless the feasts listed below are generally prominent in all calendars. Those shown in capitals were observed as principal feasts throughout the West in the Middle Ages and in the Tridentine Rite. The Latin title of a saint's day assumes the prefix 'In festo . . .' and is therefore in the genitive, except where the intention is more specific (e.g. Conversio Sancti Pauli).

Month	Day	Typical Latin Title	English Translation
January	21	S. Agnetis virginis et martyris	St Agnes, Virgin and Martyr
	25	Conversio S. Pauli apostoli	Conversion of St Paul, Apostle
February	2	PURIFICATIO BEATAE MARIAE VIRGINIS	Purification of the Blessed Virgin Mary
	5	S. Agathae virginis et martyris	St Agatha, Virgin and Martyr
	22	Cathedra S. Petri	St Peter's Chair
	24	S. Matthiae apostoli	St Matthias, Apostle
March	25	ANNUNTIATIO BEATAE MARIAE VIRGINIS	Annunciation of the Blessed Virgin Mary
April	25	S. Marci evangelistae	St Mark, Evangelist
May	1	SS. Philippi et Jacobi apostolorum	St Philip and St James, Apostles
	3	Inventio S. Crucis	Invention (finding) of the Cross
June	11	S. Barnabae apostoli	St Barnabas, Apostle
	24	NATIVITAS S. JOANNIS BAPTISTAE	Nativity of St John Baptist
	29	SS. PETRI ET PAULI APOSTOLORUM	St Peter and St Paul, Apostles
	30	Commemoratio S. Pauli	Commemoration of St Paul
July	22	S. Mariae Magdalenae	St Mary Magdalen
	25	S. Jacobi apostoli	St James, Apostle
August	1	S. Petri ad vincula	St Peter's Chains
	6	Transfiguratio domini nostri Jesu Christi	Transfiguration of our Lord [from 1457]
	10	S. Laurentii martyris	St Laurence, Martyr
	15	ASSUMPTIO BEATAE MARIAE VIRGINIS	Assumption of the Blessed Virgin Mary
	24	S. Bartholomaei apostoli	St Bartholomew, Apostle
	28	S. Augustini episcopi	St Augustine (of Hippo), Bishop
	29	Decollatio S. Joannis Baptistae	Beheading of St John Baptist

Month	Day	Typical Latin Title	English Translation
September	8	NATIVITAS BEATAE MARIAE VIRGINIS	Nativity of the Blessed Virgin Mary
	14	Exaltatio S. Crucis	Exaltation of the Cross
	21	S. Matthaei apostoli et evangelistae	St Matthew, Apostle and Evangelist
	29	S. Michaelis archangeli	St Michael, Archangel
October	18	S. Lucae evangelistae	St Luke, Evangelist
	28	SS. Simonis et Judae apostolorum	St Simon and St Jude, Apostles
November	1	OMNIUM SANCTORUM	All Saints
	2	Commemoratio omnium fidelium defunctorum	Commemoration of All Souls (not always noted in Calendars written before c. 1350, but observed from the eleventh century)
	9	S. Martini episcopi et confessoris	St Martin, Bishop and Confessor
	25	S. Katherinae virginis et martyris	St Catherine, Virgin and Martyr
	30	S. Andreae apostoli	St Andrew, Apostle
December	6	S. Nicholai episcopi et confessoris	St Nicholas, Bishop and Confessor
	8	CONCEPTIO BEATAE MARIAE VIRGINIS	Conception of the Blessed Virgin Mary
	21	S. Thomae apostoli	St Thomas, Apostle

Feasts during the week after Christmas Day are listed above in the cycle of the Temporale.

APPENDIX 2

The Psalter

Columns one and two give the Latin (Vulgate) and Hebrew (used in the Book of Common Prayer) numberings; where a psalm is sung in two parts in some Uses (e.g. monastic) it is numbered *a* and *b*. Column three gives the textual incipit; the roman numeral (e.g. [iii]) is often used in sources to distinguish psalms with the same opening words; the arabic numeral (e.g. 20)) identifies the verse of a new part. Columns four and five identify the day, the Office, and the place in the sequence of a group of psalms at which a psalm is recited; those used every day are shown as 'all'; the additional psalms at Prime on Sunday are lettered *a*★–*f*★; in secular Uses psalms (other than 118) are recited complete; Psalm 118 is recited in eight-verse units in monastic Use and sixteen-verse units in secular Use (identified as *a* and *b*).

Number		Textual Incipit	Place in Ferial Psalter	
Latin	Hebrew		Monastic	Secular
1	1	Beatus vir [i] qui non abiit	Monday Prime 1	Sunday Matins 1
2	2	Quare fremuerunt gentes	Monday Prime 2	Sunday Matins 2
3	3	Domine quid multiplicati	all Matins Introductory	Sunday Matins 3
4	4	Cum invocarem	all Compline 1	all Compline 1
5	5	Verba mea auribus percipe	Monday Lauds 3	Monday Lauds 2
6	6	Domine ne in furore [i] . . . miserere	Monday Prime 3	Sunday Matins 4
7	7	Domine deus meus	Tuesday Prime 1	Sunday Matins 5
8	8	Domine dominus noster	Tuesday Prime 2	Sunday Matins 6
9a	9	Confitebor tibi [i] . . . in toto corde	Tuesday Prime 3	Sunday Matins 7
9b		Exsurge domine (20)	Wednesday Prime 1	
	10	Ut quid domine (v. 22 of Latin Psalm 9)		
10	11	In domino confido	Wednesday Prime 2	Sunday Matins 8
11	12	Salvum me fac (i) domine	Wednesday Prime 3	Sunday Matins 9
12	13	Usquequo domine	Thursday Prime 1	Sunday Matins 10
13	14	Dixit insipiens [i] . . . sepulchrum	Thursday Prime 2	Sunday Matins 11
14	15	Domine quis habitabit	Thursday Prime 3	Sunday Matins 12
15	16	Conserva me domine	Friday Prime 1	Sunday Matins 13
16	17	Exaudi domine	Friday Prime 2	Sunday Matins 14
17a	18	Diligam te domine	Friday Prime 3	Sunday Matins 15
17b		Cum sancto sanctus (26)	Saturday Prime 1	
18	19	Caeli enarrant	Saturday Prime 2	Sunday Matins 16
19	20	Exaudiat te dominus	Saturday Prime 3	Sunday Matins 17
20	21	Domine in virtute tua	Sunday Matins 1	Sunday Matins 18

| Number | | Textual Incipit | Place in Ferial Psalter | |
Latin	Hebrew		Monastic	Secular
21	22	Deus deus meus [i] respice	Sunday Matins 2	Sunday Prime a★
22	23	Dominus regit me	Sunday Matins 3	Sunday Prime b★
23	24	Domini est terra	Sunday Matins 4	Sunday Prime c★
24	25	Ad te domine levavi	Sunday Matins 5	Sunday Prime d★
25	26	Judica me [i] domine	Sunday Matins 6	Sunday Prime e★
26	27	Dominus illuminatio mea	Sunday Matins 7	Monday Matins 1
27	28	Ad te domine clamabo	Sunday Matins 8	Monday Matins 2
28	29	Afferte domino	Sunday Matins 9	Monday Matins 3
29	30	Exaltabo te [i] domine	Sunday Matins 10	Monday Matins 4
30	31	In te domine speravi [i] . . . libera me	Sunday Matins 11	Monday Matins 5
30a		In te domine (1–6 only)		all Compline 2
31	32	Beati quorum remissae sunt	Sunday Matins 12	Monday Matins 6
32	33	Exsultate justi	Monday Matins 1	Monday Matins 7
33	34	Benedicam dominum	Monday Matins 2	Monday Matins 8
34	35	Judica domine	Monday Matins 3	Monday Matins 9
35	36	Dixit iniustus	Monday Lauds 4	Monday Matins 10
36a	37	Noli aemulari	Monday Matins 4	Monday Matins 11
36b		Declina a malo (27)	Monday Matins 5	
37	38	Domine ne in furore [ii] . . . quoniam	Monday Matins 6	Monday Matins 12
38	39	Dixi custodiam	Monday Matins 7	Tuesday Matins 1
39	40	Exspectans exspectavi	Monday Matins 8	Tuesday Matins 2
40	41	Beatus qui intelligit	Monday Matins 9	Tuesday Matins 3

41	42	Quemadodum desiderat	Monday Matins 10	Tuesday Matins 4
42	43	Judica me [ii] deus	Tuesday Lauds 3	Tuesday Lauds 2
43	44	Deus auribus	Monday Matins 11	Tuesday Matins 5
44	45	Eructavit cor meum	Monday Matins 12	Tuesday Matins 6
45	46	Deus noster refugium	Tuesday Matins 1	Tuesday Matins 7
46	47	Omnes gentes plaudite	Tuesday Matins 2	Tuesday Matins 8
47	48	Magnus dominus	Tuesday Matins 3	Tuesday Matins 9
48	49	Audite haec omnes	Tuesday Matins 4	Tuesday Matins 10
49	50	Deus deorum	Tuesday Matins 5	Tuesday Matins 11
50	51	Miserere mei deus [i] secundum	all Lauds 2	Mon.–Sat. Lauds 1
51	52	Quid gloriaris	Tuesday Matins 6	Tuesday Matins 12
52	53	Dixit insipiens [ii] . . . nonne scient	Tuesday Matins 7	Wednesday Matins 1
53	54	Deus in nomine	Tuesday Matins 8	all Prime 1
54	55	Exaudi deus [i] . . . intende	Tuesday Matins 9	Wednesday Matins 2
55	56	Miserere mei deus [ii] quoniam	Tuesday Matins 10	Wednesday Matins 3
56	57	Miserere mei deus [iii] miserere	Tuesday Lauds 4	Wednesday Matins 4
57	58	Si vere utique	Tuesday Matins 11	Wednesday Matins 5
58	59	Eripe me [i] de inimicis meis	Tuesday Matins 12	Wednesday Matins 6
59	60	Deus repulisti nos	Wednesday Matins 1	Wednesday Matins 7
60	61	Exaudi deus [ii] deprecationem	Wednesday Matins 2	Wednesday Matins 8
61	62	Nonne deo	Wednesday Matins 3	Wednesday Matins 9
62	63	Deus deus meus [ii] ad te	Sunday Lauds 4	all Lauds 3
63	64	Exaudi deus [iii] . . . a timore	Wednesday Lauds 3	Wednesday Lauds 2
64	65	Te decet hymnus	Wednesday Lauds 4	Wednesday Matins 11
65	66	Jubilate deo [i] . . . psalmum	Wednesday Matins 4	

| Number | | Textual Incipit | Place in Ferial Psalter | |
Latin	Hebrew		Monastic	Secular
66	67	Deus misereatur nostri	all Lauds 1	all Lauds 4
67a	68	Exsurgat deus	Wednesday Matins 5	Wednesday Matins 12
67b		Benedictus dominus [i] die quotidie (20)	Wednesday Matins 6	
68a	69	Salvum me fac [ii] deus	Wednesday Matins 7	Thursday Matins 1
68b		Exaudi me domine (17)	Wednesday Matins 8	
69	70	Deus in adiutorium	Wednesday Matins 9	Thursday Matins 2
70	71	In te domine speravi [ii] . . . et eripe	Wednesday Matins 10	Thursday Matins 3
71	72	Deus judicium tuum	Wednesday Matins 11	Thursday Matins 4
72	73	Quam bonus Israel deus	Wednesday Matins 12	Thursday Matins 5
73	74	Ut quid deus repulisti	Thursday Matins 1	Thursday Matins 6
74	75	Confitebimur tibi	Thursday Matins 2	Thursday Matins 7
75	76	Notus in Judaea	Friday Friday 3	Thursday Matins 8
76	77	Voce mea ad dominum [i] . . . et intendit	Thursday Matins 3	Thursday Matins 9
77a	78	Attendite popule	Thursday Matins 4	Thursday Matins 10
77b		Et dilexerunt (36)	Thursday Matins 5	
78	79	Deus venerunt	Thursday Matins 6	Thursday Matins 11
79	80	Qui regis Israel	Thursday Matins 7	Thursday Matins 12
80	81	Exsultate deo	Thursday Matins 8	Friday Matins 1

81	Deus stetit in synagoga	Thursday Matins 9	Friday Matins 2
82	Deus quis similis	Thursday Matins 10	Friday Matins 3
83	Quam dilecta	Thursday Matins 11	Friday Matins 4
84	Benedixisti domine	Thursday Matins 12	Friday Matins 5
85	Inclina domine aurem tuam	Friday Matins 1	Friday Matins 6
86	Fundamenta eius	Friday Matins 2	Friday Matins 7
87	Domine deus salutis meae	Thursday Lauds 3	Friday Matins 8
88a	Misericordias domini	Friday Matins 3	Friday Matins 9
88b	Tunc locutus (20)	Friday Matins 4	
89	Domine refugium factus es	Thursday Lauds 4	Thursday Lauds 2
90	Qui habitat in adiutorio	all Compline 2	all Compline 3
91	Bonum est confiteri	Friday Lauds 4	Saturday Lauds 2
92	Dominus regnavit [i] decorem	Friday Matins 5	Sunday Lauds 1
93	Deus ultionum	Friday Matins 6	Friday Matins 10
94	Venite exsultemus	all Matins Invitatory	all Matins Invitatory
95	Cantate domino [i] . . . cantate	Friday Matins 7	Friday Matins 11
96	Dominus regnavit [ii] exsultet terra	Friday Matins 8	Friday Matins 12
97	Cantate domino [ii] . . . quia mirabilia	Friday Matins 9	Saturday Matins 1
98	Dominus regnavit [iii] irascantur	Friday Matins 10	Saturday Matins 2
99	Jubilate deo [ii] . . . servite	Friday Matins 11	Saturday Matins 3 / Sunday Lauds 2
100	Misericordiam et judicium	Friday Matins 12	Saturday Matins 4
101	Domine exaudi [ii] . . . et clamor meus	Saturday Matins 1	Saturday Matins 5
102	Benedic anima mea [i] . . . et omnia	Saturday Matins 2	Saturday Matins 6
103a	Benedic anima mea [ii] . . . domine	Saturday Matins 3	Saturday Matins 7
103b	Hoc Mare (25)	Saturday Matins 4	
104a	Confitemini domino [i] et invocate	Saturday Matins 5	Saturday Matins 8
104b	Et intravit (23)	Saturday Matins 6	

Number		Textual Incipit	Place in Ferial Psalter	
Latin	Hebrew		Monastic	Secular
105a	106	Confitemini domino [ii] . . . quis loquetur	Saturday Matins 7	Saturday Matins 9
105b		Et irritaverunt (32)	Saturday Matins 8	
106a	107	Confitemini domino [iii] . . . dicant qui	Saturday Matins 9	Saturday Matins 10
106b		Dixit et stetit (25)	Saturday Matins 10	
107	108	Paratum cor meum	Saturday Matins 11	Saturday Matins 11
108	109	Deus laudem meam	Saturday Matins 12	Saturday Matins 12
109	110	Dixit dominus	Sunday Vespers 1	Sunday Vespers 1
110	111	Confitebor tibi [ii] . . . in consilio	Sunday Vespers 2	Sunday Vespers 2
111	112	Beatus vir [ii] qui timet	Sunday Vespers 3	Sunday Vespers 3
112	113	Laudate pueri	Sunday Vespers 4	Sunday Vespers 4
113	114	In exitu Israel	Monday Vespers 1	Sunday Vespers 5
	115	Non nobis domine		
114	116	Dilexi quoniam	Monday Vespers 2	Monday Vespers 1
115		Credidi	Monday Vespers 3a	Monday Vespers 2
116	117	Laudate dominum [i] omnes gentes	Monday Vespers 3b	Monday Vespers 3
117	118	Confitemini domino [iv] . . . dicat nunc	Sunday Lauds 3	Sunday Prime f★
118	119	Beati immaculati (1)	Sunday Prime 1	all Prime 2a
		In quo corrigit (9)	Sunday Prime 2	all Prime 2b
		Retribue servo tuo (17)	Sunday Prime 3	all Prime 3a
		Adhaesit pavimento (25)	Sunday Prime 4	all Prime 3b
		Legem pone (33)	Sunday Terce 1	all Terce 1a
		Et veniat super me (41)	Sunday Terce 2	all Terce 1b

Subdivisions of psalms are identified by number and verse (e.g. 118 (25)). As in section 2.1 above, roman numerals in the incipit are introduced to identify separate psalms with identical opening words: they are commonly identified in this way in sources (e.g. Confitemini iv).

Textual Incipit	Psalm Number (verse)
Ad dominum cum tribularer	119
Ad te domine clamabo	27
Ad te domine levavi	24
Ad te levavi oculos	122
Adhaesit pavimento	118 (25)
Afferte domino	28
Appropinquet deprecatio	118 (169)
Attendite popule	77
Audite haec omnes	48
Beati immaculati	118 (1)
Beati omnes	127
Beati quorum remissae sunt	31
Beatus qui intelligit	40
Beatus vir [i] qui non abiit	1
Beatus vir [ii] qui timet	111
Benedicam dominum	33
Benedic anima mea [i] . . . et omnia	102
Benedic anima mea [ii] . . . domine	103
Benedictus dominus [ii] deus meus	143
Benedictus dominus [i] die quotidie	67 (20)
Benedixisti domine	84
Bonitatem fecisti	118 (65)
Bonum est confiteri domino	91
Caeli enarrant	18
Cantate domino [i] . . . cantate	95
Cantate domino [iii] . . . laus eius	149
Cantate domino [ii] . . . quia mirabilia	97
Clamavi in toto corde meo	118 (145)
Confiteantur	144 (10)
Confitebimur tibi	74
Confitebor tibi [ii] . . . in consilio	110
Confitebor tibi [i] . . . in toto corde	9
Confitebor tibi [iv] quia	138 (14)
Confitebor tibi [iii] . . . quoniam	137

Textual Incipit	Psalm Number (verse)
Confitemini domino [i] et invocate	104
Confitemini domino [v] . . . confitemini	135
Confitemini domino [iii] . . . dicant qui	106
Confitemini domino [iv] . . . dicat nunc	117
Confitemini domino [ii] . . . quis loquetur	105
Conserva me domine	15
Credidi	115
Cum invocarem	4
Cum sancto sanctus	17 (26)
De profundis	129
Declina a malo	36 (27)
Deficit in salutare	118 (81)
Deus auribus	43
Deus canticum novum	143 (9)
Deus deorum	49
Deus deus meus [ii] ad te	62
Deus deus meus [i] respice	21
Deus in adiutorium	69
Deus in nomine	53
Deus judicium tuum	71
Deus laudem meam	108
Deus misereatur nostri	66
Deus noster refugium	45
Deus quis similis	82
Deus repulisti nos	59
Deus stetit in synagoga	81
Deus ultionum	93
Deus venerunt	78
Dilexi quoniam	114
Diligam te domine	17
Dixi custodiam	38
Dixit dominus	109
Dixit et stetit	106 (25)
Dixit iniustus	35
Dixit insipiens [ii] . . . nonne scient	52
Dixit insipiens [i] . . . sepulchrum	13
Domine clamavi ad te	140
Domine deus meus	7
Domine deus salutis meae	87
Domine dominus noster	8

Textual Incipit	Psalm Number (verse)
Domine exaudi [ii] . . . auribus	142
Domine exaudi [i] . . . et clamor meus	101
Domine in virtute tua	20
Domine ne in furore [i] . . . miserere	6
Domine ne in furore [ii] . . . quoniam	37
Domine non est exaltatum	130
Domine probasti me	138
Domine quid multiplicati	3
Domine quis habitabit	14
Domine refugium factus es	89
Domini est terra	23
Dominus illuminatio mea	26
Dominus regit me	22
Dominus regnavit [i] decorem	92
Dominus regnavit [ii] exsultet terra	96
Dominus regnavit [iii] irascantur populi	98
Ecce nunc benedicite	133
Ecce quam bonum	132
Eripe me [i] de inimicis meis	58
Eripe me [ii] domine	139
Eructavit cor meum	44
Et dilexerunt	77 (36)
Et intravit	104 (23)
Et irritaverunt	105 (32)
Et veniat super me	118 (41)
Exaltabo te [ii] deus	144
Exaltabo te [i] domine	29
Exaudi deus [iii] . . . a timore	63
Exaudi deus [i] . . . intende	54
Exaudi deus [ii] deprecationem	60
Exaudi domine	16
Exaudi me domine	68 (17)
Exaudiat te dominus	19
Exspectans exspectavi	39
Exsurgat deus	67
Exsultate deo	80
Exsultate justi	32
Feci judicium	118 (121)
Fundamenta eius	86
Hoc mare	103 (25)

Textual Incipit	Psalm Number (verse)
In aeternum domine	118 (89)
In convertendo	125
In domino confido	10
In exitu Israel	113
In quo corrigit	118 (9)
In te domine speravi [ii] . . . et eripe	70
In te domine speravi [i] . . . libera me	30
Inclina domine aurem tuam	85
Iniquos odio habui	118 (113)
Jubilate deo [i] . . . psalmum	65
Jubilate deo [ii] . . . servite	99
Judica domine	34
Judica me [ii] deus	42
Judica me [i] domine	25
Justus es domine	118 (137)
Laetatus sum	121
Lauda anima mea	145
Lauda Jerusalem	147
Laudate dominum [iii] de caelis	148
Laudate dominum [iv] in sanctis	150
Laudate dominum [i] omnes gentes	116
Laudate dominum [ii] quoniam	146
Laudate nomen	134
Laudate pueri	112
Legem pone	118 (33)
Levavi oculos meos	120
Lucerna pedibus meis	118 (105)
Magnus dominus	47
Manus tuae fecerunt me	118 (73)
Memento domine David	131
Memor esto verbi tui	118 (49)
Mirabilia testimonia	118 (129)
Miserere mei deus [iii] miserere	56
Miserere mei deus [ii] quoniam	55
Miserere mei deus [i] secundum	50
Misericordiam et judicium	100
Misericordias domini	88
Nisi dominus aedificaverit	126
Nisi quia dominus	123
Noli aemulari	36

Textual Incipit	Psalm Number (verse)
Nonne deo	61
Notus in Judaea	75
Omnes gentes plaudite	46
Paratum cor meum	107
Portio mea domine	118 (57)
Principes persecuti sunt	118 (161)
Quam bonus Israel deus	72
Quam dilecta	83
Quare fremuerunt gentes	2
Quemadmodum desiderat	41
Qui confidunt	124
Qui habitat in adiutorio	90
Qui regis Israel	79
Quid gloriaris	51
Quomodo dilexi	118 (97)
Retribue servo tuo	118 (17)
Salvum me fac [ii] deus	68
Salvum me fac [i] domine	11
Saepe expugnaverunt	128
Si vere utique	57
Super flumina Babylonis	136
Te decet hymnus	64
Tunc locutus	88 (20)
Ut quid deus repulisti	73
Usquequo domine	12
Venite exsultemus	94
Verba mea auribus percipe	5
Vide humilitatem	118 (153)
Voce mea ad dominum [ii] . . . deprecatus	141
Voce mea ad dominum [i] . . . et intendit	76

2.3 Variable Canticles

Monastic Matins of Twelve Lessons: Lesser Canticles Sung in the Third Nocturn

Individual monasteries did not necessarily follow the same scheme in the Middle Ages. The canticles shown below represent a consensus from English medieval houses based on the researches of J. B. L. Tolhurst. A fuller list (with more variants) may be found in his edition of *The Monastic Breviary of Hyde Abbey* (1932–42), vi, 182–4.

Sundays *per annum*

Domine miserere nostri	Isaiah 33: 2–10
Audite qui longe estis	Isaiah 33: 13–18
Miserere domine plebi tuae	Ecclesiasticus 36: 14–19

Sundays in Advent

Ecce dominus in fortitudine	Isaiah 40: 10–17
Cantate domino canticum	Isaiah 42: 10–16
Haec dicit dominus redemptor Israel	Isaiah 49: 8–13

Christmas

Populus qui ambulat	Isaiah 9: 2–7
Laetare Jerusalem	based on Isaiah 66: 10–16
Urbs fortitudinis	Isaiah 26: 1–12

Sundays in Lent (often from Septuagesima)

Deducant oculi mei	Jeremiah 14: 17–21
Recordare domine	Lamentations 5: 1–7, 15–17, 19–21
Tollam quippe vos	Ezekiel 36: 24–8

Feasts of Apostles, Martyrs, Confessors

Vos sancti domini   Isaiah 61: 6–9
Fulgebunt justi   Wisdom of Solomon 3: 7–9
Reddet deus mercedem   Wisdom of Solomon 10: 17–20

Feast of One Martyr or Confessor

Beatus vir qui in sapientia   Ecclesiasticus 14: 22; 15: 3–4, 6
Beatus vir qui confidit   Jeremiah 17: 7–8
Beatus vir qui inventus   Ecclesiasticus 31: 8–11

Feast of Virgins

Audite me divini fructus   Ecclesiasticus 39: 17–21
Gaudens gaudebo   Isaiah 61: 10 to 62: 3
Non vocaberis ultra   Isaiah 62: 4–7

Lauds (Monastic and Secular): Lesser Canticle sung before 'Laudate' Psalms

Sunday	Benedicite omnia opera	Daniel 3: 57–88, 56
Monday	Confitebor tibi domine	Isaiah 12: 1–6
Tuesday	Ego dixi in dimidio	Isaiah 38: 10–20
Wednesday	Exsultavit cor meum	1 Samuel 2: 1–10
Thursday	Cantemus domino	Exodus 15: 1–19
Friday	Domine audivi	Habakkuk 3: 1–19
Saturday	Secular:	
	Audite caeli quae loquor	Deuteronomy 32: 1–43
	Monastic:	
	(1) Audite caeli	Deuteronomy 32: 1–21
	(2) Ignis succensus est	Deuteronomy 32: 22–43

On feast-days *Benedicite* was sung (with Sunday psalms).

2.4 WEEKLY CYCLE OF PSALMS

Ferial Psalter (Secular)

Office	Day	Psalms
Matins	Sunday	94; 1–3, 6–20
	Monday	94; 26–37
	Tuesday	94; 38–41, 43–49, 51
	Wednesday	94; 52, 54–61, 63, 65, 67
	Thursday	94; 68–79
	Friday	94; 80–88, 93, 95–96
	Saturday	94; 97–108
Lauds	Sunday	92, 99, 62 with 66, *Benedicite*, 148–150
	Weekdays	50, [variable psalm], 62 with 66, Canticle, 148–150
	Variable:	Mon. 5, Tue. 42, Wed. 64, Thu. 89, Fri. 142, Sat. 91
Prime★	Sunday	21–25, 53, 117, 118 (1–32), *Quicumque vult*
	Weekdays	53, 118 (1–32), *Quicumque vult*
Terce	Daily	118 (33–80)
Sext	Daily	118 (81–128)
None	Daily	118 (129–76)
Vespers	Sunday	109–113
	Monday	114–116, 119, 120
	Tuesday	121–125
	Wednesday	126–130
	Thursday	131–32, 134–136
	Friday	137–141
	Saturday	143–147
Compline	Daily	4, 30 (1–6), 90, 133

★ After the sixteenth-century reform of the Roman Breviary, the Psalms at Prime were redistributed: in between Psalms 53 and 118 (1–32) one additional psalm was recited (except on Saturday): Sunday 117, Monday 23, Tuesday 24, Wednesday 25, Thursday 22, Friday 21. The whole *cursus* of Office psalms was revised under Pope Pius X in 1911.

Ferial Psalter (Monastic)

Office	Day	Psalms
Matins	Sunday	3, 94; 20–31
	Monday	3, 94; 32–34, 36*a*, 36*b*, 37–41, 43, 44
	Tuesday	3, 94; 45–49, 51, 52–55, 57–58
	Wednesday	3, 94; 59–61, 65, 67*a*, 67*b*, 68*a*, 68*b*, 69–72
	Thursday	3, 94; 73–74, 76, 77*a*, 77*b*, 78–84
	Friday	3, 94; 85–86, 88*a*, 88*b*, 92–93, 95–100
	Saturday	3, 94; 101–102, 103*a*, 103*b*, 104*a*, 104*b*, 105*a*, 105*b*, 106*a*, 106*b*, 107–108
Lauds	Daily	66, 50, [2 variable psalms], Canticle, 148–150
	Variable psalms:	Sun. 117, 62; Mon. 5, 35; Tue. 42, 56; Wed. 63, 64; Thu. 87, 89; Fri. 75, 91; Sat. 142
Prime	Sunday	118 (1–32)
	Monday	1, 2, 6
	Tuesday	7, 8, 9*a*
	Wednesday	9*b*, 10, 11
	Thursday	12, 13, 14
	Friday	15, 16, 17*a*
	Saturday	17*b*, 18, 19
Terce	Sunday	118 (33–56)
	Monday	118 (105–128)
	Tuesday to Saturday	119, 120, 121
Sext	Sunday	118 (57–80)
	Monday	118 (129–152)
	Tuesday to Saturday	122, 123, 124
None	Sunday	118 (81–104)
	Monday	118 (153–176)
	Tuesday to Saturday	125, 126, 127
Vespers	Sunday	109–112
	Monday	113–114, 115 with 116, 128
	Tuesday	129–132
	Wednesday	134–137
	Thursday	138*a*, 138*b*, 139, 140
	Friday	141, 143*a*, 143*b*, 144*a*
	Saturday	144*b*, 145–147
Compline	Daily	4, 90, 133

2.5. A Selection of Proper Psalms for Feast-days

In addition to proper antiphons, specific series of psalms were used on certain feast-days at the Office. A selection of some series that were used more frequently is listed below: those from the Commune Sanctorum evidently had long-established roots to be so standardized. The two individual feasts show a marked difference: the feast of Corpus Christi, a 'new' thirteenth-century feast, has a largely consistent pattern of psalmody, while the feast celebrating the Dedication of a Church shows greatest local variety. The selection demonstrates how individual Uses and foundations often had their own specific sequences: they show common patterns but with distinct

---

Proper Psalms (Secular)

Key: E English (i.e. Hereford, Salisbury, and York)
　　　H Hereford (Breviary)
　　　R Roman (1522 and Tridentine Breviaries)
　　　S Salisbury (Breviary)
　　　Y York (Breviary)

Matins

Apostle	18, 33, 44	46, 60, 63	74, 96, 98 (E, R)
Martyr	1, 2, 3	4, 5, 8	10, 14, 20 (E, R)
Confessor	1, 2, 3	4, 5, 8	14, 20, 23 (E, R)
Virgin	8, 18, 23	44, 45, 86	95, 96, 97, (E)
	8, 18, 23	44, 45, 47	95, 96, 97 (R)
Virgin Mary	8, 18, 23	44, 45, 86	95, 96, 97 (E, R)
Dedication	23, 45, 47	83, 86, 87	90, 95, 98 (R)
	23, 45, 47	83, 84, 86	87, 90, 95 (Y)
	23, 45, 47	83, 84, 86	90, 95, 96, (H, S)
Corpus Christi	1, 4, 15	19, 22, 41	42, 80, 83, (E, R)

variants. Greatest variety is found in the monastic sequences, where Matins
has a common core related to secular Use but with varying additions, and
Vespers tends to include differing selections from the secular group.

In a number of Breviaries the sequence is taken for granted: the incipit of
the first psalm may be given, or else an indication of the series (e.g. *de dominica*
or *dominicales* for Sunday series, or *de domina* for the Blessed Virgin Mary).
The principal hours to be affected are Matins and Vespers: at Lauds it was
usual to use the Sunday sequence of psalms with *Benedicite*.

Proper Psalms (Monastic)

Key: HW   Hyde Abbey, Winchester, *c.*1300 (Breviary)
      N   Norwich Cathedral Priory, *c.*1260 (Customary)
      SMY   St Mary's Abbey, York, *c.*1400 (Ordinal)

The Ordinal of St Mary's, York, lacks Commune Sanctorum, and the
Norwich Customary lacks Corpus Christi and Dedication.

Matins

Apostle	18, 21, 31, 33, 44, 46	60, 63, 64, 74, 96, 98 (HW)
	18, 33, 34, 46, 60, 63	74, 95, 96, 97, 98, 100 (N)
Martyr	1, 2, 4, 5, 8, 10	14, 20, 23, 63, 64, 91 (HW)
	1, 2, 4, 5, 8, 10	14, 20, 63, 64, 91, 96 (N)
Confessor	1, 2, 4, 5, 8, 10	14, 20, 23, 95, 96, 97 (HW, N)
Virgin	8, 18, 23, 44, 45, 47	84, 86, 95, 96, 97, 98 (HW, N)
Virgin Mary	8, 18, 23, 44, 45, 47	84, 86, 95, 96, 97, 98 (HW, N)
Dedication	23, 26, 43, 45, 47, 64	83, 86, 87, 90, 95, 96 (HW)
	10, 23, 25, 28, 45, 47	64, 83, 86, 87, 90, 95 (SMY)
Corpus Christi	1, 4, 5, 15, 19, 22	41, 42, 80, 83, 101, 103 (HW)
	1, 4, 15, 19, 22, 41	42, 80, 83, 101, 103, 104 (SMY)

Secular

Vespers

Dominicales	109, 110, 111, 112, 113 (E, R)
Laudate	112, 116, 145, 146, 147 (E, R most often at First Vespers)
Apostle	109, 110, 111, 112, 116 (R, First Vespers)
	109, 112, 115, 125, 138 (E, R, Second Vespers)
Virgin	109, 121, 126, 129, 131 (E, R)
Virgin Mary	109, 112, 121, 129, 131 (E)
	109, 112, 121, 126, 147 (R)
Dedication	109, 110, 111, 112, 147 (R)
	109, 121, 126, 146, 147 (H)
	115, 121, 126, 146, 147 (S)
	121, 124, 126, 137, 147 (Y, First Vespers)
	109, 121, 126, 131, 147 (Y, Second Vespers)
Corpus Christi	109, 110, 115, 127, 147 (E, R)

Monastic

Vespers

Dominicales	109, 110, 111, 112 (HW, N)
Apostle	109, 111, 112, 138 (HW, N)
Martyr	109, 111, 112, 115 (N)
Confessor	109, 111, 112, 115 (N)
Virgin	109, 121, 126, 129 (HW)
	109, 112, 121, 126 (N)
Virgin Mary	109, 121, 126, 131 (HW, N)
Dedication	121, 126, 146, 147 (H)
	121, 124, 126, 147, (SMY, First Vespers)
	109, 124, 126, 147 (SMY, Second Vespers)
Corpus Christi	109, 110, 115, 127 (HW)
	109, 110, 115, 147 (SMY)

2.6. The Distribution of the Psalter in the English Book of Common Prayer (following the Hebrew numbering)

The Monthly Cycle

Day	Mattins	Evensong	Day	Mattins	Evensong
1	1–5	6–8	16	79–81	82–85
2	9–11	12–14	17	86–88	89
3	15–17	18	18	90–92	93–94
4	19–21	22–23	19	95–97	98–101
5	24–26	27–29	20	102–103	104
6	30–31	32–34	21	105	106
7	35–36	37	22	107	108–109
8	38–40	41–43	23	110–113	114–115
9	44–46	47–49	24	116–118	119 (1–32)
10	50–52	53–55	25	119 (33–72)	119 (73–104)
11	56–58	59–61	26	119 (105–144)	119 (145–176)
12	62–64	65–67	27	120–125	126–131
13	68	69–70	28	132–135	136–138
14	71–72	73–74	29	139–141	142–143
15	75–77	78	30	144–146	147–150

Proper Psalms (1552)

Christmas Day   Mattins: 18, 45, 85   Evensong: 89, 110, 132
Easter Day   Mattins: 2, 57, 111   Evensong: 113, 114, 118
Ascension Day   Mattins: 8, 15, 21   Evensong: 24, 47, 108
Whit Sunday   Mattins: 48, 68   Evensong: 104, 145

In 1662 proper psalms were added for Ash Wednesday (6, 32, 38; 102, 130, 143) and Good Friday (22, 40, 54; 69, 88).

APPENDIX 3

Frequently Used Choral Texts in Latin and English

3.1. ORDINARY OF THE MASS

Kyrie

Kyrie eleison. Kyrie eleison. Kyrie eleison.
Christe eleison. Christe eleison. Christe eleison.
Kyrie eleison. Kyrie eleison. Kyrie eleison.

Gloria in excelsis

Gloria in excelsis deo. Et in terra pax hominibus bonae voluntatis. Laudamus te. Benedicimus te. Adoramus te. Glorificamus te. Gratias agimus tibi propter magnam gloriam tuam. Domine deus, rex caelestis, deus pater omnipotens. Domine fili unigenite Jesu Christe. Domine deus, agnus dei, filius patris. Qui tollis peccata mundi, miserere nobis. Qui tollis peccata mundi, suscipe deprecationem nostram. Qui sedes ad dexteram patris, miserere nobis. Quoniam tu solus sanctus. Tu solus dominus. Tu solus altissimus, Jesu Christe. Cum sancto spiritu, in gloria dei patris. Amen.

Credo in unum deum

Credo in unum deum, patrem omnipotentem, factorem caeli et terrae, visibilium omnium et invisibilium. Et in unum dominum Jesum Christum, filium dei unigenitum. Et ex patre natum ante omnia saecula. Deum de deo, lumen de lumine, deum verum de deo vero. Genitum, non factum, consubstantialem patri: per quem omnia facta sunt. Qui propter nos homines, et propter nostram salutem descendit de caelis. Et incarnatus est de spiritu sancto ex Maria virgine: et homo factus est. Crucifixus etiam pro nobis sub Pontio Pilato: passus, et sepultus est. Et resurrexit tertia die, secundum scripturas. Et ascendit in caelum: sedet ad dexteram patris. Et iterum venturus est cum gloria judicare vivos et mortuos: cuius regni non erit finis. Et in spiritum sanctum dominum, et vivificantem: qui ex patre, filioque

ORDINARY OF THE MASS

Kyrie

Lord have mercy. Lord have mercy. Lord have mercy.
Christ have mercy. Christ have mercy. Christ have mercy.
Lord have mercy. Lord have mercy. Lord have mercy.

Gloria in excelsis

Glory be to God on high, and in earth peace, good will towards men. We
praise thee, we bless thee, we worship thee, we glorify thee, we give thanks
to thee for thy great glory, O Lord God, heavenly King, God the Father
almighty. O Lord the only-begotten son Jesu Christ; O Lord God, Lamb of
God, Son of the Father, that takest away the sins of the world, have mercy
upon us. Thou that takest away the sins of the world, have mercy upon us.
Thou that takest away the sins of the world, receive our prayer. Thou that
sittest at the right hand of God the Father, have mercy upon us. For thou only
art holy; thou only art the Lord; thou only, O Christ, with the Holy Ghost,
art most high in the glory of God the Father. Amen.

Credo in unum deum

I believe in one God the Father almighty, maker of heaven and earth, and of
all things visible and invisible:

   And in one Lord Jesus Christ, the only-begotten Son of God, begotten of
his Father before all worlds, God of God, Light of Light, very God of very
God, begotten not made, being of one substance with the Father, by whom
all things were made; who for us men and for our salvation came down from
heaven, and was incarnate by the Holy Ghost of the Virgin Mary, and was
made man, and was crucified also for us under Pontius Pilate. He suffered and
was buried, and the third day he rose again according to the Scriptures, and
ascended into heaven, and sitteth on the right hand of the Father. And he shall
come again with glory to judge both the quick and the dead: whose kingdom
shall have no end.

   And I believe in the Holy Ghost, the Lord and giver of life, who proceedeth

procedit. Qui cum patre, et filio simul adoratur, et conglorificatur: qui locutus est per prophetas. Et unam, sanctam, catholicam et apostolicam ecclesiam. Confiteor unum baptisma in remissionem peccatorum. Et exspecto resurrectionem mortuorum. Et vitam venturi saeculi. Amen.

Sursum corda

v. Dominus vobiscum.   R. Et cum spiritu tuo.
v. Sursum corda.   R. Habemus ad dominum.
v. Gratias agamus domino deo nostro.   R. Dignum et justum est.

Sanctus and Benedictus

Sanctus, sanctus, sanctus dominus deus sabaoth. Pleni sunt caeli et terra gloria tua. Hosanna in excelsis.
Benedictus qui venit in nomine domini. Hosanna in excelsis.

Agnus dei

Agnus dei, qui tollis peccata mundi: miserere nobis.
Agnus dei, qui tollis peccata mundi: miserere nobis.
Agnus dei, qui tollis peccata mundi: dona nobis pacem.

Ite missa est

v. Dominus vobiscum.   R. Et cum spiritu tuo.
v. Ite missa est.   R. Deo gratias.

from the Father and the Son, who with the Father and the Son together is worshipped and glorified, who spake by the prophets. And I believe one catholic and apostolic church. I acknowledge one baptism for the remission of sins. And I look for the resurrection of the dead, and the life of the world to come. Amen.

Sursum corda

v.	The Lord be with you.	R.	And with thy spirit.
v.	Lift up your hearts.	R.	We lift them up unto the Lord.
v.	Let us give thanks to our Lord God.	R.	It is meet and right so to do.

Sanctus and Benedictus

Holy, holy, holy, Lord God of hosts, heaven and earth are full of thy glory: glory be to thee, O Lord most high.
Blessed is he that cometh in the name of the Lord: hosanna in the highest.

Agnus dei

O Lamb of God, that takest away the sins of the world, have mercy upon us.
O Lamb of God, that takest away the sins of the world, have mercy upon us.
O Lamb of God, that takest away the sins of the world, grant us thy peace.

Ite missa est

v.	The Lord be with you.	R.	And with thy spirit.
v.	Go, the mass is ended.	R.	Thanks be to God.

3.2. TEXTS FOR THE OFFICE

Te deum laudamus (Matins)

Te deum laudamus: te dominum confitemur. Te aeternum patrem omnis terra veneratur. Tibi omnes angeli, tibi caeli et universae potestates: tibi cherubim et seraphim incessabili voce proclamant: sanctus, sanctus, sanctus dominus deus sabaoth. Pleni sunt caeli et terra maiestatis gloriae tuae. Te gloriosus apostolorum chorus: te prophetarum laudabilis numerus: te martyrum candidatus laudat exercitus. Te per orbem terrarum sancta confitetur ecclesia: patrem immensae maiestatis: venerandum tuum verum, et unicum filium: sanctum quoque paraclitum spiritum. Tu rex gloriae, Christe. Tu patris sempiternus es filius. Tu ad liberandum suscepturus hominem, non horruisti virginis uterum. Tu devicto mortis aculeo, aperuisti credentibus regna caelorum. Tu ad dexteram dei sedes, in gloria patris. Judex crederis esse venturus. Te ergo quaesumus, tuis famulis subveni, quos pretioso sanguine redemisti. Aeterna fac cum sanctis tuis in gloria numerari. Salvum fac populum tuum domine, et benedic hereditati tuae. Et rege eos, et extolle illos usque in aeternum. Per singulos dies, benedicimus te. Et laudamus nomen tuum in saeculum, et in saeculum saeculi. Dignare domine die isto, sine peccato nos custodire. Miserere nostri domine, miserere nostri. Fiat misericordia tua domine super nos, quemadmodum speravimus in te. In te domine speravi: non confundar in aeternum.

Te decet laus (Monastic Matins)

Te decet laus, te decet hymnus, tibi gloria deo patri et filio, cum sancto spiritu, in saecula saeculorum. Amen.

Benedictus (Lauds)

Benedictus dominus deus Israel: quia visitavit, et fecit redemptionem plebis suae.
Et erexit cornu salutis nobis, in domo David pueri sui:
Sicut locutus est per os sanctorum, qui a saeculo sunt, prophetarum eius:
Salutem ex inimicis nostris, et de manu omnium qui oderunt nos:
Ad faciendem misericordiam cum patribus nostris, et memorari testamenti sui sancti.

OFFICE TEXTS

Te deum laudamus

We praise thee, O God; we acknowledge thee to be the Lord. All the earth doth worship thee, the Father everlasting. To thee all angels cry aloud, the heavens, and all the powers therein. To thee cherubin and seraphin continually do cry; Holy, holy, holy: Lord God of Sabaoth; heaven and earth are full of the majesty of thy glory. The glorious company of the apostles praise thee. The goodly fellowship of the prophets praise thee. The noble army of martyrs praise thee. The holy church throughout all the world doth acknowledge thee; the Father of an infinite majesty; thine honourable, true, and only Son; also the Holy Ghost, the comforter. Thou art the king of glory, O Christ. Thou art the everlasting Son of the Father. When thou tookest upon thee to deliver man, thou didst not abhor the virgin's womb. When thou hadst overcome the sharpness of death, thou didst open the kingdom of heaven to all believers. Thou sittest at the right hand of God in the glory of the Father. We believe that thou shalt come to be our judge. We therefore pray thee, help thy servants, whom thou hast redeemed with thy precious blood. Make them to be numbered with thy saints in glory everlasting. O Lord, save thy people, and bless thine heritage. Govern them, and lift them up for ever. Day by day we magnify thee; and we worship thy name, ever world without end. Vouchsafe, O Lord, to keep us this day without sin. O Lord, have mercy upon us, have mercy upon us. O Lord, let thy mercy lighten upon us, as our trust is in thee. O Lord, in thee have I trusted, let me never be confounded.

Te decet laus

Honour is thine, praise is thine, to thee be glory, O God, Father and Son, with the Holy Spirit, for ever and ever. Amen.

Benedictus

Blessed be the Lord God of Israel: for he hath visited, and redeemed his people;

And hath raised up a mighty salvation for us: in the house of his servant David;

As he spake by the mouth of his holy prophets: which have been since the world began;

That we should be saved from our enemies: and from the hands of all that hate us;

To perform the mercy promised to our forefathers: and to remember his holy covenant;

Jus iurandum, quod juravit ad Abraham patrem nostrum, daturum se nobis:
Ut sine timore, de manu inimicorum nostrorum liberati, serviamus illi:
In sanctitate et justitia coram ipso, omnibus diebus nostris.
Et tu puer, propheta altissimi vocaberis: pracibis enim ante faciem domini
parare vias eius:
Ad dandam scientam salutis plebi eius, in remissionem peccatorum eorum:
Per viscera misericordiae dei nostri: in quibus visitavit nos, oriens ex alto:
Illuminare his qui in tenebris et in umbra mortis sedent: ad dirigendos pedes
nostros in viam pacis.

Magnificat (Vespers)

Magnificat anima mea dominum.
Et exsultavit spiritus meus in deo salutari meo.
Quia respexit humilitatem ancillae suae: ecce enim ex hoc beatam me dicent
omnes generationes.
Quia fecit mihi magna qui potens est: et sanctum nomen eius.
Et misericordia eius a progenie in progenies: timentibus eum.
Fecit potentiam in brachio suo: dispersit superbos mente cordis sui.
Deposuit potentes de sede: et exaltavit humiles.
Esurientes implevit bonis: et divites dimisit inanes.
Suscepit Israel puerum suum: recordatus misericordiae suae.
Sicut locutus est ad patres nostros, Abraham et semini eius in saecula.

Nunc dimittis (Secular Compline)

Nunc dimittis servum tuum domine, secundum verbum tuum in pace:
Quia viderunt oculi mei salutare tuum:
Quod parasti ante faciem omnium populorum:
Lumen ad revelationem gentium, et gloriam plebis tuae Israel.

3.3 *PATER NOSTER*

Pater noster, qui es in caelis: sanctificetur nomen tuum: adveniat regnum,
tuum: fiat voluntas, sicut in caelo, et in terra. Panem nostrum quotidianum
da nobis hodie: et dimitte nobis debitta nostra, sicut et nos dimittimus
debitoribus nostris. Et ne nos inducas in tentationem, sed libera nos a malo.

To perform the oath which he sware to our forefather Abraham: that he would give us;

That we being delivered out of the hands of our enemies: might serve him without fear;

In holiness and righteousness before him: all the days of our life.

And thou, child, shalt be called the prophet of the highest: for thou shalt go before the face of the Lord to prepare his ways;

To give knowledge of salvation unto his people: for the remission of their sins,

Through the tender mercy of our God: whereby the day-spring from on high hath visited us;

To give light to them that sit in darkness, and in the shadow of death: and to guide our feet into the way of peace.

Magnificat

My soul doth magnify the Lord: and my spirit hath rejoiced in God my Saviour.

For he hath regarded: the lowliness of his handmaiden.

For behold, from henceforth: all generations shall call me blessed.

For he that is mighty hath magnified me: and holy is his Name.

And his mercy is on them that fear him: throughout all generations.

He hath shewed strength with his arm: he hath scattered the proud in the imagination of their hearts.

He hath put down the mighty from their seat: and hath exalted the humble and meek.

He hath filled the hungry with good things: and the rich he hath sent empty away.

He remembering his mercy hath holpen his servant Israel: as he promised to our forefathers, Abraham and his seed, for ever.

Nunc dimittis

Lord, now lettest thou thy servant depart in peace: according to thy word.

For mine eyes have seen: thy salvation.

Which thou hast prepared: before the face of all people;

To be a light to lighten the Gentiles: and to be the glory of thy people Israel.

PATER NOSTER

Our Father, which art in heaven, hallowed be thy name. Thy kingdom come. Thy will be done, in earth as it is in heaven. Give us this day our daily bread. And forgive us our trespasses, as we forgive them that trespass against us. And lead us not into temptation; but deliver us from evil.

3.4. ANTIPHONS IN HONOUR OF THE BLESSED VIRGIN MARY

Alma redemptoris mater

Alma redemptoris mater, quae pervia caeli
porta manes, et stella maris, succurre cadenti,
surgere qui curat populo; tu quae genuisti,
natura mirante, tuum sanctum genitorem:
virgo prius ac posterius, Gabrielis ab ore
sumens illud ave, peccatorum miserere.

Ave regina caelorum

Ave regina caelorum,
ave domina angelorum:
salve radix, salve porta,
ex qua mundo lux est orta:
gaude virgo gloriosa,
super omnes speciosa:
vale, o valde decora,
et pro nobis Christum exora.

Regina caeli

Regina caeli laetare, alleluia:
quia quem meruisti portare, alleluia:
resurrexit, sicut dixit, alleluia:
ora pro nobis deum, alleluia.

Salve regina

Salve regina, mater misericordiae:
vita, dulcedo, et spes nostra, salve.
Ad te clamamus, exules, filii Hevae.
Ad te suspiramus, gementes et flentes
in hac lacrimarum valle

Eia ergo, advocata nostra,
illos tuos misericordes oculos ad nos converte.
Et Jesum, benedictum fructum ventris tui,
nobis post hoc exsilium ostende.
O clemens: O pia:
O dulcis virgo Maria.

(Many medieval readings omitted 'mater' in the first line.)

ANTIPHONS IN HONOUR OF THE BLESSED VIRGIN MARY

Alma redemptoris mater

Kind mother of the redeemer, thou who art
the open door of heaven and star of the sea,
help thy fallen people, striving to rise again;
thou who gavest birth to thine own sacred creator
while Nature marvelled; thou who yet was virgin
before and afterwards, receiving that 'Hail'
from the lips of Gabriel, have mercy on sinners.

Ave regina caelorum

Hail, O queen of heaven,
hail, O lady of the angels:
hail O root, hail O gateway,
out of whom came forth
the light of the world:
rejoice, O glorious virgin,
precious above all others:
farewell, O truly fair,
and plead for us to Christ.

Regina caeli

Queen of heaven rejoice, alleluia:
he whom thou wast worthy to bear, alleluia:
is risen, as he said, alleluia:
pray for us to God, alleluia.

Salve regina

Hail O queen, mother of mercy:
our life, sweetness, and hope, hail.
To thee do we cry, exiles, children of Eve.
To thee do we sigh, mourning and weeping
in this vale of tears.

Therefore, O thou our advocate,
turn thy merciful eyes towards us.
And, after this our exile, show to us
the blessed fruit of thy womb, Jesus.
O merciful, O kind, O sweet virgin Mary.

SELECT BIBLIOGRAPHY

1. BIBLIOGRAPHY

PFAFF, Richard W., *Medieval Latin Liturgy: A Select Bibliography* (Toronto Medieval Bibliographies, 9; Toronto, 1982). An accessible guide to the literature, with useful annotations. Though medieval in focus, a substantial number of the items listed are relevant to the whole period of this study. It contains important items that address themselves to the bibliography of liturgy.

2. DICTIONARIES

CABROL, Fernand, and LECLERQ, Henri, *Dictionnaire d'archéologie chrétienne et de liturgie* (15 vols. in 30; Paris, 1907–53).

CROSS, Frank L., and LIVINGSTONE, Elizabeth A. (eds.), *The Oxford Dictionary of the Christian Church* (London, 1958; 2nd edn. 1974; rev. Oxford, 1983). An essential and exceptionally comprehensive one-volume reference book. A concise version is available in paperback.

DAVIES, J. Gordon, *A New Dictionary of Liturgy and Worship* (London, 1986). Emphasizes modern pastoral liturgy, but nevertheless useful.

SADIE, Stanley, *The New Grove Dictionary of Music and Musicians* (20 vols.; Basingstoke and London, 1980). Standard English musical encyclopaedia, containing articles on Mass, Office, liturgical books and forms. Many chant manuscripts described under 'Sources'.

The New Catholic Encyclopedia (20 vols.; New York etc., 1967).

3. EDITIONS OF PRIMARY SOURCES AND TEXTS

3.1 Series

Corpus Consuetudinum Monasticarum (Siegburg, 1963–). An important series of medieval European monastic customaries, including Cluny, Fleury, and some English sources.

Henry Bradshaw Society (London, 1891–). One of the largest collections of edited liturgical texts, including many important medieval sources, predominantly English.

Monumenta Monodica Medii Aevi (Kassel and Basel, 1956–). Edited texts of medieval chant.

Paléographie Musicale (Solesmes, Tournai, Berne, 1889–). Two series; facsimile editions of medieval sources of liturgical chant.

Rerum Ecclesiasticarum Documenta Series Latina: Fontes (Rome, 1955–). Includes René-Jean Hesbert's comparative tables of the formation of the Antiphonal (vols. 7–12).

Studi e Testi (Rome, 1900–). Includes Amalarius of Metz's formative documents on Carolingian reform of liturgy (vols. 89, 90, 95), and catalogues of liturgical manuscripts in the Vatican Library (vols. 251, 253, 260, 267, 270).

3.2 Edited Texts and Facsimiles

(* Asterisked items are dealt with in detail in Chapter 13.)

*COOKE, William, and WORDSWORTH, Christopher (eds.), *Directorium Sacerdotum* (2 vols., Henry Bradshaw Society, 20, 22; 1901–2).

*DICKINSON, Francis H. (ed.), *Missale Sarum* (4 soft-bound issues; Burntisland, 1861–83).

*FOWLER, Joseph T. (ed.), *Rites of Durham* (Surtees Society, 107; 1902).

*FRERE, Walter H. (ed.), *Antiphonale Sarisburiense* (in portfolios, London, 1901–24; repr. in 6 vols., Farnborough, 1966).

*—— (ed.), *Graduale Sarisburiense* (London, 1894).

*—— (ed.), *The Use of Sarum* (2 vols., Cambridge, 1898–1901; repr. Farnborough, 1969). Vol. i: Consuetudinary and Customary; vol. ii: Ordinal and Tonary.

*—— and BROWN, Langton E. G. (eds.), *The Hereford Breviary* (3 vols, Henry Bradshaw Society, 26, 40, 46; 1904–15).

*HENDERSON, William G. (ed.), *Manuale et Processionale ad usum insignis ecclesiae Eboracensis* (Surtees Society, 63; 1874).

*—— (ed.), *Missale ad usum insignis ecclesiae Eboracensis* (2 vols., Surtees Society, 59, 60; 1874).

*—— (ed.), *Missale ad usum percelebris ecclesiae Herfordensis* (Leeds, 1874; repr. Farnborough, 1969).

*—— (ed.), *Processionale ad usum insignis praeclarae ecclesiae Sarum* (Leeds, 1882; repr. Farnborough, 1969).

HUNT, John E. (ed.), *Cranmer's First Litany, 1544, and Merbecke's Book of Common Prayer Noted, 1550*, facsimile (London, 1939).

*LAWLEY, Stephen W. (ed.), *Breviarum ad usum insignis ecclesie Eboracensis* (2 vols., Surtees Society, 71, 75; 1880–2).

*LEGG, J. Wickham (ed.), *Missale ad usum Ecclesie Westmonasteriensis* (3 vols., Henry Bradshaw Society, 1, 5, 12; 1891–6).

*—— (ed.), *The Sarum Missal Edited from Three Early Manuscripts* (Oxford, 1916; repr. 1969).

*LIPPE, Robert (ed.), *Missale Romanum, Mediolani, 1474* (2 vols., Henry Bradshaw Society, 17, 33; 1899–1907).

*[MCLACHLAN, Laurentia (ed.)], *Antiphonaire monastique, XIIIe siècle. Codex F. 160 de la Bibliothèque de la Cathédrale de Worcester*, facsimile (Paléographie Musicale, ser. 1, vol. xii; Tournai, 1922).

*[MCLACHLAN, Laurentia] (The Abbess of Stanbrook) and TOLHURST, John B. L. (eds.), *The Ordinal and Customary of the Abbey of Saint Mary York* (3 vols., Henry Bradshaw Society, 73, 75, 84; 1936–51).

*PROCTER, Francis, and WORDSWORTH, Christopher (eds.), *Breviarum ad* *usum insignis ecclesiae Sarisburiensis* (3 vols., Cambridge, 1879–86; repr. Farnborough, 1970).

★[RASTALL, G. Richard (ed.)], *Processionale ad Usum Sarum*, fascimile (Clarabricken, 1980).

SCHIMMELPFENNIG, Bernhard, *De Zeremonienbücher der römischen Kurie im Mittelalter* (Bibliothek des deutschen historischen Instituts in Rome, 40; Tübingen, 1973).

★TOLHURST, John B. L. (ed.), *The Customary of the Cathedral Priory Church of Norwich* (Henry Bradshaw Society, 82; 1948).

★—— (ed.), *The Monastic Breviary of Hyde Abbey, Winchester* (6 vols., Henry Bradshaw Society, 69, 70, 71, 76, 78, 80; 1932–42).

★—— (ed.), with notes by Laurentia McLachlan, *The Ordinal and Customary of the Benedictine Nuns of Barking Abbey* (2 vols., Henry Bradshaw Society, 65, 66; 1927–8).

★WORDSWORTH, Christopher (ed.), *Ceremonies and Processions of the Cathedral Church of Salisbury* (Cambridge, 1901).

VAN DIJK, Stephen J. P., *Sources of the Modern Roman Liturgy* (2 vols., Leiden, 1963). Thirteenth-century documents, mostly Franciscan.

Basic texts of Roman (Tridentine) and monastic Breviaries and Missals can be obtained second-hand. Roman Breviaries published after 1911 follow the revised psalmody etc. introduced under Pope Pius X. Latin books published after 1970 follow the newly revised orders of the Second Vatican Council. The Book of Common Prayer (1662) of the Church of England is still in print.

3.3 Modern Books with Chant

Antiphonale Monasticum (Tournai, 1934).

Liber Usualis (edition with English rubrics, Tournai, 1934; rev. 1961).

Useful accessible anthologies, but both need to be used with care: they are selective in what they include, and reflect the Tridentine and monastic Rites in their twentieth-century revised forms. The editions of the chants are those made by the monks of Solesmes (based on the earliest sources available) and do not necessarily coincide with what was used between the tenth and eighteenth centuries.

The most recent editions of *Graduale Romanum*, *Graduale Triplex*, and *Liber Hymnarius* are useful for choral chants, but have been designed for the modern liturgy as reformed following the Second Vatican Council.

Processionale Monasticum (Solesmes, 1893; repr. with rev. 1983). The most comprehensive collection of monastic processional chants available.

3.4 Reconstructed Orders

LAMOTHE, Donat R., and CONSTANTINE, Cyprian G., *Matins at Cluny for the Feast of St Peter's Chains* (Plainsong and Medieval Music Society; London, 1986).

SANDON, Nick (ed.), *The Use of Salisbury* (Newton Abbot, 1984–). A conflation of available sources to produce a comprehensive usable text of the Salisbury liturgy with complete texts, chant, rubrics, and description. Available volumes include Ordinary of the Mass, and Proper of the Mass from Advent to the week following the Octave of Epiphany.

4. SOURCE STUDIES AND CATALOGUES

4.1 Source Studies

HUGHES, Andrew, *Medieval Manuscripts for Mass and Office: A Guide to their Organization and Terminology* (Toronto, 1982). A comprehensive survey of the principal liturgical books, forms, and orders of Mass and Office with analysis of the ordering of the manuscripts in which they are found; highly systematized but not always easy to use. There is also a summary list of manuscripts consulted.

LEROQUAIS, Victor, *Les Manuscrits liturgiques latins du Haut Moyen Âge à la Renaissance* (Paris, 1931).

VOGEL, Cyrille, *Introduction aux sources de l'histoire du culte chrétien au Moyen Âge* (Bibliotheca 'Studi medievali', 1; Spoleto, 1966; 2nd edn., 1975; Eng. tr. rev. William G. Storey and Niels K. Rasmussen, *Medieval Liturgy: An Introduction to the Sources*, Washington DC, 1986). Valuable bibliographical information, but very little on the Office.

4.2 Catalogues

In addition to catalogues of individual libraries the following contain information on liturgical sources. Two valuable typescripts are included.

FRERE, Walter H., *Bibliotheca Musico-Liturgica: A Descriptive Handlist of the Musical and Latin-Liturgical Manuscripts of the Middle Ages in the Libraries of Great Britain and Ireland* (2 vols., London 1901–32; repr. Farnborough, 1967).

HUGHES, Andrew, 'Forty-seven Medieval Office Manuscripts in the British Museum: A Provisional Inventory of Antiphonals and Breviaries' (typescript; deposited in Students' Room, British Library, London, 1976).

KER, Neil R., *Medieval Libraries of Great Britain: A List of Surviving Books*

(Royal Historical Society Guides and Handbooks, 3; 2nd edn. London, 1964).

—— *Medieval Manuscripts in British Libraries* (3 vols. to date; Oxford, 1969–).

LEROQUAIS, Victor, *Les Bréviaires manuscrits des bibliothèques publiques de France* (6 vols.; Paris, 1934).

—— *Les Sacramentaires et les missels manuscrits des bibliothèques publiques de France* (4 vols.; Paris, 1924).

VAN DIJK, Stephen J. P., 'Handlist of the Latin Liturgical Manuscripts in the Bodleian Library' (6 vols., typescript; deposited in Duke Humfrey's Library, Bodleian Library, Oxford, 1951).

5. SECONDARY MATERIALS

5.1 General

DIX, Gregory, *The Shape of the Liturgy* (London, 1945). Primarily but not exclusively directed to the Mass.

JONES, Cheslyn, WAINWRIGHT, Geoffrey, and YARNOLD, Edward (eds.), *The Study of Liturgy* (London, 1978). Better on the formative periods and influenced by current liturgical thinking, this is nevertheless an excellent starting point for reading on all the main areas of study which are dealt with separately by a variety of authors.

SANDON, Nick (ed.), *The Octave of the Nativity: Essays and Notes on Ten Liturgical Reconstructions for Christmas* (London, 1984). Written to accompany a series of radio broadcasts of Christmas liturgical celebrations as they might have been conducted at ten different churches between the tenth and seventeenth centuries. Also includes useful general introductory essays on liturgy.

WEGMAN, Hermann A. J., *Christian Worship in East and West: A Study Guide to Liturgical History*, Eng. tr. Gordon W. Lathrop (New York, 1985). A historical overview in clearly delineated sections; strongest on the Roman Rite.

VAN DIJK, Stephen J. P., and HAZELDEN WALKER, Joan, *The Origins of the Modern Roman Liturgy: The Liturgy of the Papal Court and the Franciscan Order in the Thirteenth Century* (London, 1960). Studies of the formation of the Romano-Franciscan liturgy, the basis of the late medieval Roman Use and the subsequent Tridentine Rite.

5.2 Liturgical Books

DE HAMEL, Christopher, *A History of Illuminated Manuscripts* (Oxford, 1986). A far more scholarly history of medieval books than either the title or the coffee-table format might suggest; includes a chapter on liturgical books.

HUGHES, Andrew, *Medieval Manuscripts for Mass and Office*, see 4.1 above.

PLUMMER, John H., *Liturgical Manuscripts for the Mass and Divine Office* (New York, 1964). An exhibition catalogue for the Pierpont Morgan Library, but a clear introduction to the main types of liturgical books.

SHEPPARD, Lancelot C., *The Liturgical Books* (Faith and Fact Books, 108; London, 1962). A concise introduction to the history of the principal Roman books.

5.3 Calendar

DENIS-BOULET, Noële M., *The Christian Calendar* (Faith and Fact Books, 112; London, 1960). A historical summary originally intended for Roman Catholic laity.

5.4 The Office

BAÜMER, Suitbert, *Histoire du bréviaire* (Fr. tr., rev. R. Biron; Paris, 1905; repr. 1967). Though old this is valuable for source readings.

GUIVER, George, *Company of Voices: Daily Prayer and the People of God* (London, 1988). A readable account of the Office which extends from earliest times to the present day. Though it has a modern pastoral bias, the historical overview is broad and even.

SALMON, Pierre, *L'Office divin: Histoire de la formation du bréviaire* (Lex Orandi, 27; Paris, 1959; Eng. tr. *The Breviary Through the Centuries* (Collegeville, Minn., 1962).

—— *L'Office divin au Moyen Âge* (Lex Orandi, 43; Paris, 1967).
These last two studies extend as far as the fourteenth century.

TOLHURST, John B. L., *Introduction to the English Monastic Breviaries*, vol. vi of *The Monastic Breviary of Hyde Abbey, Winchester* (Henry Bradshaw Society, 80; London, 1942). The most comprehensive study of medieval monastic liturgy, based for the most part on English sources.

5.5 The Mass

CRICHTON, James D., *A Short History of the Mass* (London, 1983). A brief guide for the novice.

JUNGMANN, Joseph A., *Missarum Sollemnia* (Vienna, 1948; 5th edn. 1962; Eng. tr. F. A. Brunner, *The Mass of the Roman Rite*, 2 vols., New York, 1951–5). The classic and unsurpassed study. The one-volume edition by Riepe (1959) lacks important references.

5.6 Processions and Additional Observances

BAILEY, Terence W., *The Processions of Sarum and the Western Church* (Pontifical Institute of Medieval Studies: Studies and Texts, 21; Toronto, 1971). Stronger on processions in secular rather than monastic Uses, it is the most comprehensive study available with a good deal of musical reference.

HARDISON, Osborne B., *Christian Rite and Christian Drama in the Middle Ages* (Baltimore, 1965). A sympathetic account of liturgical drama.

SMOLDON, William S., *The Music of the Medieval Church Dramas* (London, 1980).

YOUNG, Karl S., *The Drama of the Medieval Church* (2 vols.; Oxford, 1933; 2nd edn. 1951).

Smoldon's extensive work was published posthumously and can be uneven. Young includes a large number of texts (without music).

5.7 Monasticism

FRY, Timothy (ed.), *RB 1980: The Rule of St Benedict in Latin and English with Notes* (Collegeville, Minn., 1981). The best critical text with parallel English translation.

KNOWLES, David, *Christian Monasticism* (London, 1969). A useful introduction to the phenomenon and principal features of the monastic life from its beginnings to the twentieth century. See also 5.10 below.

—— *The Monastic Order in England: A History of its Development from the Times of St Dunstan to the Fourth Lateran Council, 940–1216* (Cambridge 1940; 2nd edn. 1964). Includes valuable chapters on Benedictine life and liturgy. See also 5.9 below.

LAWRENCE, Clifford H., *Medieval Monasticism: Forms of Religious Life in Western Europe in the Middle Ages* (London, 1984; 2nd edn. 1989). A concise but excellent historical survey of all the main issues and movements.

DE VOGÜÉ, Adalbert, *The Rule of St Benedict: A Doctrinal and Spiritual Commentary*, Eng. tr. J. P. Hasbrouck (Cistercian Studies, 54; Kalamazoo, Mich., 1983). An important commentary on the relationship of the Rule to Benedictine practice.

5.8 Anglican Liturgy

BRIGHTMAN, Frank E., *The English Rite* (2 vols., London, 1915; repr. 1970). Complete and precise readings of the Book of Common Prayer texts between 1549 and 1662, together with their earlier sources.

CUMING, Geoffrey J., *A History of Anglican Liturgy* (London, 1969; 2nd edn. 1982). A successor to Procter and Frere's history (see below).

HARPER, John, *A History of Music in the English Church from Bede to the Present Day* (forthcoming). With reference always to liturgical context.

LE HURAY, Peter G., *Music and the Reformation in England 1548–1660* (London, 1967; repr. Cambridge, 1978). Contains important chapters on music and the Book of Common Prayer, and on the practice of music in church, as well as a thorough study of the repertory.

PROCTER, Francis, and FRERE, Walter H., *A New History of the Book of Common Prayer* (London, 1901). Superseded but not displaced by Cuming.

TEMPERLEY, Nicholas, *The Music of the English Parish Church* (2 vols., Cambridge, 1979). Very little on the period before 1550.

5.9. Institutions

HARRISON, Frank Ll., *Music in Medieval Britain* (London, 1958; 4th edn., Buren, 1980). A pioneering study of the interaction of foundations, ritual, and music.

KNOWLES, David and HADCOCK, R. Neville, *Medieval Religious Houses: England and Wales* (London, 1953; rev. 1971). Annotated lists of all the secular, monastic, and other religious institutions known up to the mid-sixteenth century.

MOORE, James H., *Vespers at St Mark's* (Studies in Musicology, 30; Ann Arbor, Mich., 1981). Some of the best Vespers music was conceived for St Mark's, Venice, in the seventeenth century. This is a detailed study of the music in the liturgical context of the celebrations.

WRIGHT, Craig, *Music and Ceremony at Notre Dame of Paris, 500–1500* (Cambridge, 1989). A study of the organization, liturgy, and related music of a single institution.

5.10. Chant

APEL, Willi, *Gregorian Chant* (London, 1958). A thoroughgoing study of musical repertory, based mostly on recent editions.

HILEY, David, *Western Plainchant: An Introduction* (London, 1991). A starting point for those to whom the subject is unfamiliar.

WAGNER, Peter G., *Einführung in die gregorianischen Melodien* (3 vols., Leipzig, 1895–1911; repr. 1962; Eng. tr. rev. Agnes Orme and Edward G. P. Wyatt, *Introduction to the Gregorian Melodies*, London, 1901; repr. *Caecilia* 84–6, 1957–9). A classic study, more historical in perspective than Apel (above).

5.11. Ceremonial

DYKMANS, Marc, *Le Cérémonial papal de la fin du Moyen Âge à la Renaissance; i: Le Cérémonial papal du XIIIe siècle* (Bibliothèque de l'Institut historique belge de Rome, 24; Brussels and Rome, 1977). See also Schimmelpfennig, section 3.2 above.

FORTESCUE, Adrian, *The Ceremonies of the Roman Rite Described* (rev. and enlarged, John O'Connell; 7th edn., London, 1943). A detailed account of ceremonial celebration of the Tridentine liturgy in the present century.

GLOSSARY OF ECCLESIASTICAL AND LITURGICAL TERMS

Abbey: a community of monks or nuns whose superior is abbot or abbess. See Chapter 2.

Abbot/Abbess: presiding monk or nun in an abbey, elected by remainder of the community.

Ablutions: literally, acts of washing; in the liturgy the washing of the sacred vessels (chalice and paten) after the communion at the end of Mass; also the ceremonial washing of the priest's hands at the Offertory and after the washing of the vessels.

Absolution: a formal declaration of God's forgiveness, pronounced by the senior priest present at a liturgical observance; where no priest is present an alternative collective form is often used.

Acclamation: a liturgical cry of praise, most often 'Alleluia'.

Acolyte: the highest rank of secular Minor Orders. Acolytes assisted in the sanctuary at the Mass. See Chapter 2.

Advent: the period of four Sundays before Christmas when the Church prepares for the coming of Christ as man. See Chapter 3.

Advent Sunday: the first day of Advent, and the beginning of the ecclesiastical and liturgical year. Most liturgical books begin with provisions for Advent Sunday.

Agnus dei: the last of the group of choral chants in the Ordinary of the Mass; a prayer for Christ's mercy in litany form, it is recited just before the communion at Mass. See Chapter 7; text in Appendix 3.

Aisle: the part of a church on one or both sides of the nave, and separated from it by pillars.

Alb: white, full-length garment worn over cassock or habit, normally tied by a girdle at the waist; worn by ministers in sanctuary at Mass (often under other vestments). In monasteries those in choir wore albs at Mass and Office on designated important feasts.

All Saints: all Christians of outstanding holiness, both known and unknown in the Church's history, now believed to be in heaven; their feast is on 1 November, but commemorated throughout the year at daily votive observances.

All Souls: the faithful dead; formally commemorated on 2 November, but commemorated throughout the year at daily votive observances.

Alleluia: Hebrew: Praise the Lord; an acclamation of joy adopted by the Christian church. Used (1) as an appendage to another text, especially during the season of Easter; (2) as a substantial chant with verse after the Gradual (and before the Sequence) at Mass. Alleluia (1 and 2) is omitted at penitential times and commemorations of the dead. See Chapters 6 and 7.

Altar: a sacred table of wood or stone on which Mass is celebrated; it is specially consecrated at five points (where there are crosses) and often contains relics in a sealed cavity. Most churches had more than one altar, of which the most important, at the east end of the Choir, was the High Altar. See Chapter 2.

Ambo: originally a substantial raised platform from which the Gospel was proclaimed; now used to mean a lectern. In large churches the ambo was often replaced by the pulpitum sited between nave and choir.

Ambrosian: of St Ambrose, but specifically refering to the liturgical Rite used in the cathedral and diocese of Milan in northern Italy.

Ambulatory: in larger churches a walkway (often an extension of the aisles) which went around the choir and presbytery. Chapels were commonly built opening off an ambulatory.

Amen: Hebrew word meaning 'so be it', used as an affirmation especially at the end of prayers.

Anaphora: Greek: offering; the Eucharistic prayer, but often applied to the whole of the second part of the Mass from *Sursum corda* (i.e. Mass of the Faithful).

Anglican: pertaining to the Church of England, or those Churches in full communion with it.

Annunciation: of the blessed Virgin Mary. The announcement to Mary by the angel Gabriel of the conception of Christ. Feast normally celebrated on 25 March, nine months before Christmas.

Ante-communion: in the Church of England the first part of the service of Holy Communion up to the Prayer of the Church Militant. See Chapter 11.

Anthem: in pre-Reformation England, the same as antiphon. After the Reformation, the term refers specifically to the choral item (with no fixed text) sung in choral foundations after the third collect at Morning and Evening Prayer. See Chapter 11.

Antiphon: most often a proper text sung before and after a psalm or canticle. Some antiphons (e.g. Offertory and Communion at Mass, in processions, and in honour of the Virgin Mary after an Office) are sung without psalm or canticle.

Antiphonal: (1) a method of singing in which verses (or half verses) are sung alternately by the two halves of the choir sitting opposite one another; (2) a classification of chant apparently originating with (1) but which identifies those chants (and especially psalmody) which do not follow a reading. The counterpart of responsorial and direct chants. See Chapter 5. (3) a choir book containing chants for the Office; the companion to the Breviary, and the counterpart to the Gradual (containing choir chants for the Mass). Occasionally even a book of Mass chants is identified as an Antiphonal. See Chapter 4.

Antiphoner: alternative to Antiphonal (3).

Apostle: one of the twelve men originally chosen by Christ and commissioned to preach the Gospel to the world. After the crucifixion Matthias took the place of Judas Iscariot (who committed suicide), and later Paul came to be regarded as Apostle to the Gentiles.

Apse: architectural term for the rounded east end of a church (hence, apsidal).

Archbishop: a bishop who, in addition to his responsibility for a diocese, presides over a group of dioceses (known as a province).

Archdeacon: literally 'chief deacon', by medieval times he was a priest who saw to much of the administration of a diocese on behalf of the bishop; often also a statutory officer and canon of a cathedral.

Ascension: the ascent of Christ into heaven forty days after the resurrection (Easter).

Ash Wednesday: the beginning of Christ's forty-day fast in the wilderness, observed as the beginning of Lent.

Asperges: Latin: sprinkle; the opening word of the antiphon sung during the ritual sprinkling of water, normally before High Mass, and used to describe the ceremony.

Aspersion: English form of *Asperges*.

Assumption: the feast which commemorates the reception of the Blessed Virgin Mary into heaven, observed on 15 August. One of the five great Marian feasts.

Augustinian: follower of the Rule of St Augustine of Hippo. Most often refers to those canons and canonesses who lived in community under a version of that Rule. There were also Augustinian (or Austin) friars. See Chapter 2.

Aumbry: cupboard, generally in the wall near an altar, where either the sacred vessels or else (in more recent times in the Church of England) the reserved sacrament is kept.

Ave Maria: the opening words of the angel Gabriel's salutation to the Virgin Mary at the annunciation, used as a frequently recited prayer in Marian devotions and as an antiphon.

Baptism: Christian initiation into membership of the Church, consisting of profession of faith, naming, immersion into (or sprinkling with) water, and (in some Rites) marking with holy oil; a rite generally conducted at the font.

Basilica: originally one of the early Roman church buildings, but subsequently used to designate a church marked out by the Pope as of particular importance.

Benedicamus: v. *Benedicamus domino*. R. *Deo gratias*. (Let us bless the Lord. Thanks be to God.) The versicle and response recited as a form of blessing at the end of an Office and, on certain days, at Mass.

Benedictine: a monk or nun who observes the Rule of St Benedict of Nursia. See Chapters 1 and 2.

Benediction: (1) a blessing; (2) a form of devotion to the Blessed Sacrament (including a silent blessing by the priest holding the Host) which became popular in the Roman Catholic church in the seventeenth century.

Benedictional: a liturgical book containing blessings. Often part of a Pontifical.

Benedictus: (1) *Benedictus qui venit*, the text recited after the *Sanctus* at Mass. Text in Appendix 3; (2) *Benedictus dominus deus Israel*, the canticle (attributed in St Luke's Gospel to Zacharias) sung at Lauds (and in the post-Reformation English Church at Morning Prayer). See Chapter 6; text in Appendix 3.

Benefice: an endowment to provide income to support a secular cleric, often the income from a parish.

Bidding of the Bedes: a series of intercessions found in the Use of Salisbury and used most commonly at the end of the Sunday procession. Part of it was absorbed into Morning and Evening Prayer after the Reformation.

Bishop: the highest of Holy Orders above deacon and priest. A bishop has authority to confirm and ordain. A bishop normally has pastoral care of a diocese.

Black Letter Days: less important days in the liturgical Calendar, so called because of their identification by the use of black ink in manuscript and some printed Calendars. The counterpart of Red Letter Days.

Blessed Sacrament: the bread and wine consecrated at Mass as the body and blood of Christ first given at the Last Supper.

Blessing: prayer of sanctification or consecration, normally pronounced only by a priest or bishop. Blessings are often contained in a Benedictional or Pontifical.

BMV: *Beata Maria Virgo*: the Blessed Virgin Mary, mother of Christ.

Book of Common Prayer: the authorized liturgical book of the Church of England, first compiled and printed in 1549, with important revisions in 1552, 1559, and 1662.

Book of Hours: a book intended for private devotion and most often containing the Little Office of the Blessed Virgin Mary, the Office of the Dead, the seven penitential psalms, etc. They were generally used by laity, and some examples are sumptuous manuscripts.

Breviary: the composite Office book. By the fourteenth century most had complete texts of the Office. Some (Noted Breviaries) had chant as well. See Chapter 3.

BVM: Blessed Virgin Mary, mother of Christ.

Calendar: the liturgical Calendar (Kalendar) denotes the date and rank of fixed feasts. See Chapter 3.

Candle: wax light used as the main source of artificial light in churches until the nineteenth century; also as a symbol of Christ the Light (especially at the Easter Vigil).

Candlemas: the feast of the Presentation of Christ in the Temple, also the feast of the Purification of the Blessed Virgin Mary; 2 February. The Marian emphasis was prevalent in the Middle Ages. The day on which Christ was proclaimed as the Light to the Gentiles by Simeon in the words of the canticle *Nunc dimittis*.

Canon: (1) an ecclesiastical statute; (2) a man in Holy Orders bound by ecclesiastical statutes. Most often a senior member of a collegiate church funded by a benefice or prebend. Regular canons lived in community, bound by a Rule.

Canon of the Mass: the most solemn part of the Mass, the prayer during which the bread and wine are consecrated by the celebrating priest. See Chapter 7.

Canoness: a woman living in community under ecclesiastical authority, most often as a regular canoness bound by a codified Rule.

Cantatory: a book, or part of a book, containing those chants sung by the soloist(s).

Canticle: a biblical text intended to be sung in the Office. The principal three are those found in St Luke's Gospel: *Benedictus dominus deus* (Lauds), *Magnificat* (Vespers), and *Nunc dimittis* (Compline).

Cantor: a general term for a solo singer. In the Middle Ages the Precentor (chief cantor) had charge of liturgical celebration, determined the chants to be sung, and designated the singers who were to begin them or sing the solo passages.

Cantoris: the side of the choir on which the Precentor (cantor) sits, the north side (left when facing the high altar).

Capitulum: chapter.

Caput jejunii: Ash Wednesday.

Cardinal: a member of the Pope's council. Cardinals together form a college which elects the Pope from among their number.

Carol: in medieval England a sacred song, normally stanzaic with refrain (burden), either with vernacular or macaronic text; those which survive with music are predominantly scored in two- or three-part polyphony. Some carols are found in sources alongside liturgical music and may have been used in the liturgy (to substitute for other items such as *Benedicamus*) or else in the refectory.

Carthusian: a monk of the Order of the Grand Chartreuse, an austere and strict Order founded by St Bruno in 1086. Each monk lived alone and only met with the rest of the community for the liturgy in church and for chapter meetings.

Cassock: a full-length garment worn by secular clerics; most often black, and worn under other vestments (e.g. alb, surplice).

Catechumen: in the early Church, a baptized Christian who awaits full admission to the Church by confirmation; catechumens did not attend the Eucharistic part of the Mass. See Mass of Catechumens.

Cathedra: bishop's presiding seat or throne.

Cathedral: church where the bishop presides and where his *cathedra* is situated.

Cathedral Priory: a monastery which serves as a cathedral, and where the bishop is titular abbot, but the prior is the executive superior of the community. See Chapter 2.

Catholic: literally 'universal' (i.e. the main Church in the West), but after the Reformation requiring the qualification of 'Roman'.

Celebrant: the priest (or bishop) who presides at a sacramental liturgy, most often the Mass.

Cell: in the Middle Ages, a small monastic community dependent and subject to the authority of a larger monastery.

Cena domini: the Lord's supper at which Christ instituted the Eucharist (Mass): Thursday before Easter Day, the first day of the solemn *Triduum*; in English known as Maundy Thursday. See Chapter 9.

Censer: thurible, the vessel in which incense is burnt.

Centonization: the use of standardized melodic formulas to compile a longer piece of chant, particularly prevalent in Tracts.

Ceremonial: (1) the manner in which the ritual of the liturgy is carried out; especially details of gesture, movement, ornament, and vestment. See Chapter 12; (2) a book detailing the liturgical customs of collegiate and cathedral churches (e.g. the Roman Ceremonial, published 1516).

Ceremony: the practical enactment of a liturgical rite.

Chalice: the cup used to contain the wine consecrated on the altar at the Mass and generally made of precious metal.

Chancel: the eastern portion of a church reserved for clergy; an alternative to presbytery.

Chancellor: a canon and officer of a collegiate cathedral foundation, he had particular responsibility in the church's legal courts.

Chant: the vast repertory of monophonic vocal music (ranging from simple formulas to extensive and elaborate melodies) which formed the core of liturgical music in the Middle Ages.

Chantry: an institution (often within a large church) whose prime purpose was to offer prayer (Mass and Office) for the benefactor(s) who established it; often staffed by one or two priests, but in some instances a more substantial, collegiate foundation.

Chapel: (1) a place of worship with an altar, sometimes within a larger church (e.g. Lady chapel—a chapel with altar dedicated to the Blessed Virgin Mary); normally only a presbytery without nave; (2) the clergy (and sometimes lay singers) who served the liturgy within a specific chapel; (3) the clergy (and sometimes lay singers) who served a noble household, and travelled with the head of the house as part of his entourage. See Chapter 2.

Chapel Royal: the household chapel of the king. See Chapel (3).

Chaplain: a cleric employed in a chapel.

Chapter: (1) a short reading, most often in the Office and taken from the Bible; (2) a daily meeting of a community (monastic or collegiate) at which a chapter (1) was read (in monasteries, from the Rule of the Order), and at which the business of the community was conducted.

Chapter house: the place where a community (monastic or collegiate) met for its daily business.

Chasuble: the outer vestment worn by the celebrant at Mass, either elliptical or rectangular in shape with a hole at the centre for the head, and often richly decorated.

Choir: (1) the community (monastic or collegiate) in its church celebrating the liturgy; (2) after the fifteenth century, the body of trained singers (not the whole community) with responsibility for singing the choral parts of Mass and Office; (3) the part of the church with seats for the community where the liturgy is conducted (sometimes Quire). See Chapter 2.

Choir screen: a screen separating the eastern part of a church reserved for the clerical community (Choir (3)) from the nave; often substantial and surmounted by a gallery (pulpitum). See Chapter 2.

Choir-step: the step at the eastern end of the choir, separating the choir from the presbytery; frequently the site of a lectern for readings and solo chant. See Chapter 2.

Chorister: boy, the junior member of a collegiate foundation, increasingly used for musical duties from the fifteenth century onwards.

Chrism: sacred oil, consecrated at Mass on Maundy Thursday, used for anointing at baptism, confirmation, and ordination. See Chapter 9.

Christmas: the feast which commemorates the birth of Christ as man, 25 December, and the season (to 5 January) which follows it.

Church: (1) the assembly of Christendom either at an international, national, denominational, or local level; (2) an independent, consecrated building with an altar where Christians meet to worship.

Church of England: the established Church in England, separated from Rome in 1534 and with a vernacular liturgy from 1549. The monarch is head of the Church, and Parliament is responsible for the laws which regulate its constitution and liturgy.

Ciborium: (1) a cup-shaped vessel in which the bread consecrated at Mass is placed when there is a large number of communicants; (2) a canopy, usually supported by four pillars, raised over the high altar.

Circumcision: the Octave of Christmas Day, 1 January, when the Church used to commemorate the circumcision of Christ following Jewish custom. The day is now observed as the Solemnity of Mary, Mother of God (Roman Catholic Church) or the Naming of Jesus (Anglican Churches).

Cistercian: of the reformed Order of monks following the Rule of St Benedict established at Cîteaux in 1098.

Clerestory: the highest level in a church building, clear of aisle roofs, and therefore an important source of light.

Clergy: those men ordained for religious service.

Cleric: a member of the clergy, or sometimes a clerk.

Clerk: (1) a man in Minor Orders (as opposed to bishop, priest, deacon, and subdeacon); (2) one of the junior members of a collegiate foundation; from the fifteenth century onwards a lay singer engaged to undertake the duties of a clerk (hence lay clerk).

Cloister: a square or rectangular covered walkway, generally on the south side of some collegiate and most monastic churches. In a monastery it provided a dry covered way linking the principal buildings (church, chapter house, refectory, etc.) and a place for study and writing. In a collegiate church it was more often used primarily for processions. The windows (glazed or unglazed) opened on to the central open space (cloister garth).

Collatio: Latin: gathering. A short rite with a reading preceding monastic Compline, often conducted in the cloister or chapter house where the community gathered before they entered the church.

Collect: in the early Church, a prayer which summed up the prayers of the assembly; in the Middle Ages a specified prayer for a particular feast, season, time, or intention, used at Mass (before the Epistle) and at the Office (generally the last item of the main structure of the Hour), recited by the celebrant or officiating priest.

Collectar: a book, or section of a book, in which collects are found.

College: an organized society sharing common functions and instituted by legal statutes. Hence, collegiate. See Chapter 2.

Colours: liturgical colours associated with ecclesiastical seasons and feasts. They affected the colour of vestments (notably at Mass) and hangings in church (especially those on or around altars).

Comfortable Words: short quotations from the New Testament said by the priest after the Absolution in the service of Holy Communion in the Church of England.

Commemoration: (1) the lowest rank for festal observance, generally reserved for minor saints. Also known as memorial; (2) the short Proper rite (antiphon, versicle and response, collect) appended to the Office (generally Lauds and Vespers) as a means of commemorating a feast displaced by a more important observance or a specific regular intention (e.g. the Blessed Virgin Mary, All Saints). See Chapter 8.

Commemorative Mass and Office: a weekly observance which displaced the liturgy specified in the Calendar at which the main Mass and Office had a specified devotional intention (most often the Blessed Virgin Mary or a patron saint). See Chapter 8.

Commination: a service proclaiming God's wrath against sinners, found in the Book of Common Prayer for use on Ash Wednesday; a relic of the earlier rite of expelling sinners from the Church during Lent.

Common: (1) liturgical texts in the Office that are regular and unchanging; (2) liturgical texts at Mass and Office shared by a number of similar feasts (e.g. Common of Apostles, Common of the Blessed Virgin Mary).

Common of Saints: that part of a liturgical book which contains the Proper texts (and chants where relevant) shared by groups of similar feasts (see Common (2)). The counterpart to Temporale (seasonal observances) and Sanctorale (specific calendar feast-days). See Chaper 3.

Commune Sanctorum: see Common of Saints.

Communion: (1) the act of receiving the consecrated bread and wine at the Mass; the bread alone for the laity after the twelfth century; (2) the antiphon sung at the time of (1) in the Mass; (3) since the Reformation, a group of Churches which are in full doctrinal and sacramental union with one another (e.g. the Anglican Communion). See Chapter 7.

Compline: the last Office of the liturgical day, normally recited at nightfall. See Chapter 6.

Confession: (1) a liturgical prayer in which sins are formally confessed. It is followed by absolution; (2) a private rite in which an individual confesses his or her sins confidentially to a priest. It is followed by absolution.

Confessor: (1) a minor saint commemorated for his or her public confession of the Christian faith; (2) the priest to whom an individual makes private confession.

Confiteor: Latin: I confess; the opening word of the prayer of confession, and used to identify it.

Confraternity: a formal association of men (most often laymen) sharing a common religious purpose.

Congregation: (1) the Christian assembly gathered for worship; (2) the laity gathered for worship; (3) a gathering of affiliated religious representatives (e.g. a group of monasteries, or the Oratorians); (4) a council (e.g. Congregation of Sacred Rites).

Consecration: the most solemn act of sanctification by words of blessing and symbolic laying on of hands; especially the consecration of bread and wine at Mass, the consecration (i.e. ordination) of bishops, and the consecration of church buildings.

Consuetudinary: a manual of customs. See Customary and Chapter 3.

Convent: an institution where men or women lived together under a communal Rule, or its buildings; hence, conventual.

Conversi: lay brothers or sisters in some monastic (especially Cistercian) communities, who undertook most of the manual work.

Cope: a ceremonial cloak worn by an officiant at the Office. In monasteries at the most solemn feasts all those in choir were habited in copes (*in cappis*).

Corpus Christi: literally the 'body of Christ'; applied to the consecrated bread at Mass, and to the feast (celebrated on the Thursday after Trinity Sunday) commemorating the institution of the Eucharist.

Corpus Domini: Corpus Christi.

Counter-Reformation: the period in the mid-sixteenth century during which the Roman Catholic Church reviewed and consolidated its doctrine and liturgy following the Protestant Reformation. See Chapter 10.

Credo: the opening word of the Creed.

Creed: an agreed statement of Christian belief. The three creeds traditionally recited in the Western liturgy are the Apostles' Creed (recited at Prime and Compline, and privately before all the Offices), the Nicene Creed (recited at Mass), and the Athanasian Creed (recited as an appendage to Prime). Text of the Nicene Creed in Appendix 3.

Cross: the principal Christian symbol, recalling the cross on which Christ died.

Crucifix: a cross bearing a representation of the figure of Christ.

Cruciform: cross-shaped, a common formal outline for churches with presbytery, nave, and transepts.

Curate: one charged with the care of souls; normally a priest or deacon serving in a parish, often, in the Middle Ages, as a substitute for the beneficed priest.

Curia: Latin: court; most often referring to the Papal or Roman Curia, the Pope's court and centre of church administration in Rome.

Cursus: Latin: course; a fixed order of liturgical observance (e.g. psalmody).

Custom: a habitual practice, ceremonial rather than ritual.

Customary: a manual of customs describing the duties of the officers of an institution and the ceremonial actions of the liturgy, the later form of consuetudinary.

Dalmatic: outer garment worn by deacon at Mass: rectangular, generally with sleeves and tassels, often decorated to match chasuble.

Day hours: the seven Offices from Lauds to Compline, as opposed to the night Office of Matins.

Deacon: the Holy Order ranking below priest. A deacon can baptize, but not celebrate Mass or grant absolution.

Dean: the senior canon and executive officer of a collegiate foundation.

Decani: the south side of the choir on which the dean sits; the opposite to Cantoris.

Dedication: (1) in some cases interchangeable with consecration of a church; (2) the annual feast commemorating the consecration of a church; (3) the saint(s) in honour of whom a specific church is dedicated.

Dialogue: a modern term to describe a versicle and response.

Diocese: a group of parishes in a single region over which a bishop has jurisdiction.

Direct psalmody: a solo chant in which the text of a psalm is sung without antiphons (or responds), generally with ornate melody often employing centonization (e.g. Tracts). See Chapter 5.

Directorium: a guide to the interpretation of the fixed and variable elements of the liturgical Calendar.

Dirige: Latin: direct; the first word of the first psalm antiphon at Vigils (i.e. Matins) of the Dead, and often used to refer to the whole Office.

Dismissal: a modern term referring to the conclusion of Mass (*Ite missa est* or *Benedicamus domino*) or Office (*Benedicamus domino*).

Diurnale: a liturgical book containing the day hours of the Office.

Divine Office: the daily cycle of liturgical prayer (specifically excluding Mass), frequently referred to as the Office. See Chapter 6.

Doctor: a saint revered for his Christian teaching.

Dominica: Sunday.

Dominican: a friar of the Order of St Dominic.

Double: a major feast.

Doxology: a form of praise to God, especially *Gloria in excelsis* (the 'greater' doxology, recited at Mass) and *Gloria patri* (the 'lesser' doxology) recited at the end of most psalms, canticles, and hymns, and near the beginning of most Offices.

Dry Mass: in the Middle Ages a Mass at which not even the celebrating priest made his communion (generally because he had already communicated at another Mass).

Duplex: double: As in *festum duplex/duplum*, a double (i.e. major) feast.

Duty side: the side of the choir designated to undertake the duties of beginning chants, singing solo sections, reciting prayers, etc. on a weekly rota, alternately Decani and Cantoris.

Easter: the feast which commemorates the resurrection of Christ from the dead. It falls on a Sunday, but its date varies according to the phases of the moon. See Chapter 3.

Easter anthems: New Testament texts which replace the *Venite* at Mattins on Easter Day in the Book of Common Prayer.

Easter sepulchre: a place (often a tomb or sometimes a small self-contained building within a church) where in some Uses the host was ceremonially laid to rest on Good Friday and raised on Easter Day to commemorate the death and resurrection of Christ.

Easter Vigil: the last of the special rites of the *Triduum* celebrated after midday on Holy Saturday, also known as Paschal Vigil. See Chapter 9.

Elevation: the ceremonial raising of the host (the large wafer of consecrated bread) by the celebrant during the Canon of the Mass.

Ember days: three days of fasting and special prayer in each of the four calendar seasons: Wednesday, Friday, and Saturday after the first Sunday in Lent, Pentecost, Holy Cross Day (14 September), and St Lucy (13 December).

Epiphany: the feast which celebrates the manifestation of Christ to the world, and is specifically linked to the adoration by the wise men in the Gospels (6 January).

Epistle: a New Testament reading from the Epistles which follows the Collect(s) and precedes the Gradual at Mass; in some cases replaced by a reading from the Acts of the Apostles, Apocalypse (Book of Revelation), or the Old Testament. See Chapter 7.

Eucharist: Greek: thanksgiving; now generally applied to the liturgy also known as the Mass, Lord's Supper, or Holy Communion.

Eucharistic Prayer: the prayer, with a long history of formation, which is constructed with a number of independent sections and during which the bread and wine are consecrated at Mass. See Canon of the Mass.

EUOUAE: the concluding vowels of *Gloria patri*, often used in choir books to denote the ending of a psalm tone.

Evangelist: a writer of a Gospel, namely Matthew, Mark, Luke, or John.

Evangelium: Gospel reading.

Eve: synonymous with Vigil. English term for the day before a major feast (e.g. Christmas Eve).

Evensong: English term for Vespers, or more often for Evening Prayer in the Book of Common Prayer. See Chapter 11.

Exorcist: the second senior (after acolyte) of the four Minor Orders. See Chapter 2.

Exposition: a form of devotion to the Blessed Sacrament particularly popular in the Roman Catholic Church from the seventeenth century onwards, during which the Host is placed in a monstrance on an altar where the people can pray before it.

Expulsion of penitents: a rite conducted in the Middle Ages on Ash Wednesday when named sinners were expelled from the church, only to be readmitted at the end of Lent during the Easter Vigil.

Exsultet: the long proclamation of the resurrection sung by the deacon near the beginning of the Easter Vigil. See Chapter 9.

Fast: a period of deprivation (most often from rich food and drink). Wednesday and Friday were common fast days, in addition to Ember days and the penitential season before Easter.

Feast: a day of special celebration to commemorate a specific event, observance, or saint. Great feasts were celebrated not only on the day but for the week (Octave) following. See Chapter 4.

Feast of Fools: in the Middle Ages a day (either 1 or 14 January) on which clerics in Minor Orders took over the liturgy and life of a collegiate foundation. Particularly popular in France, it became so ribald and discredited that it was suppressed in the fourteenth century.

Feria: an ordinary, non-festal weekday; hence, ferial. See Chapter 4.

Festal: of or pertaining to a feast.

Festum: Latin: feast.

Font: a ceremonial basin, generally made of stone, in which water for baptism is placed, and at which the rite of baptism is conducted; particularly important at Easter when new water is blessed in the font (representing new life in the risen Christ), to which processions are made during the first week of Easter.

Fore-Mass: the first part of the Mass, now known as the Liturgy of the Word. Also referred to as synaxis or Mass of Catechumens.

Form: a bench or row of stalls in choir.

Forty Hours: a form of devotion, including exposition of the Blessed Sacrament, that became popular in the Roman Catholic Church after the Counter-Reformation.

Fraction: the breaking of the host before the communion at Mass.

Franciscan: a member of the Order of Friars Minor founded by Francis of Assisi in 1209. The Rule received Papal approval in 1223.

Frankish: the empire and Church of central northern Europe which was particularly powerful and influential in the eighth and ninth centuries. See Chapter 1.

Friar: a man living under the authority of a Rule and based in a conventual house, but committed to mission and preaching in the outside world (by contrast with an enclosed monk).

Gaudete: Latin: rejoice. The first word of the Introit at Mass on the third Sunday in Advent, and used to identify that day when the strictures of the penitential season are eased.

Genuflect: to bend one knee to the ground, generally as an act of reverence to the Blessed Sacrament.

Gilbertine: a small English Order of monks and nuns following the Rule of St Augustine, who shared the same church building and lived in adjacent conventual buildings.

Gloria: (1) *Gloria patri* (Glory to the Father); lesser doxology sung at the end of psalms and canticles etc. See Chapter 6. (2) *Gloria in excelsis* (Glory be to God on high); greater doxology, the second of the choral chants of the Ordinary of the Mass. See Chapter 7; text in Appendix 3.

Good Friday: the day when the Church commemorates the death of Christ. The second day of the solemn *Triduum*. See Chapter 9.

Gospel: (1) an account of the life of Christ. Four gospel narratives are included in the New Testament, attributed to Matthew, Mark, Luke, and John; (2) the reading from the Gospel at Mass. See Chapter 7.

Gradual: (1) the choral chant sung after the first reading at Mass. See Chapter 7; (2) the book containing all the choral chants for the Proper of the Mass. See Chapter 4.

Gradual psalms: a group of psalms recited (often privately) as an act of prayer, namely Psalms 124–134. There is some uncertainty why they are so described.

Greeting: the liturgical greeting *Dominus vobiscum* with reply *Et cum spiritu tuo* used as an introduction to many prayers and blessings. Until quite recently it could be said only by a deacon, priest, or bishop.

Gregorian: associated with Pope Gregory I (*c.*540–604); e.g. Gregorian chant, the collection of Roman chant codified at the end of the sixth century.

Gregorian calendar: the astronomical calendar introduced by Pope Gregory XIII in 1582 to compensate for errors in the earlier calendar of Julius Caesar. Gradually adopted throughout Europe (not until 1752 in England).

Hebdomadarius: Latin: weekly. The priest responsible for certain weekly duties in the conduct of the Office.

High Mass: the principal Mass of the day, generally celebrated solemnly with elaborate ceremonial and music; hence, *Missa solemnis* or *Missa solemniter*. See Chapters 7 and 11.

Historia: books of the Old Testament and Apocrypha read at Matins during the summer months; i.e. Kings, Wisdom, Job, Tobias, Judith, Maccabees, Ezekiel, Esther.

Holy Communion: the title of the Eucharist in the Book of Common Prayer of the Church of England. See Chapter 11.

Holy Orders: the senior orders to which the clergy are ordained: in ascending order subdeacon, deacon, priest, bishop. Contrast with Minor Orders. See Chapter 2.

Holy Saturday: the day when the church commemorates Christ's period in the tomb after his death on the cross. The last of the three days of the solemn *Triduum*. See Chapter 9.

Holy Week: the week immediately preceding Easter Day, between Palm Sunday and Holy Saturday. The last three days are the solemn *Triduum*. See Chapter 9.

Homily: (1) a reading from the writings of the Church Fathers (e.g. St Augustine of Hippo) used during the third nocturn of Matins; (2) an authorized sermon text intended to be read at Holy Communion in the Church of England after the Reformation.

Horarium: (1) a timetable for the day, especially in a monastery; (2) a book containing the Hours (i.e. Divine Office).

Hosanna: Hebrew word meaning 'save now' used as a cry at Christ's entry to Jerusalem on Palm Sunday, and now used as an acclamation of praise (e.g. *Hosanna in excelsis* in the *Sanctus* and *Benedictus* at Mass).

Hospital: in the Middle Ages, a conventual establishment where pilgrims stayed or the poor and aged were cared for.

Host: the large wafer of bread consecrated, elevated, and consumed by the priest at Mass.

Hour: a term used to identify one of the Office services since each was celebrated at a fixed time of day (e.g. Prime, Terce, Sext, None, but applied to the whole cycle). Hence Book of Hours, the book containing selected cycles of services from the Office.

Household chapel: a religious establishment within the household of a noble-
man, prince, or bishop. It was generally an organization which accompanied
the head of the house on his travels. In the later Middle Ages it included lay
musicians as well as clergy. See Chapter 2.

Humble Access: a prayer introduced by Cranmer into the service of Holy
Communion immediately before the consecration.

Hymn: Greek: a song of praise to God; liturgically a metrical, stanzaic text
recited at an Office. The Western repertory was mostly compiled between
about the fourth and thirteenth centuries.

Hymnal: the book, or section of an Antiphonal or Breviary, containing
hymns for the Office.

Improperia: Latin: reproaches. Reproofs spoken by Christ, and sung in a
formalized version with the Trisagion ('thrice holy', sung in Latin and
Greek) during the ceremony of veneration of the cross in the Good Friday
liturgy (described in Chapter 9).

In medio chori: Latin: in the middle of the choir; the place where the lectern
used by the rulers of the choir was situated, between the two sets of facing
stalls. See Chapter 2.

Incense: mixture of aromatic gums and spices burnt on charcoal in a thurible,
and used in solemn rituals (i.e. High Mass and Solemn Vespers) as a
symbol of prayer and sanctification.

Incipit: Latin: it begins. The initial word or phrase of a more substantial text,
often all that is shown to denote the use of a text which is commonly used
or found elsewhere in a liturgical book.

Intercession: a prayer on behalf of others.

Introit: the choral chant sung at the beginning of the Mass, originally during
the entry of the ministers. The first of the sequence of proper choral chants.
See Chapters 5 and 7.

Invitatorium: the section of an Antiphonal or Breviary containing the texts
(and chants) to be used in the opening section of Matins with Psalm 94.

Invitatory: an antiphon used as a refrain to Psalm 94 in the opening section
of Matins, or the whole item (antiphon and psalm). See Chapter 6.

Ite: first word of *Ite missa est* used as the dismissal at the end of Mass, with
reply *Deo gratias*.

Jesuit: priest subject to the authority of the Society of Jesus, a missionary and
educative Order founded in 1534 by Ignatius Loyola during the Counter-
Reformation.

Julian calendar: astronomical calendar established during the time of Julius
Caesar (*c.*40 BC); displaced by the Gregorian calendar from 1582.

Kalendar: See Calendar.

Kiss of peace: a rite of conciliation before communion at Mass, symbolically passed from the celebrant to the assisting clergy and then to all in choir during *Agnus dei*. See Chapter 7.

Kyriale: the book, or that section of a Gradual or Missal, containing the choral chants of the Ordinary of the Mass (i.e. *Kyrie, Gloria in excelsis, Credo, Sanctus* and *Benedictus, Agnus dei, Ite*, and *Benedicamus*).

Kyrie: Greek: *Kyrie [eleison]* (Lord have mercy), the first of the choral chants of the Ordinary of the Mass. See Chapter 7.

Lady Chapel: a chapel within a church with an altar dedicated to the Blessed Virgin Mary; often the place where Lady Mass and Lady Office were celebrated.

Lady Mass: Mass celebrated in honour of Our Lady (i.e. the Blessed Virgin Mary, Mother of Christ); generally a daily observance in the later Middle Ages. See Chapter 8.

Lady Office: Office recited in honour of the Blessed Virgin Mary. Two forms: the daily Little Office (*officium parvum*) and the full Commemorative Office (*plenum servitium*) used weekly. See Chapter 8.

Laetare: Latin: rejoice. The first word of the Introit at Mass on the third Sunday of Lent when the strictures of Lent were relaxed (known in England as Refreshment Sunday).

Last Gospel: the first fourteen verses of St John's Gospel which it became customary for the celebrant to recite at the very end of Mass after the dismissal.

Laudate: Latin: praise. Applied to groups of psalms beginning *Laudate*. (1) Psalms 148–150 recited at the end of the psalmody at Lauds; (2) the sequence of proper psalms often used at First Vespers of feasts: Psalms 112, 116, 145, 146, 147.

Lauds: the first of the seven day Hours of the Office, recited immediately after the night Office of Matins in the secular Uses. Full Latin title: *Laudes Matutinales* (morning praises). See Chapter 6.

Lay: of the people; non-clerical. Frequently applied to posts intended for clergy but occupied by an unordained person, often a musician (e.g. lay clerk, lay vicar).

Lectern: free-standing reading desk, large enough to take substantial books.

Lectio: Latin: a reading, generally scriptural.

Lectionary: the table indicating the distribution of readings according to the requirements of the Calendar of liturgical seasons and feasts.

Lector: a reader. One of the Minor Orders of the clergy.

Lent: the period from Ash Wednesday to Holy Saturday: the major portion of the penitential season (normally beginning at Septuagesima in the Middle Ages), it recalls Christ's forty days in the wilderness.

Lesser canticle: a canticle other than the three canticles from St Luke's Gospel (*Benedictus, Magnificat, Nunc dimittis*), especially those used at Lauds in the psalmody and those used in the third nocturn of monastic Matins.

Lesser litany: *Kyrie eleison* (Lord have mercy) as used in the Office preces. See Chapters 6 and 11.

Lesson: a reading, generally scriptural.

Liber: Latin: book.

Liber Usualis: Latin: book of use (best understood in this context as 'useful book'). A late ninteenth-century compilation of texts and chants for Sundays and feasts from Breviary, Antiphonal, Missal, and Gradual.

Litany: prayer in the form of a series of petitions recited by a minister with a series of repeated refrains interjected by choir or people.

Little Hours: the Offices without a canticle (i.e. Prime, Terce, Sext, and None).

Little Office: most often the Little Office of the Blessed Virgin Mary, recited daily, but also applied to comparable Offices (e.g. of All Saints).

Liturgy: Greek *leitourgia*: literally, people's public service (originally in a civil sense); (1) the whole of the formalized, written-down worship of the Church intended primarily for celebration and recitation in church; (2) the Eucharist; (3) specific written texts of the Eucharist (e.g. Liturgy of St James); (4) the study of worship (or liturgiology). See Prologue.

Liturgical drama: a sung dialogue heightened by some dramatic action (e.g. the Easter dialogue *Quem quaeritis in sepulchro*). More extended forms were organized in separate scenes.

Lord's Prayer: the prayer beginning *Pater noster* (Our Father) which Christ taught to his disciples and instructed them to use.

Lord's Supper: an alternative title for Holy Communion.

Low Mass: a simple celebration of Mass said by a priest with one assistant.

Lucernarium: the lighting of the lamps which marked the beginning of the service of evening prayer in the early centuries of the Church. It died out in the West.

Lutheran: an adherent to the doctrine of Martin Luther whose challenge to the Church in 1517 instigated the Protestant Reformation. The Lutheran church is strongest in Northern Germany and Scandinavia.

Magnificat: Latin: magnifies; the first word of the Song of Mary. The second of the canticles found in the nativity narrative in St Luke's Gospel, and sung at Latin Vespers and English Evening Prayer. See Chapter 6; text in Appendix 3.

Maior: Latin: greater. Used to distinguish more important or principal feast-days: *festum duplex maior* (greater double feast).

Mandatum: Latin: commandment. The first word of the antiphon used at the ceremony of washing the feet, and used to describe the ceremony which itself recalls Christ washing the feet of his disciples at the Last Supper on the night before his crucifixion. See Chapter 9.

Manuale: a book containing services used in a parish church (e.g. baptism, marriage). Often known as Rituale abroad.

Marian: of Mary, i.e. the Blessed Virgin Mary.

Martyr: one who dies by violence for the sake of the Christian faith.

Martyrology: an official register of martyrs, from the eighth century onwards often enlarged by narratives of the martyrdom. Recited at Prime.

Mary: mother of Christ, generally referred to as the Blessed Virgin Mary. Not to be confused with Mary Magdalen, a follower of Christ.

Mass: the Latin title for the principal sacramental service of the Church. The central action is the consecration of bread and wine, recalling the words and actions of Christ at the Last Supper with his disciples on the night before his crucifixion. See Chapter 7.

Mass of Catechumens: in the early Church, the first part of the Mass to which those aspiring to be full members of the Church were admitted.

Mass of Chrism: the Mass on Maundy Thursday morning at which the oils for use at baptism, confirmation, ordination, etc. are consecrated. See Chapter 9.

Mass of the Dead: the fixed form of Mass used on the day of burial and as a daily or occasional commemoration of those who have died, either collect-ively or individually. See Chapter 7.

Mass of the Faithful: in the early Church, the second part of the Mass during which the bread and wine were consecrated and consumed, and to which only full members of the Church were admitted (see Mass of Catechumens).

Mass of the Pre-Sanctified: a form of Mass used on Good Friday when the Host consecrated on the preceding day is consumed. See Chapter 9.

Matins: the night Office, also known as Vigils or Nocturns. See Chapter 6.

Mattins: used in this book to distinguish the Latin night Office of Matins from the service of Morning Prayer (Mattins) in the Church of England. See Chapter 11.

Maundy Thursday: Thursday before Easter Sunday. The day on which the Church commemorates the institution of the Eucharist (Mass, Holy Communion) by Christ with his disciples at the Last Supper on the night before his crucifixion. See Chapter 9.

Memoria: Latin: remembrance. (1) a day which commemorates a minor saint without disturbing the normal pattern of the ferial liturgy; (2) Memorial.

Memorial: an observance consisting of antiphon, versicle, and collect for a specific intention or saint, and usually said after a complete Office. Closely related to commemoration and suffrage. See Chapter 8.

Mendicant: friar, or of friars.

Metrical psalm: a translation of a psalm into the vernacular and into metrical verse, generally strophic.

Milanese: of Milan (liturgically more often Ambrosian).

Minister: an officiant, not necessarily in Holy Orders, at a liturgical service.

Minor Canon: a cleric who serves in a collegiate church but is not a member of the governing body of canons, the Chapter. Sometimes known as Vicar Choral.

Minor Orders: the junior clerical Orders, and counterpart to Holy Orders. In ascending order the Minor Orders consisted of Porter, Lector, Exorcist, and Acolyte. See Chapter 2.

Missal: the book containing the priest's texts for the Mass. Later Missals often had complete Mass texts even with music (Noted Missals). See Chapter 4.

Mitre: a form of headgear worn by a bishop (and certain abbots) in the shape of tongues of fire, recalling the descent of the Holy Spirit at Pentecost.

Mode: a unit of melodic classification applied to the repertory of liturgical chant.

Monastery: a convent of monks. More widely applied to any community in which religious live in enclosure and under the authority of a Rule: hence, monastic.

Monk: a man who has sworn vows of obedience, celibacy, and common sharing of property under a religious Rule.

Monstrance: an open or transparent vessel of precious metal in which the Host is placed to be visible for devotion.

Morrow Mass: the first of the two main Masses celebrated daily in choir. See Chapters 3 and 7.

Motet: a polyphonic setting of a text without a specific liturgical place; used to replace prescribed liturgical texts from at least the sixteenth century onwards.

Mother house: in centrally organized monastic Orders, the principal monastery (e.g. Cluny, Cîteaux) whose customs the other monasteries follow.

Mozarabic: properly that part of Spain conquered by the Moors, but liturgically used to refer to the Hispanic Rite.

Nativity: birth, especially the birth of Christ. Other feasts commemorate the Nativity of John the Baptist and the Nativity of the Blessed Virgin Mary.

Nave: the main, central body of a church building, west of the choir.

New Testament: the Christian section of the Bible, consisting of gospels, Acts of the Apostles, epistles, and the Apocalypse (Revelation of St John the Divine).

Nocturn: the main unit of the Office of Matins, consisting principally of psalms, readings, and responds. See Chapter 6.

None: the last of the Little Hours of the daily Office (literally at the ninth hour of the day). See Chapter 6.

North side: the north end of the altar at which the Book of Common Prayer directs the priest to stand to celebrate Holy Communion.

Noted Breviary: a Breviary including notated choral chant.

Noted Missal: a Missal including notated choral chant.

Novice: a prospective member of a religious community who has not taken solemn (life-long) vows.

Nun: a woman who has sworn vows of obedience, celibacy, and common sharing of property under a religious Rule.

Nunc dimittis: the third of the canticles from St Luke's Gospel, the Song of Simeon, sung at the Office of Compline; text in Appendix 3.

'O' antiphons: the collection of *Magnificat* antiphons, each beginning 'O . . .', sung at Vespers between 16 and 23 December, the last days of Advent.

O sapientia: the first of the O antiphons, often marked in the Calendar.

Oblation: literally, 'offering'. The Prayer of Oblation, largely extracted from the text of the Latin Canon of the Mass, follows the communion in the Church of England rite. See Chapter 11.

Octave: (1) the eighth day after a feast, often celebrated as a feast in its own right (e.g. Octave of Corpus Christi); (2) the whole week following a principal feast (e.g. Octave of Christmas).

Offertory: (1) the offering of bread and wine at Mass; (2) the choral chant in the Mass sung after the *Credo* and before the Secret and *Sursum corda* during (1). See Chapter 7.

Office: (1) the daily round of prayer of the Church consisting of the services Matins, Lauds, Prime, Terce, Sext, None, Vespers, and Compline. Sometimes referred to as the Divine Office; (2) used to identify one of the constituent services of the whole Office (e.g. the Office of Matins also known as the night Office). See Chapter 6.

Office of the Dead: the fixed texts of the Offices of Vespers, Matins, and Lauds recited on the day of burial, or as a daily or occasional commemoration of the dead. See Chapter 6.

Officium: (1) Latin: Office; (2) an alternative title for the Introit at Mass.

Old Testament: the pre-Christian part of the Bible, primarily an account of the Jewish people and their relationship with God.

Opus dei: Latin: the work of God; the Divine Office.

Oratory: place of prayer. From the later sixteenth century in Italy, a hall adjacent to a church in which paraliturgical celebrations took place, especially during Lent when there were restrictions on music in church.

Oratorian: a priest in the community around St Philip Neri in Rome (1562), established as a religious congregation (1612), who used Oratories as a place for popular devotional services and oratorios.

Order: (1) as in Holy Orders and Minor Orders, above; (2) a group of religious communities conforming to an agreed Rule and set of customs (e.g. the friars); (3) a service or the ritual sequence it follows.

Ordinal: the book which established ritual order of the liturgy (i.e. which specific items were to be recited, and often by whom). See Chapter 4.

Ordination: the sacramental conferral of spiritual authority on a cleric, especially the principal Holy Orders of deacon and priest. The ordaining of a bishop was formerly generally referred to as consecration.

Ordinary: (1) a general term for Mass texts that are fixed and unchanging; (2) the unchanging choral chants of the Mass: *Kyrie*, *Gloria in excelsis*, *Sanctus* and *Benedictus*, *Agnus dei*, and *Ite* or *Benedicamus*.

Ordo: Latin: order; specifically a liturgical order of service.

Ordo Missae: Order of Mass; generally applied to the priest's ordinary texts in the Mass, within which the Canon (Canon Missae) may be separately identified. See Chapter 7.

Ordines Romani: a series of some fifty documents describing the customs of liturgical observance in Rome, and dating from about the eighth to the tenth centuries.

Organum: a medieval practice in which a second voice (or more) embellished the chant, often (in the tenth and eleventh centuries) moving conjunctly and in parallel motion with the original melody.

Our Father: the opening words of the Lord's Prayer, which Christ gave his disciples as a pattern for prayer.

Palm Sunday: the Sunday before Easter Day on which the Church commemorates the entry of Christ into Jerusalem in the week of his crucifixion. The first day of Holy Week.

Paraliturgical: a modern term to describe Christian observances which are not part of the prescribed liturgy, but which relate to it in structure or intent.

Parasceve: Jewish day of preparation for the Sabbath. Used to identify Good Friday in Holy Week. See Good Friday above.

Parish: a district served by a priest who has spiritual care for the people living within it, with a parish church. A constituent part of a diocese. See Chapter 2.

Paschal: originally, of the Jewish Passover, but in Christian terminology an alternative term for Easter.

Paschal candle: the candle blessed and lit at the Easter Vigil as a symbol of the risen Christ, light of the world. See Chapter 9.

Passion: (1) the account in the gospels of Christ's arrest, trial, crucifixion, and death; (2) musical settings of (1).

Passion Sunday: two weeks before Easter Day; the fifth Sunday of Lent. (In the modern Calendar, Passiontide begins on Palm Sunday.)

Passiontide: the period between Passion Sunday and Holy Saturday.

Paten: the plate on which the Host is placed at Mass; of precious metal and often fashioned to match the chalice.

Pater noster: Latin: Our Father; used to identify the prayer Christ taught his disciples. Text in Appendix 3.

Patron: in the Christian sense, a saint after whom a church is named.

Pax: Latin: peace. (1) a short dialogue in the Mass: *Pax vobiscum. Et cum spiritu tuo* (Peace be with you. And with thy spirit) recited before the *Agnus dei*; (2) the kiss of peace. See above and Chapter 7.

Peace: see *Pax* and Kiss of Peace.

Penitential: repentant, used to describe the season of Advent and between Septuagesima and Easter. See Chapter 3.

Penitential psalms: a sequence of seven: Psalms 6, 31, 50, 101, 129, 142.

Pentecost: Greek: fiftieth day. Seven weeks after Easter Day, the Sunday on which the Church celebrates the descent of the Holy Spirit on to the apostles.

Per annum: Latin: through the year; used to describe the normative periods of the liturgical calendar which fall between Epiphany and Septuagesima, and Corpus Christi and Advent. See Chapter 3.

Pew: wooden bench, especially in an English parish church from the thirteenth century onwards.

Pica, Pie: see Directorium.

Piscina: a stone basin with drain near the altar where the ablutions took place.

Placebo: Latin: I will please. The opening word of Vespers in the Office of the Dead, by which it is often known. See Chapter 6.

Plenum servitium: Latin: full service. The full cycle of the Office as opposed to a Little Office. See Lady Office.

Polyphony: music scored with more than one independent line; as opposed to monophony.

Pontifical: the book containing the rites conducted by bishops (e.g. confirmation, ordination, consecration of a church), also blessings used by a bishop. See Chapter 4.

Pope: the presiding bishop of the Church; since the Reformation, of the Roman-Catholic Church. The Pope is elected from among and by the cardinals. See Chapter 2.

Porter: the most junior of the Minor Orders of the clergy; doorkeeper.

Postcommunion: the proper prayer recited by the celebrant after the Communion at Mass.

Prebend: the endowment (often income from a part of the estate or a parish) in a secular collegiate church or cathedral which supported a senior member of the institution.

Prebendary: a cleric supported by a prebend; an alternative title for a canon in a collegiate church. See Chapter 2.

Precentor: literally, 'chief cantor'; the cleric or monk with charge of the direction of the liturgy. In medieval times, often he also had charge of the scriptorium. In secular cathedrals, a senior canon and officer. See Cantor and Chapter 2.

Preces: Latin: prayers; a fixed sequence of Lesser Litany, *Pater noster*, and versicles and responses used at the end of Prime and Compline. See Chapter 6.

Preface: the introduction to the Eucharistic Prayer, beginning with *Sursum corda* and leading to *Sanctus*. See Chapter 7.

Premonstratensian: a religious Order; essentially an austere form of the Augustinians influenced by the Cistercians. Founded in 1120 and named after their first house at Prémontré. Known in England as White Canons.

Pre-Sanctified: see Mass of Pre-Sanctified.

Presbytery: the part of the church reserved for ordained clergy; in medieval churches the part of the church east of the choir, and including the high altar.

Priest: a cleric in Holy Orders who has authority to absolve sins and celebrate Mass. See Chapter 2.

Prime: the first of the Little Hours of the Divine Office (literally at the first hour of the day). See Chapter 6.

Primer: a devotional book popular among the medieval laity, generally including Little Office of the Virgin, Office of the Dead, Gradual Psalms, Penitential Psalms, Litany of the Saints. Often synonymous with Book of Hours. Later versions were written in the vernacular.

Principal feast: the most important class of feast-day (*festum principalis*) celebrated with greatest solemnity (e.g. Christmas Day, Easter Day, Nativity of the Blessed Virgin Mary).

Prior/Prioress: (1) the senior monk or nun in a monastic community next in rank after the abbot or abbess; (2) the presiding monk or nun in a monastic community where there is no abbot or abbess.

Priory: a monastic community headed by a prior or prioress.

Private Mass: a Low Mass celebrated with only a priest and clerk present.

Processional: the book containing the chants and prayers for liturgical processions.

Profession: the commitment of a member of a religious community to vows to observe the Rule.

Proper: (1) describing a liturgical text that is particular to a specific feast or observance; (2) collectively all the items as in (1) in the Office or the Mass that are changeable and particular to a feast or observance. The opposite of ferial in the Office and Ordinary in the Mass. Especially used to identify the variable choral chants of the Mass: Introit, Gradual, Alleluia, Offertory, and Communion. See Chapters 3, 6, and 7.

Prosa: Latin: prose. A term used in some instances to describe either a Sequence (see below) or a hymn sung in procession with a refrain (see Chapter 8).

Psalm: one of the collection of 150 poetic religious texts found in the Book of Psalms in the Old Testament. See Chapter 5.

Psalm-tone: the melodic formula, essentially a decoration of a monotone, in two sections, to which each verse of a psalm is intoned (in two halves). The formula is repeated for every verse of a psalm. There are eight principal psalm-tones.

Psalmi idiotici: Latin, non-scriptural texts used in the early Church. Some have survived in the liturgy (e.g. *Gloria in excelsis* in the Mass, and *Te deum laudamus* at Matins).

Psalmody: a group of psalms, often those used in a specific Office service.

Psalter: the book, or part of a Breviary or Antiphonal, where the texts of the psalms and canticles (and some related common items) are found. See Chapter 5 and Appendix 2.

Pulpitum: in large medieval churches, the gallery above the choir screen from which the Gradual, Alleluia, and Gospel were sung. Some foreign examples are somewhat closer to an ambo. See Chapter 2.

Purification: see Candlemas.

Pyx: a receptacle to contain the reserved Host. In England the pyx often hung on a chain from the roof in the sanctuary.

Quadragesima: Latin: fortieth day; applied to the whole season of Lent, though originally just the first Sunday of Lent, forty days before Easter.

Quem quaeritis: Latin: whom do you seek [in the sepulchre]?; the opening of the dramatic dialogue on Easter Day. See Chapters 8 and 9.

Quicumque vult: Latin: whosoever wishes [to be saved]; the opening words of the Athanasian Creed recited at Prime.

Quinquagesima: Latin: fiftieth day. The Sunday before Lent.

Quire: see Choir (3).

Reader: see Lector.

Rector: Latin: ruler. A title given to some parish priests because of the nature of their income from tithes.

Rector chori: Latin: ruler of the choir. On days when the choir was ruled, two or four rulers directed the choral chants from the lectern in the middle of the choir (*in medio chori*). See Chapter 2.

Red Letter Days: important feast-days indicated in the Calendar by the use of red (rather than black) ink.

Refectory: in a monastery, the place where the community ate together.

Regular: bound by vows to a Rule; regular clergy included friars, monks, nuns, and Augustinian canons. The opposite of secular. See Chapter 2.

Relics: material remains of a saint after death.

Religious: a member of an Order or Congregation bound by vows. See Regular above, and Chapter 2.

Reliquary: a receptacle (often a casket) for relics.

Requiem: Latin: rest; the opening word of the Introit to the Mass of the Dead, and often used to identify the whole Mass. See Mass of the Dead.

Reredos: a decorative panel or panels behind an altar, of either wood or stone.

Respond: (1) a form of responsorial chant which follows a lesson at Matins or a short chapter in the other Offices. Those at Matins have elaborate, melismatic chant; those at the other Hours are generally set to simple melodic formulas. See Chapter 6; (2) used by some writers to distinguish the portion of the respond repeated (in whole or part) as a refrain.

Response: the answer recited by the whole choir to a versicle said by a minister.

Responsorial: choral chant which follows and therefore responds to a reading in the Office or Mass. Its distinctive characteristics are described in Chapter 5, its liturgical placings in Chapters 6 and 7.

Responsory: Respond (1).

Rhymed Office: a medieval Office written for a special feast or observance with text in verse.

Rite: (1) the broad classification of a whole pattern of liturgical observance, within which there may be variant regional or local Uses (e.g. Roman Rite); (2) the form, structure, and text of an individual liturgical service (e.g. Eucharistic rite); See Introduction and Chapter 12.

Rite of Peace: see Kiss of Peace and *Pax*.

Ritual: pertaining to the rite (2); see Ordinal and Chapter 12.

Rituale: *Rituale Romanum*, the Tridentine replacement for the medieval Manuale with parish rites of baptism, confirmation, marriage, etc.

Rogation: special days of prayers and fasting in early summer with intercession, especially for the next harvest: originally 25 April and three days before Ascension Day. See Chapters 3 and 8.

Roman: of Rome. Often used loosely to mean 'of the Papal Curia' in relation to late medieval liturgy, or to the Roman Catholic Church after the Reformation.

Rood: cross (thus Holy Rood); applied to the large cross often found at the east end of the nave near the choir screen. Hence, rood beam, rood loft, rood screen—all surmounted by a cross.

Rubric: an instruction originally written in red (where the main text was in black).

Rule: code of behaviour by which a religious community is regulated (e.g. the Rule of St Benedict). See Chapters 1 and 2.

Ruler: see *Rector chori*.

Sacrament: 'an outward and visible sign of an inward and spiritual grace' (Book of Common Prayer) or 'the sign of a sacred thing in so far as it sanctifies men' (Thomas Aquinas). All have origin and authority in Christ's actions or the teaching of the Apostles. The principal sacraments are baptism and the Eucharist; the remaining five are confirmation, ordination, marriage, penance and absolution, and anointing of the sick.

Sacramentary: the liturgical book used by the celebrant at the Mass until about the twelfth century when it was supplanted by the more comprehensive compilation of the Missal.

Sacrist: the officer of the church responsible for the liturgical books, vessels, and vestments.

Sacristy: the room in or close to the church where the liturgical books, vessels, and vestments are kept.

Saint: a holy man or woman formally recognized as such by the Church by canonization. The medieval saints include apostles, martyrs, confessors, doctors, and virgins, as well as the angels. In the New Testament the term refers to any baptized believer.

Sanctorale: the portion of the Calendar and of liturgical books with material related to the observance of dated feast-days, mostly of Saints; sometimes referred to as the Proper of the Saints. The counterpart to the Temporale. See Chapter 3.

Sanctuary: the area immediately surrounding an altar in a church or chapel.

Sanctus: Latin: Holy. The opening of the acclamation in praise of God's holiness sung at Mass at the end of the Preface and before the Canon of the Mass. Generally followed by the *Benedictus qui venit* in the Latin Rites. See Chapter 7; text in Appendix 3.

Sarum: an abbreviation used extensively in the nineteenth and twentieth centuries to denote Salisbury. It is in fact an erroneous and spurious reading of the medieval abbreviation of Sarisburiensis (Salisbury).

Schola cantorum: Latin: school of singers; (1) a select body of able singers; (2) the place where singing was taught; song school.

Screen: a partition separating two parts of a church or chapel. See Choir Screen and Chapter 2.

Season: a part of the year, but the liturgical seasons do not follow the calendar seasons. The most important liturgical seasons are Advent, Christmas, Epiphany, Lent, and Easter. See Temporale and Chapter 3.

Secret: the prayer recited silently by the celebrant after the Offertory and before the *Sursum corda* at Mass.

Secular: the adjective used to describe the ecclesiastical foundations and clergy 'in the world', as opposed to those subject to the authority of a Rule. The opposite of regular or religious. See Chapter 2.

Sedilia: Latin: seats. A row of three seats (often set into the wall with carved canopies) on the south side of the sanctuary where the celebrant, deacon, and subdeacon sat during parts of the Mass (e.g. Epistle).

Semiduplex: Latin: half double. A classification of feast between simple (*simplex*) and double (*duplex*); the principle is widespread, but the term is especially used in the medieval Roman Use and later Tridentine Rite. See Chapters 3 and 10.

Septuagesima: Latin: seventieth day. The Sunday nine weeks before Easter, three before Lent; in the Middle Ages and in the Tridentine Rite the beginning of the penitential season. See Chapters 3 and 6.

Sequence: a medieval, non-scriptural text composed in verse sung after the Alleluia (or Tract) on most important liturgical days; the same melody is generally used for a pair of stanzas. See Chapters 7 and 10.

Sequentiary: the book, or part of the Antiphonal or Missal, including Sequences and also Tropes. See Chapter 3.

Sermon: a discourse, generally delivered by a priest or bishop in church, as a means of Christian instruction or exhortation; the ambo, *cathedra*, pulpit, or pulpitum were commonly used to deliver it.

Server: a non-specialist term to describe one of those assisting the principal clergy in the ceremonial at Mass, in processions etc.; includes taperer, thurifer, crucifer (cross-bearer).

Sexagesima: Latin: sixtieth day. The Sunday eight weeks before Easter.

Sext: the third of the Little Hours of the Office, recited literally at the sixth hour of the day. See Chapter 6.

Simplex: Latin: simple. A classification for lesser feasts with Matins of either nine (twelve in monastic churches) or three lessons. See Chapters 3 and 6.

Solemn: an adjective used to describe liturgical observances with the most elaborate ritual and ceremonial as a mark of their importance.

Stall: a seat in choir. Stalls were arranged in facing rows on the two sides of the choir. The most senior clerics or monks sat in the back row of stalls. See Chapter 2.

Station: a place where people assembled; in medieval churches a point where a procession halted, usually for the recitation of antiphon, versicle, and collect. See Chapter 8.

Statutes: a legal document which defined the nature, purpose, and character of an institution. All collegiate (and thus secular cathedral) churches were established and regulated by statutes. See Chapter 2.

Subdeacon. until the thirteenth century, the most senior of the Minor Orders; thereafter the most junior of Holy Orders. See Chapter 2.

Suffrages: a standard series of memorials (consisting of antiphon, versicle, and collect) used as an appendage to an Office (especially Lauds and Vespers) in honour of a regular group of saints or for peace; sometimes known as *memoria feriales*.

Superior: a general term for the senior member of a religious community.

Surplice: a white linen vestment worn over a cassock or habit; generally with full sleeves, yoke at the neck and less than full length (in these respects contrasting with the alb).

Sursum corda: Latin: Lift up your hearts. The dialogue at the beginning of the Preface in the Mass, marking the beginning of the Eucharistic prayer.

Synaxis: Greek: assembly. Properly relates to an early rite of psalms, readings, and prayers, but often used to describe the first part of the Mass before the Eucharistic prayer. See Mass of Catechumens.

Tabernacle: an ornamental receptacle (basically a small cupboard with locking doors) in which a Host consecrated at Mass is kept (for use at Exposition of the Blessed Sacrament, or for the dying), placed on the altar or to one side of it; from the sixteenth century it replaced the pyx in the Roman Catholic church.

Tabula: Latin: table. The weekly rota of assigned duties in a monastic house, and the list where they were written down; important here for the allocation of duties in the liturgy. See Chapter 2.

Taperer: an assistant at Mass or in procession, who carries a ceremonial candle.

Te deum: Latin: [We praise] thee O God. The opening words of the prose hymn sung near the end of Matins. See Chapter 6; text in Appendix 3.

Te igitur: the opening words of the Canon of the Mass, said by the priest immediately after the *Sanctus* and *Benedictus*.

Temporale: the portion of the Calendar and of liturgical books with material related to the observance of the seasons of the Church year (thus excluding feasts of saints for the most part); sometimes referred to as the Proper of the Time. The counterpart to the Sanctorale. See Chapter 3.

Tenebrae: Latin: darkness. The name given to the night Office of Matins (and Lauds following) during the solemn *Triduum*, when candles were ceremonially extinguished. See Chapter 9.

Terce: the second of the Little Hours of the Office, literally at the third hour of the day. See Chapter 6.

Thurible: the ceremonial vessel (a covered bowl suspended on metal chains) in which charcoal and incense are burnt.

Thurifer: the assistant to the principal clergy who carried (and swung) the thurible especially at Mass and in processions.

Time: see Temporale.

Tonary: the book, or part of larger liturgical book, which contained a guide to the use of the antiphonal repertory and psalm tones according to modal classification. See Chapter 4.

Tone: a melodic formula used to chant a large range of different items (e.g. psalm tone, gospel tone, tone for collects).

Tonus peregrinus: Latin: wandering tone; the only psalm tone with two reciting notes, one for each half verse, it is traditionally associated with Psalm 113.

Tract: the choral chant sung in place of the Alleluia at Mass (i.e. after the Gradual) especially during the penitential season from Septuagesima to the end of Holy Week, and at Masses of the Dead; a through-composed setting of psalm verses without refrain. See Direct psalmody and Chapters 5 and 7.

Transept: the transverse part of a cruciform (cross-shaped) church building at the eastern end of the nave; the two wings on either side of the crossing are often referred to independently as north and south transepts.

Transfiguration: the feast which commemorates the change in the appearance of Christ before some of the apostles on the mountain; celebrated on 6 August, but not formally established until 1457, and therefore placed in the Sanctorale.

Treasurer: a senior canon and officer in a collegiate or cathedral church (canon or prebendary) with responsibility for the finance of the institution, and in church for the precious ornaments and vessels.

Tridentine: of Trent, i.e. of the sixteenth-century Council of Trent. Used to describe the reformed Roman Church and its liturgy from the later sixteenth century until the Second Vatican Council (1962–5); hence Tridentine Rite, Tridentine Breviary, Tridentine Missal. See Chapter 10.

Triduum: often *sacrum triduum*, Latin: three holy days; the three days before Easter Day on which the Church commemorates the institution of the

Eucharist (Maundy Thursday), the crucifixion of Christ (Good Friday), and his resting in the grave (Holy Saturday). See Chapter 9.

Triforium: the second level of arcading (often without windows) in the nave (and choir) of a church building above the main arches and below the clerestory; often at the height of the aisle roofs.

Trina oratio: a form of devotional prayer in three sections, based around the penitential psalms, and normally recited privately.

Trinity: (1) God the Father, God the Son, God the Holy Spirit–three Persons but one God. A central belief of the Christian Church; (2) the Sunday after Pentecost observed as the feast of the Holy Trinity from the Middle Ages (formalized in 1334).

Trope: a medieval text, text and melody, or melody interpolated into an existing choral chant, especially in the Ordinary and Proper of the Mass; generally allocated to soloists. Tropes tended to be highly localized repertories.

Troper: a book, or section of an Antiphonal, Cantatory, or Missal, including tropes and Sequences. See Chapter 4.

Tunicle: the outer vestment worn by the subdeacon at Mass; similar to but simpler than the dalmatic.

Use: the variant form of a normative Rite used in a particular region, diocese, or monastic Order (e.g. Use of Salisbury and Use of the Papal Curia are variants of the medieval Roman Rite). See Introduction.

Veneration of the cross: the ceremony of venerating (by kneeling before and kissing) a cross during the Good Friday liturgy. See Chapter 9.

Venite: Latin: come; the opening word of Psalm 94, sung near the beginning of Matins as part of the Invitatory.

Verse: (1) the basic unit of a psalm or canticle, divided into two parts by a caesura; (2) a solo section within a choral chant, especially a responsorial chant (e.g. respond at Matins, Gradual and Alleluia at Mass).

Versicle: (1) the first part of a short dialogue recited by a minister to which there is a collective response; namely, versicle and response; (2) a shorthand reference to the whole unit of versicle and response.

Vespers: the evening Office at which the canticle *Magnificat* is sung. See Chapter 6.

Vestment: an ecclesiastical garment, especially chasuble, dalmatic, and tunicle worn by celebrant, deacon, and subdeacon at Mass, and the cope worn by the clergy.

Vicar: from Latin *vicarius*: substitute; (1) a cleric in a collegiate church who acted as substitute for a canon or presbendary; effectively one of the junior clergy who undertook the daily conduct of the liturgy in choir (hence vicar choral, or, in the case of a lay singer taking on the duties, lay vicar). See Chapter 2; (2) a priest appointed to take charge of a parish as a substitute for the rector (especially where a monastery had charge of the parish); (3) in the Church of England, a priest in charge of a parish.

Vigil: the day before a feast-day (generally beginning after midday). See Chapter 3.

Vigils: an alternative name for Matins, especially as in Vigils of the Dead.

Virgin: a celibate female saint. Also applied to the Blessed Virgin Mary, mother of Christ, often referred to simply as the Virgin.

Votive: an adjective to describe an Office, Mass, or other observance that is not part of the liturgy laid down by the Calendar, but is additional to the main course of daily liturgy; usually for a special intention. See Chapter 8.

Votive Antiphon: a modern term applied to the ceremony of antiphon, versicle, and collect commonly recited after the end of Vespers or Compline, most often in honour of the Blessed Virgin Mary. See Chapter 8.

Votive Mass: a Mass offered for a special intention, in addition to and not as part of the prescribed liturgy of the day. See Lady Mass and Chapter 8.

Votive Office: a single hour of the Office or a group of hours recited in addition to and not as part of the prescribed Office of the day. See Little Office, Lady Office, and Chapter 8.

Vulgate: the Latin text of the Bible in most common use (hence *Biblia Vulgata*); a translation mostly undertaken in the late fourth century by St Jerome.

Whitsun: an English alternative to Pentecost; hence, Whitsunday and Whitsuntide.

INDEX